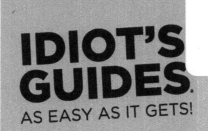

Zen Living

by Domyo Sater Burk

A member of Penguin Group (USA) Inc.

To Bob Orman, without whose encouragement I would probably never have written this book,
and to John Burk, my companion in this life.

ALPHA BOOKS

Published by Penguin Group (USA) Inc.

Penguin Group (USA) Inc., 375 Hudson Street, New York, New York 10014, USA • Penguin Group (Canada), 90 Eglinton Avenue East, Suite 700, Toronto, Ontario M4P 2Y3, Canada (a division of Pearson Penguin Canada Inc.) • Penguin Books Ltd., 80 Strand, London WC2R 0RL, England • Penguin Ireland, 25 St. Stephen's Green, Dublin 2, Ireland (a division of Penguin Books Ltd.) • Penguin Group (Australia), 250 Camberwell Road, Camberwell, Victoria 3124, Australia (a division of Pearson Australia Group Pty. Ltd.) • Penguin Books India Pvt. Ltd., 11 Community Centre, Panchsheel Park, New Delhi—110 017, India • Penguin Group (NZ), 67 Apollo Drive, Rosedale, North Shore, Auckland 1311, New Zealand (a division of Pearson New Zealand Ltd.) • Penguin Books (South Africa) (Pty.) Ltd., 24 Sturdee Avenue, Rosebank, Johannesburg 2196, South Africa • Penguin Books Ltd., Registered Offices: 80 Strand, London WC2R 0RL, England

International Standard Book Number: 978-1-61564-424-7
Library of Congress Catalog Card Number: 2013945254

17 16 15   8 7 6 5 4 3 2

Interpretation of the printing code: The rightmost number of the first series of numbers is the year of the book's printing; the rightmost number of the second series of numbers is the number of the book's printing. For example, a printing code of 14-1 shows that the first printing occurred in 2014.

Printed in the United States of America

Note: This publication contains the opinions and ideas of its author. It is intended to provide helpful and informative material on the subject matter covered. It is sold with the understanding that the author and publisher are not engaged in rendering professional services in the book. If the reader requires personal assistance or advice, a competent professional should be consulted. The author and publisher specifically disclaim any responsibility for any liability, loss, or risk, personal or otherwise, which is incurred as a consequence, directly or indirectly, of the use and application of any of the contents of this book.

Most Alpha books are available at special quantity discounts for bulk purchases for sales promotions, premiums, fund-raising, or educational use. Special books, or book excerpts, can also be created to fit specific needs. For details, write: Special Markets, Alpha Books, 375 Hudson Street, New York, NY 10014.

Publisher: *Mike Sanders*
Executive Managing Editor: *Billy Fields*
Executive Acquisitions Editor: *Lori Cates Hand*
Development Editor: *John Etchison*
Senior Production Editor: *Janette Lynn*

Cover/Book Designer: *William Thomas*
Indexer: *Johnna VanHoose Dinse*
Layout: *Ayanna Lacey*
Proofreader: *Jeanne Clark*

Contents

Introduction

If you've picked up this book, you're at least a little curious about Zen. Over the last 20 years, it's become more and more likely that your curiosity was piqued because you know someone who practices Zen, or because you encountered references to Zen in popular culture. This book contains just about everything I could think of to tell you about Zen, but I hope it won't satisfy your curiosity. As the title of this book suggests, Zen is about *living*, so ideally you will always maintain your sense of curiosity about it.

Many books about Zen are wary of telling you about all the wonderful ways Zen practice can change your life, because they don't want to hook you in with promises and then have you find out Zen takes a lot of work. Zen doesn't actually offer you any solutions or answers; it just teaches you how to find them for yourself. In the end, it's up to you, and no guru, book, or seminar can unlock the potential of your life unless you actively participate in a long, sometimes arduous, process.

Still, many of us who practice Zen can remember the first time we picked up a book about Zen that really made sense to us: it was like a ray of sunshine had broken through all the clouds and illuminated our life. Alternatively, your first real encounter with Zen may feel like a breath of fresh air, or finding a life boat when you're stranded in the middle of the ocean.

Zen gives you practical instructions for how to engage your life in a way that results in a sense of meaning, relief from stress and suffering, more freedom, and confidence that you have the tools you need to deal with whatever comes. I love to think that this book will end up in the hands of someone who will find in it the ray of light they needed in their life. Perhaps that someone is you.

How This Book Is Organized

This book is divided into five parts, each dealing with a different aspect of Zen.

Part 1, Getting Started with Zen, explains what Zen is, how it relates to Buddhism, and what benefits you can get from practicing it. This part walks you step by step through finding out more about Zen, trying out the most basic and essential Zen methods (meditation and mindfulness), and visiting a Zen group if that's what interests you. There's also a chapter in this section about how to establish and maintain a Zen practice of your own, in case you want to get started right away or want to know ahead of time what it might look like.

Part 2, Zen Tools, gives you detailed instructions for how to use the important Zen methods for building awareness and understanding. These include zazen (meditation), mindfulness, moral precepts, working with habits, cultivating insight, and the various things that Zen practitioners do together, like meditation retreats and chanting. Armed with what you learn in this part, you can get to work on your life.

Part 3, Essential Zen Teachings, explains in down-to-earth language the most important Zen and Buddhist teachings for you to know, including the Four Noble Truths, no-self, emptiness, and enlightenment. Don't worry if you don't completely understand them right away! Zen teachings are meant to give you questions to explore and contemplate in your life.

Part 4, The Zen Path, describes how you use Zen tools and teachings to transform your life. This includes how you identify and let go of attachments, gain insight into the true nature of self, and learn to face the truth of your life. The whole idea is that the truth sets you free.

Part 5, Living Zen, helps you see how Zen practice functions in your relationships, work, and daily life. This part includes advice on how to find opportunities for practice in your everyday activities, how to use Zen practice to face challenges, and how to make the most out of your life the Zen way.

At the end of the book, you'll find a glossary and a list of resources that includes books and websites.

Zen Supplements and Tidbits

Throughout the chapters of this book, you will find four types of additional information, set apart in sidebars, to help you better understand the information in the chapter, or to enrich your learning process:

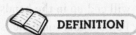

DEFINITION

Specialized Zen terms will be italicized in the main part of the chapter text and defined in a definition sidebar.

CONSIDER THIS

These sidebars offer supplemental information, or present a Zen idea or practice for you to consider in the context of the chapter you are reading.

POTENTIAL PITFALL

When there's something discussed in the text that you might misunderstand, or some typical trap you might want to avoid, it will be presented in one of these sidebars.

ZEN WISDOM

> Quotes from Zen teachers and practitioners are offered in these sidebars, to enrich your reading experience, give you different perspectives, and point you toward other books you might want to read.

Acknowledgments

My first thanks must be extended to my Zen ordination and transmission teacher, Gyokuko Carlson Roshi, who may have sacrificed years off her life span to train me. I hope that I demonstrate enough understanding and generosity in this life to make her sacrifice worth it. Thanks also to my other Zen teacher, Kyogen Carlson Roshi, for helping me understand Zen and for giving me respect for a wide variety of viewpoints and ways of practice.

Thanks also to the Bright Way Zen sangha, for their unwavering support of my writing this book, even though it meant I neglected some of my priestly duties while doing it. They are a source of deep inspiration and learning for me. Special thanks to Bright Way Zen member Lorna Simons, who volunteered her time to edit every page with her eagle eye before I submitted it. Special thanks also to member Cindy Rinchin McKinley, whose calm wisdom about the relationship between Zen practice and mental health care informed my chapter on this subject, and member Mary Fushin Payne, whose cheerful and generous teachings on practicing with intense and chronic pain informed my chapter on Zen when life is tough.

Gratitude must also go, of course, to my parents. They generously supported and encouraged my education from the beginning. The thousands of hours of writing I had to do over the course of all that schooling have paid off in this book.

Thanks of course to my husband John. His companionship, honest feedback, and generous support make all of my work possible. Finally, gratitude to Bob Orman. He insisted that I write, inspiring me to put aside the excuse that I was too busy to do so. His encouragement led directly to this book.

Trademarks

All terms mentioned in this book that are known to be or are suspected of being trademarks or service marks have been appropriately capitalized. Alpha Books and Penguin Group (USA) Inc. cannot attest to the accuracy of this information. Use of a term in this book should not be regarded as affecting the validity of any trademark or service mark.

Getting Started with Zen

If you only read one part of this book, read this part. Here I give you just enough details about Zen as a tradition to put it into context, but also try to give you a good sense of the *spirit* of Zen. I also offer some reasons why you might want to make it a part of your life.

You'll also find instructions for doing just that: how to find out more about Zen when you're done with this book, how to make sense out of Zen teachers and groups, how to meditate, and how to start a mindfulness practice. There's also some encouragement to go ahead and try Zen for yourself, because you don't need to worry about not doing it right. In Zen, it's considered ideal to approach everything with "beginner's mind," or the open, attentive attitude you have when you know you don't have it all figured out (because none of us actually do).

Part 1 also includes instructions for how to develop a Zen practice of your own, in case you want to get started right away. Even if you don't, these instructions can give you a picture of what ongoing Zen living looks like.

1

Getting Started with Zen

Introducing Zen

These days, when I tell someone I'm a Zen Buddhist, the response is usually, "Cool." People don't necessarily understand exactly what it means to be a Zen Buddhist, but they know there's a certain level of respect for Zen in Western culture.

Over the last 50 years, Zen has become well established in the West. There's a Zen Center in most major cities in the United States, most bookstores have a Zen section, and thousands of Americans and Europeans identify themselves as Zen practitioners. Still, if you ask most people—even Zen practitioners—what Zen is, they'll find it difficult to give you a simple answer. That's at least in part because it's the nature of Zen to be difficult to define, but this chapter will give you a basic understanding of what Zen is and why some people are so enthusiastic about it.

In This Chapter

- What is Zen, anyway?
- Zen as a method to master the art of your life
- Can you just have a Zen philosophy?
- How does Zen relate to Buddhism?
- Reasons you might want to practice Zen

Zen Is the Art of Living

Zen is not concerned with the afterlife, or whether or not there is one. It is not concerned with fulfilling obligations to a God, or whether or not there is a God. No matter what you believe, Zen is a method you can use to make the most of your life: noticing it, appreciating it, understanding it, learning how to cause happiness instead of misery, and hopefully even becoming a master in the art of living it fully.

You've ended up with a human life—why not master the use of your own mind and body as you might master any skill or art, so you can maintain your dignity while being ready for anything that happens in your life?

Life Is a Great Opportunity

It may not always feel like it, but your life is precious. Viewed without any expectations whatso-ever, your heartbeat is miraculous and lifting your teacup to your lips is an amazing experience. Small children know this. So do people near the end of a terminal illness. To someone with only two weeks to live, even an argument or waiting at a red light are experiences to be relished. So what about the time in between childhood and the end of life? Why does life so often seem monotonous, frustrating, vaguely disappointing, or downright painful?

According to Buddhism, the way you experience life depends largely on your views about the world. These views include the way you see your relationship to things and people, what happiness is and how to achieve it, and the apparent permanence of your existence.

As you grow up you accumulate lots of views, and this is only natural. You have things you want to get done, and you need to navigate a complex world; your views help you generalize, predict, and make sense of things. However, many of your views are outdated, limited, and down-right erroneous. Because of your views, you experience life through many filters rather than in the direct, appreciative way of someone with no expectations or agendas. The goal of Zen is to awaken to life as it is, rather than stay in the comparative dream world of our ideas about it.

Yet Zen is not about returning to the point of view of a child. Buddhist teaching says that it is a rare and precious opportunity to be born a human being precisely because, as a human being, you have such a capacity for messing things up in your head. That capacity can also be used for refining your understanding and coming around to a much fuller appreciation of reality than a child is capable of.

The metaphor of Genesis from the Bible is quite apt here: when the descendants of Adam and Eve turn toward God, it is a much more profound devotion than that of Adam and Eve before they lost their innocence. When you have lost touch with the preciousness of life and then found your way back to it, your appreciation becomes more conscious and mature.

ZEN WISDOM

"Therefore, your living body is a fortunate, rare, and precious gift, and your human mind—consciousness risen to the point where there can be identity and value and thought and beauty and autonomous choice—is dear beyond compare ... how is it that up to now you haven't thought about the best and highest way of fulfilling your human purpose, you haven't resolved to go beyond your self-centeredness and self-concern so that you can begin to manifest wisdom and compassion—or whatever you consider to be the highest of human purposes? Considering deeply the preciousness of human life, you feel inspired to begin to do something more with your life."

—Zen Teacher Norman Fischer, from *Training in Compassion: Zen Teachings on the Practice of Lojong*

It's Like Learning to Drive

Somehow we think that by the time we turn 18, or 21, or 30, or *at least* 45, we should know how to live this human life. However, learning to live well is a bit like learning to drive—except that the human body and mind make up the most complex machine in the world, that daily negotiates a multidimensional, ever-changing environment.

Imagine you're sitting behind the wheel of a car for the first time. You have no idea what all the levers and buttons and pedals are for. Maybe someone explains these things to you, but the first time you turn the key and put the car into the gear it's exciting and somewhat terrifying. Everything is awkward and requires care and planning. Even when you perform all the steps correctly, the car's movements are jerky and inelegant.

Once you've mastered the art of driving a car, there seems to be little separation between you and the car. You've learned how to navigate the road safely and efficiently, and your intentions are translated smoothly into the behavior of the vehicle. Because driving has become a natural activity for you, you can merge onto a highway, turn on your windshield wipers, and carry on a conversation all at the same time.

It takes much longer to master the art of living than it takes to master the art of driving. In fact, the art of living is so complex and nuanced that mastering it takes a lifetime—and even then you won't have reached perfection. A car has one function, while a human being has infinite ways to function. Cars are standardized, while each human being is unique and changes throughout his or her lifetime.

> **CONSIDER THIS**
>
> Deciding to master the art of your life isn't about comparing yourself to others, or
> identifying your current life as inadequate. It's about acknowledging your vast po-
> tential. You can see clearly how much an apprentice or journeyman has yet to learn
> compared to the master craftsman, but you don't look down on them just because
> they're still learning. Instead, you respect their effort.

In essence, Zen is the art of living. All the teachings and practices of Zen are aimed at helping
you live more wisely, more compassionately, and more fully. A Zen master has become adept at
simply living her life, but she is not so much a master of her life as she is a master of the art of
Zen study and practice.

Zen makes no claim to have an exclusive handle on all the wisdom and practices that help you
live a better life; in fact you will find similar teachings and methods in all the major religions
and in any program, such as Alcoholics Anonymous, that aims to help people benefit themselves.
What is unique about Zen is its singular focus on the art of living, in combination with its incredibly comprehensive approach.

Discovering Your Own Answers

No one can tell you how best to live your life. Be they a Zen master, your mother, or your therapist, others can only tell you what has worked well for them or what they've observed working
well for others. Your genetics, upbringing, experiences, personality, aspirations, and circumstances contribute to your being an incredibly complex person; no one but you knows what it's
like to be you, no one knows what will work best for you, and no one except you can ultimately
change your mind or behavior. Even if you found a perfect guru to prescribe teachings and
actions for you, you would still have to enact them yourself.

In its purest form, Zen does not give you answers. Instead, it gives you means to find answers. It
gives you tools for settling your mind so you can see more clearly, practices for working toward
goals of your own choosing, and teachings to help you raise the most important questions within
your own mind.

Of course, the Zen tradition has been maintained over the centuries by human beings, and
human beings love to tell one another how it is. Don't be surprised if during your exploration
of Zen you run into some advice or some statements about the way the universe functions. Just
remember this is not the essence of Zen; it's just more food for thought.

Dignified and Ready

So here's some food for thought: when you experience your life directly, without the filters of your views—the goal of Zen practice—you are at your best. You are dignified and as ready as you can be for whatever arises the next moment.

The dignity you experience when you are living the Zen way involves being self-sufficient, centered, and fearless. You are self-sufficient because you understand the impermanent nature of the self and are no longer casting about for things to make you feel substantial or safe. You are simply awareness meeting flow, and that's enough. You are centered because you know the answers can't come from anywhere else but right where you are. You are fearless because fear is based on a worry that an enduring self-nature might come under threat in the future, and while you are facing the future, you know only the present exists.

 CONSIDER THIS

Japanese samurai warriors practiced Zen in order to remain fearless, centered, and effective in the midst of battle. Whatever you think of a samurai's goals, this argues for the potential of Zen practice to result in increased self-possession and readiness.

Living the Zen way means you're as ready as you can possibly be because, as described above, you're not grasping, worrying, or anticipating. This leaves you open and aware. When you aren't trying to guess what's going to happen next, you don't constrain your possible responses. Anticipation causes tenseness and just slows you down. If you remain dignified, all you've learned and practiced previously is accessible to you in an instant, without your having to worry about it.

The Zen Tradition

The Zen tradition is over a thousand years old and is rich in history, literature, stories, art, and practices. If you're interested, you could spend your life studying it. However, you don't have to learn much about Zen as a tradition in order to start making it a part of your life. Here I'll just try to give Zen some context—particularly what Zen means, how it came to be, how it relates to Buddhism, and how you can engage with it.

The word *Zen* originally just meant meditation. In India the word for meditation was *dhyana*, in China the word was *chan*, and in Japan the word was *zen*. Over time Zen has come to refer to a number of things:

- Meditation itself

- The school (or sect) of Buddhism that uses meditation as its primary method, or Zen Buddhism

- An adjective describing a spare, clean, elegant, and/or nature-based aesthetic
- An adjective describing the mind-state or approach to life that is supposed to be the result of meditation or Zen practice

People generally don't use the word Zen to refer to meditation itself anymore, so I'll work on the other meanings of the term.

Zen Buddhism arose in China in the sixth and seventh centuries, when various Buddhist sects were starting to differentiate themselves from one another. At the time there were many different types of study and practice presented by Buddhists as a means of cultivating insight and attaining enlightenment. These included reading and reciting certain scriptures, devotional practices, and esoteric rituals. The Zen folks believed that simple meditation was the most effective and authentic method of Buddhist practice. They cited not only the results of their own meditation, but the scriptures that described the original Buddhist, Siddhartha Gautama, attaining his insight and liberation through meditation.

Probably the most widespread use of the word "Zen" in popular culture is as an adjective referring to a particular aesthetic. Furniture, clothing, and perfumes are labeled and sold as "Zen." This largely reflects the historical association of Zen with Japanese culture. Many aspects of the Japanese aesthetic have evolved to favor simplicity, clean lines, and minimal adornment. While it's true that some of this aesthetic is due to Zen's influence, it's still quintessentially Japanese. Zen's influence on other cultures, including Korean, Chinese, and Western cultures, has yielded different results. As usual, the reality is much more varied than the popular conceptions, so beware of equating Zen with things like rock gardens or a lack of clutter.

What about *Zen* as a description of the supposed results of meditation, such as an imperturbable state of mind, a quiet wisdom, self-restraint, or non-attachment? This use of the term reflects some of the ideals and goals of Zen practice. However, only a handful of the ideals and goals of Zen practice have made it into the popular culture, and many of those are misunderstood. For example, people often equate non-attachment with the aloofness of dissociation, but this is not the Zen ideal at all. This book will help clarify and expand your idea about what is *Zen*.

 POTENTIAL PITFALL

It's important to make a distinction between ideals and people. Just as a good Christian aspires to be Christ-like but would never claim to have fully achieved that goal, a Zen practitioner aspires to Zen ideals but doesn't necessarily make any claim about always manifesting them.

How Zen Relates to Buddhism

If you're not already a Zen Buddhist, you're probably wondering, "Do I have to be Buddhist to practice or appreciate Zen?" The answer is debatable. It's impossible to clearly separate Zen and Buddhism; Zen developed as a form of Buddhism, and many core Zen practices and teachings are pre-Zen Buddhist in origin. At the same time there are many Buddhist practices, teachings, rituals, and so on that are not essential to Zen practice.

If you're hoping for a simple explanation of how Zen relates to Buddhism, you're likely to be disappointed. In comparison to the Abrahamic faiths with their one God and their authoritative texts, Buddhism can seem like a many-headed, many-legged beast. It's not just that there are different sects of Buddhism, it's also that there is no deity guiding its practice, no authoritative text held commonly amongst all Buddhists, and no restraints put on the proliferation of its teachings and practices except this: does the teaching or practice reduce suffering?

Basically, the only thing all Buddhists have in common is the goal of attaining liberation from delusion and suffering. Buddhist masters of every generation are actually encouraged to interpret and adapt teachings and practices to fit their audiences. Most Buddhists acknowledge that there are many different methods for attaining liberation, and which one you choose is your own concern.

In a sense, then, Zen is just a method to use to attain the Buddhist goal of liberation, a goal that is set out in the Buddhist mythology describing the spiritual journey of Siddhartha Gautama. In brief, Siddhartha lived the first part of his life in the lap of luxury but was still troubled by the prospect of unavoidable suffering in the form of disease, old age, and death. He subsequently spent six years doing ascetic spiritual practice in the Indian style of the time, but did not come to the peace or understanding he longed for.

Finally he settled on the middle way between indulgence and asceticism and decided to sit in a calm, balanced meditative state until he resolved the problem of human suffering. The way the story goes, he *did* resolve the problem—by realizing in what sense human beings create their own suffering, and how they can stop doing it.

After his realization (which is much more complicated than what is described here), Siddhartha was called a *Buddha*, which simply means "awakened one." The idea is that he woke up to the truth. It doesn't matter so much, here, exactly how early Buddhists described that truth, or whether the truth you might be trying to wake up to is Buddhist.

I'll go more into Buddhist teachings that are relevant to Zen practice later. The important thing is that a Buddha is liberated by *truth*, and all Buddhists subsequent to Siddhartha have striven to either wake up to truth themselves, support those who are trying to wake up, or in some way demonstrate their devotion to the Truth Which Liberates (even if they don't expect to attain it).

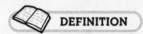 **DEFINITION**

> **Buddha**, literally "one who is awakened," means a person who has completely woken up to the truth and dispelled all of his or her delusions. Whether there has ever been a human being who is a complete Buddha is a matter of debate, although many Buddhists believe there was at least one: Shakyamuni Buddha, originally Siddhartha Gautama, who lived over 2,500 years ago.

When you distill Buddhism down to its basics, it doesn't make a lot of sense to divorce it from Zen. However, in true Buddhist style, Zen has reinterpreted, rephrased, and even built on pre-Zen Buddhism, so unless you want to you don't need to go back to the pre-Zen stuff. Other Zen teachers may differ with me here, but I think that would be less of a comment on the inadequacy of Zen in and of itself and more a comment on the richness of the Buddhist tradition as a whole: why not avail yourself of it?

Still, if aspects of the Buddhist tradition turn you off (mythology, supernatural imagery, teachings on reincarnation, and so on), please disregard what doesn't ring true to you and concentrate on what does. This is entirely consistent with Buddhist teaching; before his death, Shakyamuni Buddha's last admonitions to his students were that they should rely on their own conviction about what is true, rather than on what someone else tells them is true.

Practice Versus Philosophy

Many people ask whether they can just have Zen as a philosophy. The answer, of course, is, "Sure! Use Zen in whatever way is beneficial to you and others." However, if you're thinking you'd like to stick to Zen-as-philosophy, you might want to ask yourself why. Is it because you don't want to make any changes in your life? That's fine, of course. But if you *do* want to make changes but you're just wary of having to join a group or be told what to think or do, consider identifying with Zen as *practice*.

All it means to have a Zen practice (as opposed to just having a Zen philosophy) is that you *do* things in order to get yourself to think and act more in accord with your own Zen ideals. Zen philosophy alone can mean you just try to think about things in a Zen way. This might actually change how you act, which is great. If you're like most people, though, just knowing "you should let it go" or "there's really no separation between self and other" doesn't help all that much. Knowing or believing something intellectually can be very, very different from actually being able to enact what you know.

Zen practice is simply employing tools and methods to slowly but surely change your mind and behavior. You get to pick the goals and the tools, so in essence it is just as independent as a personal philosophy. However, you can get some good ideas about how to best use Zen tools and methods from other people, and you can get together with people to use them. You don't generally "have a philosophy" with anyone else, so a Zen practice can be richer in this aspect, too, if you're so inclined.

Dispelling Some Myths About Zen

I don't know what your ideas about Zen are; maybe you don't even have any. However, I know what mine were before (and after) starting Zen practice, and what kinds of Zen or Buddhist images are presented in popular Western culture. For me the stereotype of the Zen master looked like this: male, the strong silent type, in control of himself, aware of his superiority and strength relative to others, and above simple human desires like those for comfort, affection, pleasure, and social contact. This stereotyped Zen master could also do kung fu, of course.

Thankfully this stereotype is untrue, or lots of us would be out of luck when it comes to trying to practice Zen. In reality, there's no ideal Zen person! The goal of Zen is to become more fully and completely ourselves, whether we're male or female, strong or weak, silent or talkative, aloof or thoroughly engaged in all kinds of human activities. What people often do, despite this, is set up some ideal that is usually not what they are, but rather what they think they should be.

 POTENTIAL PITFALL

What kinds of changes would you like to make in your life? How many of those changes would truly result in more happiness for yourself and others, and how many of them are about ideals you've gotten from outside—from parents, friends, or popular culture? Zen asks you to examine your goals carefully; some of them you just might want to drop!

Zen practice can indeed give you more strength and help you keep your mouth closed when it would be better not to say anything. Zen can help you find a reliable and accessible source of peace and joy that's not dependent on your access to things like food, alcohol, or the company of others. The thing is, if you achieve some of these things, you'll probably end up being surprised by how these changes look in your life and by how much of your resistance to change was due to a misunderstanding about what change really entailed. For example, you don't become less dependent on others by breaking free of the natural human need for intimacy; you become less dependent on others by recognizing that nothing separates you from intimacy except your own mind.

What Zen Practice Has to Offer

You won't hear many Zen teachers talking at length about the great things you can get out of Zen, or what Zen can help you achieve. This isn't because Zen practice doesn't have benefits, it's because thinking about the benefits causes problems in your practice. As long as you're thinking about what's (hopefully) going to happen in the future, you can't be fully present with what's happening now. (At least, not as completely present as Zen practice requires.) As long as you're hoping to become different, you can't clearly see and accept yourself as you are, which is a Zen prerequisite for lasting change. Still, diligent Zen practice is likely—although never guaranteed—to have some super benefits, and some of them are described here.

Waking Up to Your Life

How many times have you arrived somewhere, usually somewhere you go all the time, and realized you can't remember anything about the drive there? Have you ever been listening to someone talking and suddenly realized you haven't heard what they've been saying for the last couple of minutes?

It's very easy to spend a majority of your time "up in your head"—worrying, planning, judging, analyzing, fantasizing—rather than being present in your body. You can miss, or be only partially aware of, what's actually going on around you. Hurrying to get to the next thing, you're likely to be oblivious to the pleasant sensation of warm dishwater on your hands, or your spouse's subtle gesture of apology. Not only do you miss out on experiences as your limited time on Earth ticks inexorably by, you aren't functioning at your best when it comes to responding to people and situations.

The Zen practices of *zazen* and mindfulness first increase your awareness of your own mind states, and then build up your attention "muscles" so you choose what you want to pay attention to. The awareness of your mind states has to come first, because you can't make the choice to be present if you aren't even aware your mind is wandering. Then you practice over and over bringing your mind back to the object of your attention, whether it's just sitting, your breath, the sensations in your hands, or a conversation. Eventually, if you really do the practice, you get better at it.

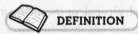 **DEFINITION**

> **Zazen**, literally "seated (*za*) meditation (*zen*)," is a silent, introspective form of meditation that is the central practice of Zen.

All this paying attention to what's actually going on results in another kind of waking up to your life: you wake up to—and are therefore able to appreciate and take care of—the specifics of your life. This includes the subtle dynamics of your relationships, your limitations, and your deep aspirations. You can get used to saying, "Wow, I never realized before …."

Less Controlled by Emotions

Unfortunately, many people think Zen is about gaining control over your emotions, or even about attaining some state of mind where you don't feel your emotions as intensely. This way of thinking about Zen makes the practice attractive to some. To others, who value the emotional aspects of their lives, it can make Zen practice seem problematic or even repellant. Fortunately, Zen practice is not about deadening your emotions or even gaining control over them. Instead, it's about increasing your awareness of your emotions, accepting them, and learning a new way to relate to them.

It's typical to believe emotions are legitimate reactions to, or feelings about, beings or situations that have an inherent, enduring reality. You feel anxiety; therefore, there's something to be anxious about. You feel as if you will never be complete without a particular person as your mate; therefore, you must obtain said mate or face a lifetime of despair. When you interpret emotions this way, they become imperatives you would be foolish not to take seriously and act on. In reality, emotions are simply a response arising within you to your *perceptions*. Sometimes your perceptions are fairly accurate, sometimes they are not; and they always apply to a fluid and dynamic reality.

By watching your emotions carefully over time, you can see how they arise and fall—they don't last forever, even if conditions don't change. You also see how sometimes they give you valuable information and sometimes they do not. Some emotional reactions are based on faulty perceptions, false assumptions, unfounded fears, or simple conditioning. When you act based on this kind of emotional reaction, you usually cause problems for yourself and others. When you gain some perspective on your emotions, you're less controlled by them and have more freedom in the way you choose to respond to things.

Stress Relief

There are physiological aspects to the way practices like Zen meditation and mindfulness can relieve stress. The very act of turning the awareness toward bodily sensations changes the functioning of the mind and body. Physical, mental, and emotional changes are caused by the simple act of paying attention to exactly what's going on in front of you without analysis or judgment.

It may be that human beings are too smart for their own good, and spend too much time and energy thinking about events in the past that they can do nothing about—or anticipating an infinite number of possible future events, most of which will never happen. It's natural to want to feel safe and in control—and the only thing you can actually control is yourself, right here, right now. By practicing the ability to return your awareness to the present, you become able to center yourself in a much more manageable field of operation (here and now) at any time, no matter what's going on around you.

CONSIDER THIS

In 1979, Jon Kabat-Zinn created a secular program based on Buddhist practice called Mindfulness Based Stress Reduction (MBSR). The program is used widely in medical and professional settings all over the world, and over 30 years of research has shown profound positive effects for people with chronic pain, anxiety, depression, stress, and a number of other serious challenges.

Whatever techniques you use, however, you can't bear an infinite amount of stress. Stress is pressure, whether it arises from deadlines, expectations, debts, illness, loss, or ambition. Too much pressure and something's going to give. The good thing is, other Zen practices can help you cultivate acceptance, patience, and compassion for your own limitations, so if you succumb to stress you can give yourself a break. And a break might be just what you need.

Greater Authenticity

Who are you, really? If you think you know the answer to that question, how many people regularly get to see and interact with that person you really are?

The irony of the questions above is that there is no fixed, "real" you, and understanding the truth of this is a key to greater authenticity. You think, act, and express yourself differently in different situations, at different times, depending on your surroundings and the people you are with. This doesn't make you flaky or characterless; it makes you alive and responsive. What we're looking for in Zen is not the authentic person (a thing) but the authentic *response*. You're responding to the world constantly, and the flavor and skillfulness of your responses is what makes you *you*.

POTENTIAL PITFALL

Sometimes when people are aiming for greater authenticity, they think it involves saying whatever they "really" want to say, or doing what *they* want to do as opposed to what others want them to do. There's a time and a place for these approaches, but authentic does not mean self-centered. Being authentic to your deeper self includes sensitivity to others, generosity, and the willingness to put off short-term gratification for longer-term benefits to yourself and others.

A fixed idea about the person you are only constrains and impedes your authentic responsiveness. You work on greater authenticity in your responses by gradually deconstructing your ideas about yourself and about life, including your fears, the opinions you hold that you know are absolutely right, and the behaviors you know are absolutely the best or only way. You don't deconstruct these ideas in order to destroy them, you deconstruct them in order to understand them better. Maybe you reconstruct and keep them, maybe you don't. If you keep certain ideas or behaviors around, you relate to them in a new way. You know they aren't *true*, and they aren't the essence of who you are.

And what is the essence of who you are? No essence, only living function. You know an authentic response when you give one; it arises without a lot of worry or forethought, and afterward you can rest in knowing you've done your best. It feels clean and wholehearted, even if its effects aren't exactly what you'd hoped for.

Being a Nicer Person

There's a Zen chant that begins, "Beings are numberless, I vow to save them all." And what are you saving all beings from? A Zen teacher I have studied with, Jan Chozen Bays, answers that question like this: you are trying to save all beings from *you*. As mentioned earlier, the only thing you really have any control over is yourself (and even that control is limited). You can significantly help the world by sparing it your anger, judgment, self-centeredness, rudeness, and insensitivity, to name just a few things.

Just intending to be a nicer person is usually not enough. Ideals and "shoulds" are easy to come by and take you part of the way, but whatever your aspirations, you probably find yourself not quite able to be as kind, generous, or patient as you'd like to be. That's why Zen approaches this from a different angle than most religions, practices, or self-help programs: Zen starts with the premise that in your heart of hearts you really are compassionate, and it's misunderstandings and habits that get in the way of you manifesting that compassion. Therefore, if you work on clarity and unraveling some of those habits, you'll naturally end up a nicer person.

According to Zen, the fundamental misunderstanding, the one that's at the root of most of your problems, is about the nature of your self. At some level you think you have an inherent, enduring self-essence. Because you believe that, you have a deadly serious mission to protect that self-essence and watch out for its best interests. This leads to all kinds of self-absorption and selfishness, even when you're trying to have a self that's really nice to others.

If you personally see how this inherent, enduring self-essence is an illusion, you recognize that your "self" is actually an amazing phenomenon of dynamic interaction and change. This kind of self is better taken care of by dancing with life than maintaining boundaries against it. No self-essence you can protect? Suddenly the world is full of beings just like you and not separate from you; what benefits them benefits you. Just like that, you're inclined to be a nicer person.

Satisfaction and Gratitude

Try this premise on for size: any dissatisfaction you feel about life is due entirely to your expectations that life should be a particular way.

When you consider this premise, chances are you can think of some of your expectations about life that are either entirely reasonable or, even better, righteous. How can you help hoping life will be relatively free of mean people, disappointment, illness, trauma, or loss? What's wrong with expecting life to be free of incredible pain, injustice, prejudice, war, or environmental degradation? Fortunately, dissatisfaction is not caused by simply acknowledging that we prefer happiness over suffering, or by the sincere desire to make the world a better place.

Dissatisfaction *is* caused by carrying a subtle but pervasive expectation that life should conform to your preferences and ideals. It's one thing to hope you don't get sick; it's another to feel like you've made some kind of deal with life so when you get sick anyway you feel somehow betrayed. Why you? What did you do to deserve this? Now you've entered dissatisfaction territory.

It's one thing to work tirelessly for justice in the world, but it's another to resent the injustice you encounter just for being there. "This just *shouldn't be,*" you think. Internally you strain against the injustice's very existence, rather than acknowledging that, yes indeed, there it is (and then doing your best to end it). With internal straining against what is, dissatisfaction arises (and probably burn-out, too).

It may sound bleak to live life without any expectations, but it's not. When you give up your insistence that life be anything other than what it is, it ironically frees up a lot of energy that you can put to use on improving life. It also results in a satisfaction with your life just as it is; challenges become part of an ongoing dance that lets you stretch, learn, and improve your skills.

In place of a laundry list of complaints about life, you now have a sense of gratitude. If you don't expect to get a bigger house, you can appreciate the one you have. If you don't expect to have an exciting social life, you can be grateful for the opportunity to sit and sip your tea. When you know life doesn't owe you anything, you are naturally grateful for what you have.

Of course, dropping—or even recognizing—your expectations is not at all easy. In Zen practice you cultivate the ability to do this by carefully examining your mind moment after moment, day after day, year after year. You start to notice the space between thoughts, and eventually develop the ability to use that space in order to make a different choice. Rather than embrace one of your expectations, it occurs to you to enter the next moment without it. Lo and behold—life looks better!

The Least You Need to Know

- You can always get better at living your life fully, wisely, and compassionately.
- Zen is a method for finding your own answers.
- Zen can be beneficial whether you practice Zen Buddhism, practice Zen without Buddhism, or just have a Zen philosophy.
- If you practice Zen, you'll change—but maybe not in the ways you expect.
- Zen practice can have many positive effects on you, but it will take some hard work.

Trying Out Zen Practice

Beyond reading this book—a good start—what can you do if you want to explore Zen further, or actually try out some Zen practices? If you didn't grow up Buddhist—or even if you did—it can be daunting to start your investigation into this activity you know next to nothing about. How can you know which sources or authorities to trust? How do people usually go about this?

This chapter will suggest some books and other resources for learning more, and give you some tips on how to discriminate amongst the many Zen or Buddhist websites, organizations, writers, and teachers you will encounter in your explorations. This chapter will also walk you through the first steps of trying out meditation, mindfulness, and Zen practice with others.

In This Chapter

* First steps to take if you want to explore Zen

* How to find resources for Zen study and practice

* Encouragement for giving Zen a try

* What you can expect the first time you meditate, practice mindfulness, or visit a Zen group

* Some tips for absolute beginners

Finding Out How to Do Zen

Only a few decades ago you would have had a hard time finding out much about Zen, and your options would have been limited in terms of authors, teachers, and approaches to the practice. Nowadays you might feel overwhelmed by all the possible directions you could go in your investigation of how to do Zen. This section can help guide your investigation with a brief explanation of the different types of Zen practiced and taught in the West, some recommended resources, and some tips on how to make wise decisions about which Zen teachings or teachers you want to engage with more deeply.

A Brief Overview of Zen in the West

Zen and other forms of Buddhism came to the West with the first Asian immigrants, but it wasn't until the mid-twentieth century that westerners from other religious backgrounds started studying and practicing Zen in substantial numbers. Around that time a number of Zen teachers arrived in the West to found practice centers and *lineages* that still persist. A thorough history of how Buddhism arrived and developed in the West can be found in Rick Fields' *How the Swans Came to the Lake: A Narrative History of Buddhism in America.*

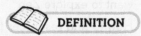 **DEFINITION**

Lineage refers to the transmission of Zen teachings and practices from teacher to student over time. Lineage is emphasized in Zen because of the idea that true understanding and manifestation of Zen can only be recognized by a person who has attained them herself; the teacher recognizes the student's attainment and empowers her to carry on the tradition.

Now, for the first time in history, all the different kinds of Buddhism and Zen that have developed across the world can be found in the same place at the same time: in the West, particularly in the United States and Europe. This can be a little mind-boggling at first, but it helps if you realize there are at least as many different kinds of Buddhism as there are different kinds of Christianity, and they differ just as much in flavor and emphasis.

In terms of Zen, in the West the major lineages are Soto and Rinzai through Japan, Seon through Korea, Ch'an through China, and Vietnamese Zen primarily through the teacher Thich Nhat Hanh. You'll find many books written by authors in these various lineages that can give you a sense of what kind(s) of Zen you resonate with most. Major cities will often have practice groups representative of all of these different types of Zen.

Many of the major practice centers and lineages in the West identify as either Rinzai or Soto Zen. These types of Zen first arose as distinct schools in China in the ninth and tenth centuries. The Rinzai school tends to emphasize dramatic awakenings to the true nature of reality and employs traditional teaching stories, or *koans*, to facilitate such awakening. The Soto school emphasizes that there is nothing separate from your experience to awaken to, and eschews koans in favor of a themeless, goalless approach to meditation.

Although a given lineage may technically be Soto or Rinzai, in reality there has been a great deal of cross-pollination between the two schools over the centuries. In addition, few lineages take a purely Rinzai or purely Soto approach to practice, because each approach actually complements and balances out the other. Still, Rinzai versus Soto has a strong effect on the flavor of the teachings and practice center, so if you've tried one and it didn't fit, you might want to try the other.

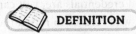 **DEFINITION**

> **Koans** are teachings to contemplate and engage intensively until one reaches a deep personal understanding of them. Formal koans are usually stories of historical interactions between teacher and student, and present an essential, nonintellectual teaching. Informal koans are challenges that arise in life and practice that require you to *live* out the answer; it's not enough to just have an idea about what the answer is.

A Few Recommended Resources

People who want to learn more about Zen often ask, "Where do I start?" It depends on what you're interested in, but I usually recommend starting with Shunryu Suzuki's *Zen Mind, Beginner's Mind* or Charlotte Joko Beck's *Everyday Zen*. These books give you a good taste of what day-to-day Zen practice is like. They're very down-to-earth, perhaps even too much so for some tastes, but it's better to get a sense early on of how Zen is just about *your* everyday life. Other classics include Thich Nhat Hanh's *The Miracle of Mindfulness*, Robert Aitken's *Taking the Path of Zen*, Master Seung Sahn's *Only Don't Know*, and Philip Kapleau's *The Three Pillars of Zen*.

If you're interested in primary sources, check out the writings of Zen Master Rinzai (or Linji in Chinese), father of the Rinzai school. Burton Watson has translated a book of his teachings titled *The Zen Teachings of Master Lin-Chi*. For the Soto school, read some of the writings of Zen Master Dogen; a good place to start is the collection translated and edited by Kaz Tanahashi titled *Moon in a Dewdrop*. One of the ancient classics common to both Rinzai and Soto is the Sutra of Hui Neng (see the translation by A. F. Price and Wong Mou-lam titled *The Diamond Sutra and The Sutra of Hui Neng*).

There's a valuable website where you can learn more about the goings-on in contemporary Zen: www.sweepingzen.com. Sweeping Zen includes a directory of Zen teachers with bios, and a directory of Zen practice places and groups. On the website you can also find news, reviews of new books, and blogs by Zen teachers. Another website you may find interesting is www.accesstoinsight.org. This is a great introduction to the Pali Canon, a pre-Zen collection of the oldest Buddhist teachings.

Author/Teacher Credentials

As you explore Zen, it's important to consider someone's Zen credentials when you're reading something they wrote, listening to one of their talks, or interacting with them in a practice center. While anyone can practice Zen, and ultimately it's about becoming more fully who you are, there are established ways within the tradition to rigorously train and study.

There are also established ways to acknowledge a person's mastery of Zen methods and their fitness to teach them. Examining Zen credentials is no different from investigating the education and credentials of your doctor, therapist, or any other professional to whom you're planning to entrust part of your life. Once you know what someone's training and credentials are, you can make your own decisions—but you might be extra wary of someone who refuses to reveal them to you.

CONSIDER THIS

Regarding teachers, you will inevitably fall somewhere on the spectrum between a devotee looking for a master to guide them, and a ruggedly independent skeptic who won't listen to anyone. As long as you're aware of your attitude, you're welcome to think what you like about teachers. However, the most constructive place is in the middle—taking responsibility for yourself, but willing to hear and try new things.

Documentation of training and teacher certification varies among the different types of Zen, but here are some things to consider no matter what Zen lineage someone is from:

How long have they been practicing Zen? Great respect is given to sheer time spent in practice. Look for 10 or 15 years of practice; many good teachers have practiced for 20 years or more. This isn't to say, of course, that you can't learn something valuable from someone who has only been practicing a little longer than you have, or even from a peer. It's just that the longer someone has been practicing, the more insight they tend to have about Zen as a *practice*—as opposed to personal insights they've developed on their own.

How and where have they practiced? Lay practice—where someone practices Zen in their daily life, without becoming a priest or monk, or spending time in a monastery—is entirely valid and respected in Zen. However, one person's year of lay practice might be much more intensive than another's. Indications of practice intensity can be gotten from time spent in intensive meditation retreats, living in residential practice centers or monasteries, or working with a teacher on a formal series of koans.

Who is their teacher or teachers? Has a legitimate teacher empowered them to teach? As mentioned earlier, Zen is a lineage tradition. You are welcome to learn from a book and practice by yourself, but if you want to call yourself a Zen teacher you need to demonstrate your practice and understanding to another qualified person in order to have them verified. You don't certify yourself; that can lead to all kinds of problems. Someone may or may not be formally empowered in their lineage, but if they mention their teacher(s) you at least have context and could always investigate their training further.

CONSIDER THIS

You're going to encounter teacher titles as you study Zen, particularly sensei, roshi, and Zen master. These are honorifics that are usually bestowed by a teacher's community or students, and the significance of the titles varies widely. Sensei is just a Japanese term for teacher. Roshi implies a mastery of Zen that's generally understood to come only with many decades of practice, and therefore is rarely applied to someone under 60, no matter how brilliant they are. People are rarely called Zen master until after their death.

What kinds of ongoing connections do they have? Beware of Zen teachers or experts who have no membership in any group whatsoever outside of one they might lead. Zen in the West is young, but professional and collegial organizations of Zen teachers have been developed. Membership is voluntary, but it encourages mutual accountability and attention to standards.

The American Zen Teacher's Association (AZTA) includes all Zen lineages, and lay as well as ordained teachers. The Soto Zen Buddhist Association (SZBA) members are ordained Soto Zen teachers. Both organizations have websites and directories. A few lineages have ended up quite large and have formed collegial organizations of their own (the Mountains and Rivers Order, the Diamond Sangha, and the Order of Buddhist Contemplatives, to name a few). The important thing is that the teacher engages in some way with peers and the larger Zen community.

Trust Your Intuition

No matter what someone's credentials, however, you should always trust your own intuition about what is true, helpful, and appropriate. It doesn't matter if a teacher is surrounded by dozens of adoring students, or an author is a ninth-century so-called Zen master; if you hear, read, or experience something that seems wrong to you, pay attention to your response. Some Zen teachings or people are going to be helpful to you as an individual, and only you can know which ones those are. In addition, Zen teachers and practitioners are fallible human beings, so feel free to use your judgment when it comes to things Zen, just as you would with anything else.

At the same time, it can be worth investigating further a Zen teaching or practice that makes you confused or uncomfortable. (Note: this does not include disrespectful, harmful, or immoral behavior on the part of Zen teachers or leaders!) Sometimes your first reaction to something can point you toward an opportunity to learn something new.

ZEN WISDOM

"So why do we take teachers and join sanghas? Just as the truth of Zen is unobscured and available to us, so are Newton's principles of physics, or the theory of relativity. Nothing stands between us and any truth. But why is it we resist learning from others when it comes to matters of inner Truth, yet understand perfectly the necessity of learning mathematics or physics from those qualified to teach them?"

—Zen Teacher Kyogen Carlson, from *Zen in the American Grain: Discovering the Teachings at Home*

For example, perhaps you initially react negatively to the Buddhist concept of non-attachment, thinking it means being emotionless. Just recognizing that fear of being emotionless can lead to a greater understanding of the role emotions play in your life. Think of Zen practice as a process of trial and error. You try something, and if it either makes you feel better or it makes you think, keep it around. If not, go ahead and move on.

On the flip side of noticing your aversion or discomfort, pay attention to when someone helps make Zen seem clear, accessible, or inspirational to you. If Zen sounds good to you in theory but the teachings and teachers you've encountered seem to confuse the issue, keep searching. Many people end up finding their "Rosetta Stone" of Zen in the form of some book or teacher that makes them finally think, "Oh! I get it now! Is *that* what they were talking about all this time?" Each one of us is unique, and what's going to get through to each person differs greatly. Fortunately, every Zen practitioner is encouraged to express it their own way, so there are almost as many expressions as there are people studying Zen.

Actually Doing Zen

Whether or not you want to think of yourself as a Zen practitioner, join a Zen group, or become a Buddhist, it's well worth taking a step beyond just reading or thinking about Zen. This is because the point of Zen is to make changes in your mind and in your life, and these changes are unlikely to happen unless you put Zen into practice.

Just reading or thinking about Zen is a little like just reading about exercise. It may be very inspiring to read about a method of training the body. You may want to explore different exercise options before committing to one, or fully understand the history or philosophy of an exercise regimen. At some point, however, the exercise program is not going to do you any good if you don't start actually doing it. You also aren't really going to understand the exercise method if you haven't experienced it for yourself.

POTENTIAL PITFALL

Never before in history have there been so many options open to people regarding their choice of spiritual path. This is great because you can explore different paths and find one that works for you. On the other hand, it can encourage "spiritual window shopping," where you never settle on a path because none of them seem perfect, and all of them seem interesting. If you only do spiritual window shopping, you never discover the lessons and rewards of spiritual practice that are only possible with commitment and prolonged effort.

Zen includes philosophy—which you might find very helpful in and of itself—but first and foremost it is a method for training the mind and body. Your experience of the method can further develop your appreciation for the philosophy, and the philosophy can inform and inspire your practice of the method.

Beginner's Mind

Fortunately, as a beginner you are in the perfect situation to practice Zen! That's because Zen is *not* like exercise, or just about any other discipline or subject. Beginner's mind is revered in Zen and is actually an attitude that expert practitioners try to cultivate.

When you first sit down in meditation, read a Zen text, or walk into a meditation hall, your eyes are wide open. You don't know what comes next or what your experience is going to be like, so your sense of curiosity is very alive. You have to stay on the lookout for clues that will tell you what this is about, and what to do. You can't rest in any sense that you "know how to do this." You can't even evaluate whether you're good at this or not, or whether you understand or not, because you just started!

ZEN WISDOM

"In Japan we have the phrase *shoshin*, which means 'beginner's mind.' The goal of practice is always to keep our beginner's mind. Suppose you recite the Prajna Paramita Sutra only once. It might be a very good recitation. But what would happen to you if you recited it twice, three times, four times, or more? You might easily lose your original attitude towards it. ... In the beginner's mind there are many possibilities; in the expert's mind there are few."

—Shunryu Suzuki Roshi (1904-1971), from *Zen Mind, Beginner's Mind*

The beautiful irony of Zen is that this beginner's way of being in the world is exactly what Zen students are trying to manifest all the time. In reality we don't know what's going to happen next, we just think we do. In reality every moment is new and different, so we are shortchanging the present any time we base our actions and responses on past experience. Unfortunately, the natural attitude of an actual beginner is difficult to maintain over time. We have to work very hard to see and engage the world with beginner's mind once we're not a beginner anymore, so enjoy it while you have it and don't feel inadequate for a moment.

Anxiety About Change

Like many things, Zen has the potential to help you change, but the decision to change has to come first. If you've picked up this book, chances are you're a curious and fairly open-minded person; but like many people, you may feel somewhat apprehensive or ambivalent about actually attempting to make changes in your life. If you're successful in your effort to change, who knows what will happen? What else will have to change? Maybe you're opening up a whole can of worms. On the other hand, if you're not successful at change, you may face frustration and disappointment. Few things are more aggravating than a friend saying, "Hey, why are you still getting so angry? Aren't you studying Zen?"

Studying Zen (or anything) takes humility and courage. According to an old Zen analogy, if you already think you know everything, you can't learn anything, just as you can't add any tea to a cup that's already full. Admitting there might be something you don't know takes humility; letting in ideas or recommendations from others takes courage. It helps to be patient with yourself.

Giving It a First Try

So the moment comes when you set down this book to give one or more Zen practices a try for the first time. In this section I'll suggest what you should do. See Part 2 of this book for detailed how-to instructions for various Zen practices; here I'll describe which practices to start with, and how to go about approaching them when you've never done them before.

Meditating for the First Time

Start by reading the section titled "Basic Instructions for Zazen" in Chapter 4. This will tell you how to position your body for comfortable and effective meditation, and what to do with your mind. If you decide to sit in a chair, sit on the front edge of a chair tall enough so that your knees end up slightly lower than your hips. If necessary, put a pillow on the chair to make it higher.

If you want to sit on the floor, you'll need to improvise a cushion. You want to sit on something fairly firm that raises the bottom of your pelvic bones off the floor at least 3 to 5 inches. You may have to stack a couple of pillows to achieve this, or fold one in half. Try sitting on the corners of the pillows, as this will avoid cutting off blood supply to your legs.

Now, decide how long you want to sit. Try 10 minutes to begin with, although if you like you can certainly sit longer. Set a timer so you don't have to keep looking at the clock (and make sure there's no clock in your field of view—it can be very distracting). Face a wall or an uncluttered patch of floor; avoid facing books, pictures, elaborate patterns, or vistas, as you want to hold your eyes fairly still instead of looking around.

Then ... just observe what happens. The whole point of zazen is to cultivate more awareness of what is, and whatever happens during your meditation is exactly what is. Just be aware of it, and try not to judge it. The only way to do this wrong is to willfully not bother to be aware, and seeing as you'd have to be aware to willfully let your mind wander, it's doubtful whether that's even possible.

 CONSIDER THIS

> Meditation is actually quite a simple, natural state. According to the ancient story, Siddhartha Gautama—the future Buddha—reached a point of utter frustration after six years of ascetic spiritual practice. Then he remembered a calm, pleasant meditative state he had spontaneously experienced as a small child, and he realized this type of meditation was the key to understanding and liberation.

After you meditate you'll probably be inclined to evaluate whether it was useful. After all, you need to decide whether to do it again, right? Well, back to the exercise analogy: you might not feel better after your first workout session. You might actually feel sore, and doubtful about the whole routine. It's going to take a series of sessions to decide whether or not a form of exercise, or zazen, is going to be helpful to you.

And how do you know if zazen is helpful? You might feel a little calmer and more centered as you go about your day, even if you didn't feel calm and centered during the meditation itself. You might also find that regular zazen lets you see your life more clearly and gives you more freedom of choice when it comes to your responses to things. Note that these benefits are described with the modifiers "a little" and "more." The results of zazen are almost never dramatic, all-or-nothing transformations, so be attentive to more subtle positive effects.

Paying Attention to Simple Tasks

One of the great things about Zen is that you can practice it anytime, anywhere. Simply returning your attention to whatever you're doing is the Zen practice of *mindfulness*. Whether you're cooking, cleaning, driving, or talking, the goal is to be aware of what's going on. This "what's going on" includes your physical posture and movements, your sensations and perceptions, and your thoughts and feelings. Beginning mindfulness practice, though, concentrates on physical movements and sensations, because we can end up getting too carried away by our thoughts and feelings until we learn to observe them in a similarly objective way.

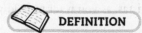 **DEFINITION**

> **Mindfulness** is the practice of returning your attention to what's in front of you and keeping it there, particularly when you're engaged in some kind of movement or task. It turns out to be more difficult than it sounds, because that's not often what we feel like doing.

It's good to start mindfulness practice with simple tasks that you do often, like sweeping the floor, eating your lunch, or taking a shower. Look for short tasks so you can aim to stay attentive the entire time. Choose activities that involve some movement and lots of physical sensations and that don't require conversation or planning.

As you set about your mindfulness task, pay particular attention to your hands and/or the physical sensations on your skin or tongue. Just notice. You might find it's almost like watching someone else's movements as you see yourself hold a dish with one hand and deftly scrub it with a dishrag held in the other. You may become aware of sensing things that you usually don't even register—the warmth of the water, the suds bursting on your skin, the sound of water running down the drain.

Mindfulness practice is its own reward, even as it helps you strengthen the ability to consciously and willfully direct your attention. Every moment that you're mindful is a moment of your life that you have appreciated! It's a shame if the bulk of your time is spent worrying, planning, fantasizing, or thinking about the past. Thinking is fine, but do you really want to devote that much of your time to it? Especially when you find yourself thinking about the same things over and over? At first glance activities like cleaning your kitchen might not seem worth paying attention to, but you'd be surprised how rich and enjoyable things can be when you're fully present for the experience.

If you end up feeling discouraged because you can't seem to concentrate in meditation or when you're practicing mindfulness, don't give up trying! It's a common experience to feel a little shocked and chagrined at the busy, chaotic state of your mind once you pay attention to it. Over time you can get better at keeping your attention in one place, but even more importantly you're becoming more aware of your own mind. Try to just observe rather than judge.

Visiting a Zen Group

There are many reasons to consider making a visit to a local *sangha*, or Zen group, if you're lucky enough to live near one. Just as joining a gym or having a personal trainer can motivate and focus your exercise, practicing Zen with a group can help you stick with the Zen practices you want to do. There's a delightful positive peer pressure that occurs when you're surrounded by other folks trying to do the same thing you want to do. In addition, of course, a group is likely to have some people in it who are more experienced than you are at Zen. You are very likely to learn something about the *Dharma*.

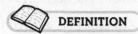

DEFINITION

> A **sangha** is a community of Zen or Buddhist practitioners. From the beginning of Buddhism, the value of practicing and studying with others has been strongly emphasized. Sangha is considered one of the three central things in Buddhism, called the three jewels, along with buddha and dharma. You can practice Zen without a sangha, but it's worth checking out the benefits of participating in one. **Dharma** refers to the Buddhist teachings, but also simply fundamental truth. The Buddhist or Zen Dharma includes all of the teachings and practices in those traditions that point to the truth, but dharma as truth itself is larger than any particular tradition.

If you feel any trepidation about venturing out to a Zen group, it may relieve you to know that Zen does not proselytize. In fact, if you show up at a group, people are likely to be friendly and happy you are there, but they generally won't try to get you to join or even encourage you to come back. Don't take this as a lack of friendliness; it's just that your practice is considered your business. If you come back, it should be because you really want to, not because Joe's going to wonder where you are.

If a group has a meeting place of its own, it may be called a Zen center or a Zen temple. There are many groups that get together to meditate and study that don't have their own spaces, though—they gather in church basements or people's homes. Although big practice centers offer more types of activities, the benefits of practicing with others can be experienced pretty much no matter the size or nature of the group.

A group may or may not use this term, but all sizes of groups practicing together qualify as a sangha. Find a sangha by searching online; most groups have a web page and can be found with search terms like zen, zazen, meditation, buddhist, or sangha. There are also various directories of Zen groups out there, organized by state and country, including those on the Sweeping Zen, AZTA, and SZBA websites.

What can you expect the first time you visit a Zen group? A Zen meeting generally has a predictable schedule of activities, just as you might expect at a church, synagogue, or mosque. If the schedule isn't obvious on a website or flyer, you can call ahead or arrive early and ask someone about it.

A Zen schedule almost always includes some meditation, usually in periods of 20 to 40 minutes (you'll know ahead of time how long). There may be more than one period of meditation, and if there is, there may be a shorter period of walking meditation in between. At any group open to the public, you will almost always be able to sit in a chair instead of on the floor if you need to, and people will be happy to show you around and answer your questions.

A Zen meeting may also include a study period, which can be a lecture-style talk, a class, or a discussion. This is an opportunity to get more of a sense of the group, and there's usually a chance to ask questions. Don't be shy, ask! (Remember what I said earlier about beginner's mind.)

You might also be surprised by some of the things that happen at a Zen gathering, especially one at a Zen center or temple. Chanting, ritual, and bowing are traditional parts of Zen Buddhism, so you may find yourself swept along into such activities even if you just went for the meditation or the study. If you are uncomfortable about this, you can ask ahead of time if there's a way for you to politely step out before these activities begin or arrive after they're over.

Even if you attend the chanting or ritual or participate in the bows, you aren't obligating yourself to anything, and generally speaking no one is going to ask you to embrace those aspects of the practice other than just being respectful of others. Who knows, you might even find you like this kind of practice!

The Least You Need to Know

- Every type and lineage of Zen has a different flavor and style.
- Read and explore different things and use your own judgment about what works for you.
- Zen is primarily a method of training the body and mind, so it's good to actually give it a try for yourself.
- It takes courage and humility to try something new, but in Zen, beginner's mind is considered very precious.
- You can try Zen practice today by sitting a few minutes in meditation and paying attention when you wash the dishes.

A Zen Practice of Your Own

If you're the kind of person who likes to jump right into doing, read this chapter for instructions on how to get yourself a Zen practice of your very own. As you meditate and try other practices for yourself, you'll have some personal experience as a context for the rest of this book.

If you're not sure you even want a Zen practice, skip this chapter and read more about Zen methods and teachings in the next two parts of this book. You can always come back to learn about how to work zazen and mindfulness into your everyday life in an effective and sustainable way.

In This Chapter

- How to make Zen an ongoing part of your life
- Establishing new Zen habits
- Integrating, not adding, Zen
- Making everything practice
- Sustaining the effort and intention

What Is a "Zen Practice"?

If you read any Zen texts or talk to any Zen practitioners, chances are good that you will hear the word "practice" over and over again. Zen Master Dogen will remind you that "practice" and enlightenment are one. "How's your practice going?" one student will ask another. Someone else will confess, "I haven't been practicing much lately." What does practice mean in a Zen context?

Practice is a wonderful English word for what Zen students and teachers are trying to talk about because it has several different meanings. In one sense, a practice is a discipline, such as a martial arts practice or a medical practice. In this sense Zen practice is your engagement with the tradition as a whole, including its goals, methods, and standards of behavior. However, this is the shallowest interpretation of the word practice in Zen. Most Zen practitioners would agree that you don't have to be doing explicitly Zen stuff to be practicing.

At another level, practice refers to something you decide to do regularly. In this sense you "make it a practice" to always eat a good breakfast, or you "make a practice of" always telling the truth. Interpreted this way, a Zen practice is about choosing to make certain activities, ideals, or approaches a regular part of your life. Such things include explicitly Zen activities like meditation, but they also include your intention to be patient with your kids, or your effort to be alert and aware as you go about your day. This is where another meaning of the English word practice becomes relevant: practice to become better at something. There's a kind of humility communicated by the term Zen practice, because it acknowledges you never reach perfection.

CONSIDER THIS

In case you feel a little inhibited about making the decision to start a Zen practice, consider doing it on a trial basis, or even secretly. No one ever has to know you gave it a try or that you decided to give it up. Your practice is entirely your own business.

At an even more subtle level, Zen practice is approaching each moment of your life with awareness and the intention to decrease suffering for yourself or others. At this level, you don't even decide ahead of time how you want to act or how you want things to go. You just meet the next thing with as much attention and openness as you can muster, and try to see clearly what response will relieve suffering or increase real happiness. Then you do your best to offer that response. Although this aspect of practice is subtle, it's also something you can do at any time, no matter what else you're doing or what's going on around you.

Making Zazen a Habit

Even though Zen practice can be a subtle, way-you-approach-each-moment practice, it helps to have a few specific things to start working on if you'd like to develop a Zen practice of your own.

The one explicitly Zen activity that a Zen practice needs is zazen, the Zen form of seated meditation. There's no rule that says how often you have to meditate, but if you don't sit zazen at all you won't really know what Zen practice is about. The reasons for this may not be immediately obvious to you, even if you start meditating! Suffice it to say that zazen develops a part of you that is usually highly neglected. How often do you deliberately settle into just being, without any agenda at all—even the agenda to enjoy yourself?

The simple act of sitting down to do zazen, even for a short session, reorients your day. Everything else you experience ends up being seen from the perspective of someone who is looking for something deeper in life than just getting by. Sitting zazen regularly shifts the frame of reference for your life. If you want to make a habit of it, here are a few things to try.

Regularity over Session Length

Because zazen can have such a positive influence on your day, it's valuable to do it every day you have the time. Most people find 20 to 40 minutes is a good length for a meditation session because it gives their mind some time to settle. However, if you aren't going to sit because you don't have 20 minutes to spare, sit for 10. If you are very busy and find yourself resisting even 10 minutes, try 5. Actually, sitting zazen for 30 seconds is better than nothing.

What can you achieve in 10 minutes, 5 minutes, or 30 seconds? On the one hand, you can't achieve much—but then, we're not trying to achieve anything in zazen, so that's okay. On the other hand, each time you sit, you're building the habit of taking the zazen posture. You start to notice the difference sitting makes in your life. Chances are good that you'll actually enjoy certain moments of your meditation, too—like when your body finally catches up with your mind and you think, "Oh, hello life! *There* you are!"

A Designated Time and Space

In developing a habit of zazen, some people find it's helpful to choose a regular time of day to sit. The time you choose depends on your schedule and responsibilities, of course, but it also depends on what time of day you find it easiest to settle the mind and body but still stay alert. Some people prefer the morning, others the evening. Few people prefer the afternoon (it tends to feel like siesta time once you sit down), but any time of day is fine if it works for you.

You may need to sit quietly in your bedroom in the morning before you let the kids know you're up, or you might sit as soon as you get home from work because that's when there's no one else in the house. Get creative if you need to, and don't be shy about letting other people know you're sitting zazen; your effort can lend a vicarious calm to the other people you live with.

If you have the space to do it, it can be very helpful to designate a place just for zazen. I once moved some furniture so I could have a tiny, private meditation space in a corner of the bedroom

I shared with my husband. Some people are able to set up a meditation room. It helps if the space can be free from clutter, but all it needs to accommodate is a rectangular meditation mat about 2 feet by 3 feet. You can buy one of these online to lend an air of specialness to your meditation space, but you can also just use a folded blanket. Even if you sit in a chair, a mat of some kind under the chair helps designate the space for meditation.

If you like, you can set up a simple altar with a Buddha statue, a picture of someone you admire, or something natural like a beautiful stone; an altar can help focus your intention. Some people also find burning incense during meditation becomes a mnemonic device; when they smell the incense, they remember the meditative frame of mind. If you have a space where you always meditate and burn incense, the space will usually end up having a pleasant smell that reminds you of meditation, even when the incense isn't burning.

CONSIDER THIS

Some people new to Zen feel uncomfortable with the use of altars, whether this is because they are non-religious or because they perceive a Zen altar as somewhat sacrilegious. However, altars are a natural human expression of reverence for something. You probably have one in your home, although you may not call it an altar: a clean, special, attractive, elevated space for objects or pictures that portray or represent important things to you. A Zen altar is usually about honoring meditation, wisdom or compassion, and it can be a meaningful addition to your meditation space.

On the other hand, don't let a chaotic schedule or the lack of a designated space keep you from sitting. Grab opportunities wherever you can! I've known people who sit a little zazen behind the wheel of their parked car during their lunch hour. You can keep your meditation mat or blanket in a closet and pull it out to make a little meditation space whenever you find a quiet ten minutes. The important thing is that you do it.

The Right Equipment

If you can sit zazen for a prolonged period without discomfort, no problem! If you can't, consider investing in a meditation mat (often called a *zabuton*), cushion, or bench, which can be found online.

Many people are amazed when they first sit on a proper meditation cushion, often called a *zafu*, after having improvised with pillows and blankets at home. Zafus are much sturdier than most pillows you have lying around the house. They're often stuffed with kapok, a cottonlike substance that resists compression, or with buckwheat hulls. A substantial meditation cushion can give you 3 or 4 inches of loft off the ground, whereas most pillows are going to compress down to 1 or 2 inches under your weight. Stacks of pillows might give you loft but are unstable. Zafus are also round, which reduces the chance that the blood supply to your legs will get cut off while you sit.

You might also find a *seiza bench* a liberating addition to your meditation practice. (You can find an illustration of someone using a seiza bench in Chapter 4.) These short little benches sit over your calves as you kneel on the floor, so you can sit down on them rather than resting your weight on your feet. They don't require much physical flexibility to use, and they support a good, upright alignment of the spine.

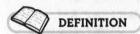

> **DEFINITION**
>
> A **zabuton** is a rectangular mat you sit on during meditation. It's usually about 2 feet by 3 feet and stuffed with cotton to cushion your legs from the floor. A **zafu** is a sturdy round cushion made specifically for sitting in a cross-legged posture. A **seiza bench** is a short bench you sit on while kneeling on the floor.

Joining a Zen Group

Many people feel wary about joining a group of any kind, especially one that might be considered spiritual or religious. You might have had a negative experience with organized religion, or suspect group membership might become oppressive or compromise your ability to think clearly and independently. Fortunately, the professed function of a Zen group is to support your own process of awakening to truth, not to provide you with a dogma to accept. If you encounter a Zen group that seems to discourage questioning, disagreement, and thinking for yourself, find a different group.

If you have visited a group that feels right to you, consider making a habit of practicing regularly with them, particularly for meditation. It can help a great deal with maintaining a regular sitting practice on your own. For one thing, if you participate with a group every week or two, you will at least sit zazen that often! For another, the experience with the group will probably inspire you to sit at other times.

Whether or not you enjoy socializing, there's no way around the fact that you are a social being. Humans inspire, encourage, and influence one another. When you spend time with other people who are making zazen and Zen practice part of their lives, you know it's possible, and you might even get some good ideas about how to maintain your own practice in the midst of a busy life.

A group will also usually have a teacher or a leader—or at least some practitioners more experienced than you are—who can give you personalized advice about your zazen. Be sure to ask them about any physical discomfort you experience during meditation. They may be able to suggest a better posture for you. Also ask for ideas about things like how to better calm your mind, how to let go of persistent thoughts or feelings, or how to know whether you're making the right kind of effort. You may be surprised to find that any struggles you're having with zazen are not at all unique to you, and that there are all kinds of different things you can try to improve your zazen.

ZEN WISDOM

"... when visiting a teacher or a center examine the teacher's students. Are they simply clones-in-training of the teacher? This is probably not a good thing—after all, Zen is about becoming more fully yourself, not becoming more like your teacher. On the other hand, do the students seem to be people you like, and might like to be with? Can you recognize the values they advocate? Are they independent and engaged in the world? Can they joke about themselves? And, importantly, can they joke about their institution and teacher? ... Do they seem to be genuinely on a path that is freeing them from their suffering?"

—Zen Teacher James Ishmael Ford, from *Zen Master Who? A Guide to the People and Stories of Zen.*

Attending a Retreat

Just as it's valuable to take an intensive course in something you want to understand or master, it's very useful to attend a meditation retreat to deepen and improve your zazen. At a Zen retreat you will end up sitting in meditation for 4 to 8 hours a day, and you will usually also receive guidance in your meditation through lectures, workshops, or personal interviews with a teacher.

Retreats can last a single day or up to a week or even 10 days. The longer a retreat, the more likely your mind and body will eventually settle, despite themselves, and you will experience a more still and spacious meditation than you usually do in the midst of daily life. This can instruct you as to what is possible in meditation, and give you an idea of what to work toward in your daily zazen.

If you can't attend a retreat because of physical discomfort during zazen or because of your life responsibilities, don't be discouraged in your zazen practice. Still, if you get the opportunity, there's nothing like a retreat to energize and clarify your efforts in meditation. You can often attend a retreat for just a single day, so you may be able to work it into your life even if you're very busy.

Zen off the Cushion

Actually, not only is Zen not limited to zazen, it shouldn't be. There's an essay on zazen by Zen Master Dogen that's recited in Zen centers and temples across the world, and it states that zazen is not meditation practice! It also asks how becoming a buddha, or awakening, could be limited to sitting or lying down. This is because the mind-body posture you take in zazen—alert, upright, still, and open—is the mind-body posture you want to take in all aspects of your life.

It's relatively easy to be still and open when you're seated in meditation. It's not easy, but it's much easier than it is when you're driving in heavy traffic, deciding how to get by on a slim budget, or arguing with a significant other! It's when you get up off the cushion that your practice is really tested. While sitting you may have a pleasant experience of calm or a nice insight about how everything is interconnected, but that calm and insight can disappear in an instant when you're challenged by life. Therefore, you need to study and experiment with how Zen practice looks and feels in all kinds of different circumstances.

POTENTIAL PITFALL

Most people only have so many hours in a week that they can devote to explicitly Zen activities, whether they spend it meditating, reading about Zen, listening to talks, practicing mindfulness in the garden, or volunteering with their Zen group. All of these things can be useful, but when you choose how to spend your Zen hours, beware of wanting them to be *productive*. The most useful Zen practice is taking the time to put everything down and be still.

After all, even if you sit zazen every day for an hour or more, the bulk of your waking hours are going to be spent off the meditation cushion. How do you practice Zen while going about your day—eating, working, playing, or interacting with others? How do you integrate Zen into your life, rather than letting it make things busier or more complicated than they already are? Fortunately Zen is *about* living your life, so there are all kinds of ways to take Zen off the cushion.

Practice Applies to Everything

To illustrate how Zen practice can apply to everything in your life, it may help to describe how Zen practice might look throughout a typical day. More details about Zen methods can be found in Part 2 of this book, so here I'll just mention which ones are relevant and how they might be used in a given circumstance.

As soon as you turn off the alarm in the morning, you have an opportunity to work with your habits. Do you greet the coming day with some enthusiasm, or do you have a sense of dread or being overwhelmed? Primarily you just notice how you feel, but you can also work on clarity by looking deeper. Do you really feel overwhelmed, or is that just a habit of mind? Can you try on a different state of mind, and if so, how does that feel? All of this reflection can happen as you get out of bed and stand brushing your teeth in the bathroom; there's no need for your movements to become ponderous.

As you stretch away the stiffness of a night's sleep, there's an opportunity for mindfulness. You notice your breath and the sensations in your body. As your mind leaps on the chance to worry about whether you are getting enough exercise, you cultivate mindfulness by letting the thoughts pass and returning your attention to your bodily sensations. Then, as you arrive in the kitchen for breakfast, you have a chance to work on not indulging anger when you notice your roommate has left dirty dishes in the sink again.

On the drive to work you notice your apprehension about a meeting you have later in the day, and decide to take some time to work on clarity. You examine your thoughts and feelings more closely. What is it about your boss that makes you feel defensive? You realize that your boss reminds you of your mother, and that she triggers in you a sense that you're not qualified to be in charge of things. This realization opens up a possibility that you can react differently to your boss by noticing how your job situation is nothing like your childhood.

> **CONSIDER THIS**
>
> Get creative with your Zen, and see if you can practice it in the most unlikely places, at the most unlikely times. When waiting at the doctor's office, notice your impatience and the way your mind would rather avoid the thought of how serious illness can get. When drinking wine and eating cake at a friend's wedding, be mindful of the vicarious joy you get from the love being experienced by others, and the fluffiness of the frosting on the cake!

At work you have many chances to work on behaving morally and compassionately—not being dishonest, not gossiping about others, being generous. Throughout the day you return to the sensations of your breath in order to be more present; you begin to recognize how worrying about the future actually makes you less efficient.

After work you get to observe a habit of eating and drinking too much. You know your patterns won't change overnight, but you at least try to increase your awareness of the choices you make and their repercussions. You acknowledge the energy it took to at least have the salad instead of the fries. Later you practice mindful appreciation of a friend who spends some time with you, and as you meditate before bed you get a sense that life is about continually learning.

There you go—Zen practice from dawn to dusk. It doesn't have to be burdensome; it can be a constant companion that can turn otherwise boring, annoying, or difficult experiences into opportunities.

It's Not Practice Versus Life

It's not unusual to feel some friction when you start practicing Zen. To the extent that you're able to change your mind and behavior, you may find others frustrated with you—especially if you're spending lots of time meditating that you used to spend with your partner, or you're suddenly trying not to abuse intoxicants while your friends still partake liberally.

Ideally your Zen practice is about waking up to, embracing, and more fully living your life. Some changes are necessary, but it's good to be a little gentle with your life and the other people in it. Try not to neglect your relationships, but instead adapt your Zen practice to include them.

Also try not to annoy people with too much talk about Zen or the great things you've realized since you started studying it. (Look for other Zen practitioners to talk to about these things; they can go on for hours about it.) Instead, try to quietly manifest what you've learned, and practice listening to others. You'll know you've hit the right balance between taking care of your life and changing it when someone suggests you take some time to go do your meditation because it makes you happier or nicer.

A sense of friction may also arise between the explicitly Zen parts of your life and the rest of it, which can seem chaotic, demanding, and agitating in comparison. People often find that while they're meditating, or spending time with a Zen group, or reading Zen books, they can access a still, centered, and appreciative state of mind that evades them at most other times. When this is the case, it's natural that some aversion arises to aspects of your life that tend to knock you off your Zen center.

Aversion or frustration is especially likely to arise if you have to put up with dysfunctional work or family situations, or have so many demands on your time that you can hardly think straight. It may be time to address the situations that are bothering you, but these situations are also extremely rich fields for practice. After all, you won't always be able to set things up the way you'd like them, so you might as well get some practice trying to be Zen in the midst of less-than-conducive conditions. Just understand that it *is* difficult to practice in these situations, and don't expect to feel as connected to Zen there as you do on your meditation seat.

Keeping It Up over Time

Hopefully you will feel some immediate benefits from Zen practice so you will feel inspired to continue. Still, if you do keep it up, there will inevitably come a time when practice starts to feel a little dull or fruitless. You need to know how to keep your practice going through these times, because mastering the art of living takes a lifetime! Think of practicing 10, 20, or 30 years; how can you approach Zen in order to be able to sustain your practice that long?

Patience, Patience, Patience

Your path of learning and development—in life as well as in Zen practice—is rarely straightforward. Sometimes it can seem like the harder you want to change something, do something, or understand something, the less likely it is to happen. Sometimes the goals you had a year ago, or 10 years ago, morph into something different as you go along, so it's not really clear where you're going in the long term.

It's best to think of your Zen practice like baking a loaf of bread or cultivating a garden. In both of these examples, you're depending on living organisms (yeast or plants) to bring about the desired result. Depending on the materials you start out with—your altitude and climate, your oven or soil—the amount of time it takes to produce what you want differs, as does the resulting product. Sometimes your bread rises quickly, sometimes it doesn't. Sometimes it's done in an hour, other times you take it out after an hour and it's still not fully baked. You may have planted a certain kind of flower in your garden but then find it doesn't thrive, while another kind takes off.

If you want to be a good gardener or bread baker, you work on understanding your own circumstances and adapt. Perhaps you even choose a slightly different goal—still a garden, still bread, but something you will be able to achieve beautifully given your materials, skills, and conditions. You also come to appreciate how these things can't be rushed; more water and fertilizer is only going to help a plant grow faster up to a point, past which they will actually kill the plant. If you turn up the heat on your bread, you will just wreck it. If you come to view your own practice and development like bread baking or gardening, you naturally become more patient and flexible. After all, the material for your Zen practice is a living organism—you.

Not Judging Your Practice

While it's true that you may be too hard on yourself, or unable to accurately evaluate the "good" of your Zen practice, neither of these is the most important reason to avoid judging your practice. The most important reason is that evaluating the effectiveness or rewards of your practice involves exactly the discriminating mind that you are seeking liberation from! This is why Zen Master Dogen spoke of the "goal of goallessness." However, it can be hard to be goalless about a practice like Zen, which takes lots of effort and sets out plenty of ideals for you to set your sights on.

Imagine this approach: you simply practice, meditating and incorporating Zen teachings and methods into your life. You do this in a steady, dedicated way, without constantly asking, "Is it worth it? Is the payoff of this effort outweighing the costs?" You go about practice the way you would go about taking care of anything that's your responsibility. When you take care of your children, clean your house, brush your teeth, or support a good friend, do you consider whether the effort is worth it? No, because these are just things you have to do. You don't even do them because you *want* to; it's not a matter of wanting to or not wanting to. It's a matter of living your life.

> **POTENTIAL PITFALL**
>
> Spiritual materialism is approaching spiritual practice with the same sense of gain or loss with which you might approach your career or your material wealth. When you are caught up in spiritual materialism, you base your actions on the idea that you lack something, and therefore strive to obtain it (such as a particular insight). Alternatively, you may think you have it while others don't, and you strive to keep it. Spiritual materialism obscures the reality that wisdom and liberation are reached by realizing your sufficiency here and now, that this sufficiency is the same for everyone, and that it cannot be possessed.

In the West many people suffer from a deep sense of inadequacy, so many Zen students carry around a sense that their practice is small, half-hearted, less than it should be, or at least less than the practice of some other people. This is unfortunate, because thinking like this can put a glass ceiling on your practice. If you've written yourself off as a halfway practitioner, you'll probably remain that way. Yet Zen, as the art of living, is unlike any other kind of discipline or skill. It's not about getting good at something else, it's about wholeheartedly embracing your life as it is. No matter what your practice or life looks like, fully embraced and lived it is perfect Zen.

Learning to Shrug

It's great to be able to avoid taking yourself and your Zen practice too seriously. I once got a fortune in a cookie that summarized this perfectly: "The beginning of wisdom is the ability to shrug." At the time that seemed to me like a very high expectation, because I was in the middle of some acute personal suffering. What on earth could it mean, to shrug? Wouldn't that require a callous disinterest? How can you possibly cultivate a disinterest in your own experience of suffering?

Fortunately, the ability to avoid taking yourself too seriously is not a matter of cultivating disinterest in yourself, it's a matter of broadening your perspective. Here's an analogy: a small child breaks his favorite crayon. He is devastated and comes to you crying uncontrollably. You don't judge him for being upset, you feel empathy for his pain, but you also know that a broken crayon is not the end of the world. There will be other crayons, and there will be a time in the not-so-distant future when the child will be able to move beyond the pain of the broken crayon and be engrossed in something else. You comfort the child, let him cry it out, and gently encourage him by reassuring him that you can get him another crayon or by distracting him with another activity.

In this scenario there is (hopefully) no point where you think, "Stupid child, getting upset about something so insignificant." The crayon is not insignificant to him, and if you were in his situation it wouldn't be insignificant to you. Yours is not a superior view, it's just a bigger view.

Our adult trials, tribulations, and longings are similar to this child's lament for his crayon. There's no way to judge our concerns as being ultimately worthy of attention or not; if we experience them as challenging, then they are. Over time, however, we can cultivate a larger view—particularly one that's not limited to the world of our small sense of self. The farther out we can place our boundaries in time and space, the more we can contain with some equanimity.

For example, if you don't feel so separate from other people, your own misfortune is contained in a broader landscape and there's a chance life won't appear so utterly bleak when things are going badly for you. Or if you've watched your own mind states carefully over time, you realize how completely they arise and fall, so even in the middle of anguish you understand it won't last forever.

It's never appropriate to shrug when it comes to someone else's pain, or your own experience of trauma or loss—after all, you don't shrug off the child who has broken his crayon. There's a time for empathy, sympathy, and healing. The shrug comes in when you start to evaluate your own practice and response to things. When the thought occurs to you, "I shouldn't be so upset about this," you shrug because you recognize this is just impatience arising. Naturally, you'd rather have achieved the ability to maintain more equanimity, but you know that by simply being present with your feelings they will pass away more quickly.

When you feel inadequate and frustrated because you want to understand a Zen teaching, or experience liberation, or achieve whatever improvement of character or understanding strikes your fancy, there comes a time in life or practice when you are able to shrug about your own longing. You are able to see the longing as a feeling that arises within a much larger sense of who you are, so it can be observed and dealt with instead of becoming all-consuming.

 ZEN WISDOM

"Magnanimous Mind is like a mountain, stable and impartial. Exemplifying the ocean, it is tolerant and views everything from the broadest perspective. Having a Magnanimous Mind means being without prejudice and refusing to take sides ....
Do not get carried away by the sounds of spring, nor become heavy-hearted upon seeing the colors of fall. View the changes of the seasons as a whole ...."

—Zen Master Dogen (1200-1253), from "Instructions for the Zen Cook," as translated by Thomas Wright in *From the Zen Kitchen to Enlightenment: Refining Your Life* by Uchiyama Roshi

A Sense of Curiosity

Finally, to sustain a Zen practice over time, it is very valuable to maintain a sense of curiosity about yourself and your life. If you approach your practice with the attitude of a scholar or scientist, you will find yourself fascinating. After all, every human being is fascinating; we have incredibly complex minds, influenced by genetics, experience, and culture. The variations in our manifestations and the ways we can experience our lives are without limit.

It may sound a little weird, but it is possible to maintain a sense of curiosity through anything. For example, let's say you suddenly experience anxiety attacks, and you've never had them before. Naturally you would like the anxiety to end, and you get to work on ways to relieve it. At the same time, however, you look deeply at your life. What is this anxiety about? Why is it coming out now? Have you been pushing away or avoiding something for too long? What ways of living might you need to reconsider?

However uncomfortable the experience, it provides an opportunity to learn something more about yourself and about how life works. Some Zen students will confess the rather unnerving experience of a slight sense of excitement when trouble hits as they wonder, "Hmmm … what am I going to learn?"

The Least You Need to Know

- If you'd like a Zen practice, pace yourself. It takes time, effort, and patience to build a practice.
- The most important thing is to make zazen—seated meditation—a regular habit, but this doesn't have to take a lot of time.
- Most of Zen practice occurs off the meditation cushion, and it's something you can do throughout your day.
- Zen is about living your life as it is, so it doesn't have to make life busier or conflict with other things you are doing.
- To make a Zen practice sustainable, it helps to approach it with patience, curiosity, a lack of judgment, and a certain lightheartedness.

Zen Tools

Zen is primarily a method. Using Zen tools, you can work toward the benefits described in Part 1, including waking up to your life, stress relief, greater authenticity, and being a nicer person. You don't get these things by reading about them, wishing for them, or having a Zen master explain how to attain them. You get these things by using the Zen method to find your own answers and solutions.

The Zen toolkit includes too many things to mention in this book, but six essential tools are described here in enough detail that you should be able to start using them. Zazen is the Zen form of seated meditation, which is the core of the whole Zen method. Mindfulness is the effort to pay attention to your life no matter what, and it has the potential to transform your daily life. Precepts are the Zen moral guidelines, which keep your life in order and also give you a great way to notice where you tend to be self-centered. Karma work is understanding and changing your habits of body, speech, and mind. Insight is seeing the truth, whether that truth is personal or universal. Finally, Sangha is practicing Zen with other people, where you might engage a Zen teacher, attend a meditation retreat, or participate in a ceremony.

Zazen: Seated Meditation

While there are countless techniques and methods people will recommend to you that are supposed to improve your life, meditation is one that has withstood the test of time. Humans have been practicing meditation for thousands of years, and probably will always do so. There are images of people seated cross-legged in meditation, carved in stone, that predate recorded history, so you're pretty safe in assuming there's something useful about the practice.

The central Zen method is zazen, or seated meditation. It's a relatively simple kind of meditation that in its pure form doesn't involve visualizations, chanting, special breathing techniques, or attempts to work yourself into an altered state. In fact, zazen is so simple it can be very difficult! Many people find that the first several years of meditation practice involve just figuring out, through personal experience, what it even means to do zazen. The basic instruction is "just sit," but when you try to do that you will probably find yourself wondering what that really means. Does it mean to be without thoughts? Does it mean to feel calm? Does it involve a profound experience, or is it inherently boring? If you think you're just sitting, you might wonder, is this it?

In This Chapter

- How to take the posture of zazen
- What to do with your mind during zazen
- Different aspects of mind and how to relate to them
- How you can improve your zazen
- Tips for when meditation seems difficult

Zazen is a multifaceted practice and experience. There's no perfect description of the method or final way to judge whether it's being done "correctly." This is because it's about *attentively being*, and your attentively being is going to keep changing depending on how long you've been practicing zazen, your conditions, your life experience, and your understanding.

In one sense your zazen is exactly the same the first time you sit and when you sit after 30 years of daily practice. In another sense it's different every time. So if you feel a little overwhelmed by trying to wrap your mind around zazen, don't be surprised or discouraged. This chapter will be a good introduction to the practice itself, techniques you can use, some potential pitfalls, and some of the reasons zazen is beneficial. It will be enough to get you started on your own exploration of this simple but elusive practice.

Physical Instructions for Zazen

The practice of zazen has physical and mental aspects. I'll first describe the physical process. Once you're in the right position, I'll tell you how to get started with the mental part.

The bottom line for zazen is that you want to be seated in a position in which you are both comfortable and alert, in a setting that is not too distracting. Our goal in zazen is simply to *be here now*, so it doesn't require a special posture, special equipment, or a special setting. In fact, if you think zazen requires such things, you may have a ready excuse not to do it very often.

A Straight, Upright Spine

In terms of posture, the most important thing is to have an erect spine. This allows you to maintain the spirit of zazen: alert, dignified, and collected. If you slouch or lean against something, you'll become drowsy or your mind will become dull or lazy. Try it! There really is no separation between mind and body; it's very difficult to keep the spirit of zazen if you're slouching.

When your spine is in the correct alignment for zazen, there is a slight concave curve in your lower back. You shouldn't be stiff, and your stomach muscles shouldn't be overly tight. At the same time, there should be energy in your spine; it should feel like there's space between each vertebra. Try taking a full breath of air and then letting the air out without allowing your body to shrink. That's the kind of erectness you want!

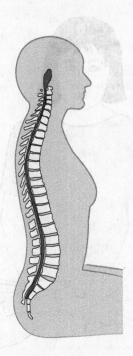

Proper alignment of the spine in zazen

Positioning the Rest of Your Body

There are many different ways to position the rest of your body in order to get this nice, erect spine. Choose a posture that's right for your body. Whether seated on the floor, on a chair, or on a kneeling bench (more on those later), your knees should ideally be below your hips. This causes your hips to rotate forward a bit, which in turn encourages that natural curve in your lower back.

If you can't get your knees lower than your hips, they at least shouldn't be any higher! I've seen lots of people with limited hip flexibility determined to sit down on the floor; their knees end up in the air and their back ends up convex and slouched. In this case they would do better to sit on a bench or a chair.

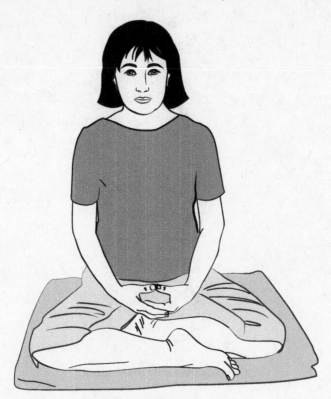

Burmese cross-legged position from front

If you have the flexibility to sit cross-legged on the floor, sit on the front edge of a substantial cushion or pillow. This tilts your body forward so your knees end up lower than your hips. Don't sit on the floor without a pillow, because you will either slouch or end up with a sore back from all the effort you're making to stay upright.

You can tuck your legs together in front of you in whatever way is comfortable as long as your spine remains in alignment and your legs and feet don't fall asleep. It helps to avoid tucking your feet under your legs. A popular position for crossed legs is called Burmese, where the calves are pulled in close to the body, but one is in front of the other (as opposed to one being on top of the other).

POTENTIAL PITFALL

Many people think meditation requires you to sit cross-legged on the floor, but that's not the case. If you are capable of such a posture, you may appreciate the sense of stability you get from being down on the floor. If you cannot sit cross-legged on the floor without pain, or without compromising the erectness of your spine, please don't do it! Almost all Western Zen centers provide benches and chairs for zazen in addition to the traditional floor cushions.

You can also maintain the proper erect spine while sitting in a chair or on a kneeling bench. If you sit in a chair, make sure you aren't leaning backward. Use a folding chair rather than a stuffed one, or put a pillow behind your back so you sit upright, or sit forward on the edge of the chair. Kneeling (or seiza) benches are specially made meditation benches about 6 to 8 inches high that you place over your calves while you're in a kneeling position. Then you sit down on the bench, and your knees end up lower than your hips and your spine lines right up.

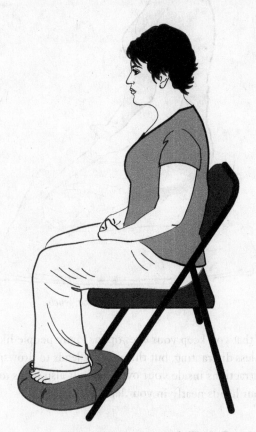

Zazen while sitting on a chair

Physical discomfort during zazen is not unusual. Some discomfort is your body getting used to the posture, and will go away over time. However, if the pain doesn't go away, pay attention. Try a different posture, or get some advice on your posture from a meditation or yoga teacher. Zazen is not meant to be painful.

Sitting on a kneeling, or seiza, bench

I strongly recommend that you keep your eyes open. Many people like meditating with their eyes closed because it feels less distracting, but this usually leads to drowsiness or daydreaming (there are plenty of distractions inside your own head). It also helps to support your effort to meditate if you fold your hands neatly in your lap.

Where and When to Do Zazen

You can "do" zazen anywhere: indoors, outdoors, in a formal meditation hall, or in your bedroom. I've done zazen on the floor of a bathroom because it was the only truly private place in my house! What's important is that there are minimal distractions. Noise or clutter might be fine; the question is, what's a distraction for *you?* What's going to pull you away from just being there? For most of us such things include television, music, computers, cell phones, and nearby conversations. Traditionally we do zazen facing a wall so we can't even distract ourselves with the scenery.

Sit zazen regularly, even daily, if you can. The classic zazen period is 30 to 40 minutes, but it's fine if you can't sit that long (or don't have time to do so). The longer you sit the more likely your mind will settle, but it's better to sit regularly for 10 or 15 minutes at a time than to sit for 40 minutes only once a month, because sitting that long feels burdensome.

CONSIDER THIS

It can be very helpful to talk to a Zen teacher or long-term practitioner about your experience of meditation. He or she can give you advice about posture and mental techniques that is specifically tailored to your physique, personality, history, and circumstances.

Mental Instructions for Zazen

This brings us to the mental aspects of zazen: how do you just sit? The next section goes into greater detail about what we are trying to do with our minds (or, more appropriately, what we are trying *not* to do with our minds). This section gives the basic instructions for what to do once you've taken your zazen posture.

First, notice where you are and what you are experiencing. Try to do this with a minimum of commentary or analysis. Just notice: it's afternoon … it's warm … there's some traffic noise … there's an itch on my leg …. Just be where you are, when you are, how you are.

Most things that attract your attention also inspire some commentary or analysis, so it can be helpful to rest your attention on some simple, relatively constant sensory input from the present. One of the best sources of such input is your own breath. When you find your mind wandering, you can just return your attention to your breath. There's nothing magical about concentrating on the breath or other physical sensations, but at least it brings you back to the present.

Don't forget that your thoughts are also just part of what's happening. According to Buddhist teachings, the mind is the sixth sense organ, and what it senses is thoughts. Thoughts are not a problem, nor are the emotions associated with them. Unless you either get caught up in them or try to push them away, they just arise and pass away. The thought may occur to you, "I've got to get groceries." No big deal. Just try not to let the thought lead to an elaborate supper plan.

And that's it. Except that you will return to the present over and over and over. Zazen can be frustrating or boring at times, but you need to keep working on your ability to return to the present, to what's really in front of you, instead of continually mulling over what only exists in the abstract in your mind. This ability can be extremely useful when you're faced with challenges or traumatic experiences.

"Meditation is a discipline because you cannot depend upon quiet mountainsides or a trip to the seashore for your peace of mind .... Meditation is the practice of finding the still point of balance within your own being in the midst of all kinds of conditions. Its purpose is not to escape, not to duck responsibility or involvement in daily life, but to know with certainty exactly where the center of your own being is."

—Zen Teacher Kyogen Carlson, from *Zen in the American Grain: Discovering the Teachings at Home*

Exercise for Your Attention

Unless you pay attention to something, you can't fully perceive, understand, or remember it. It's incredibly useful to have the ability to put your attention on something and hold it there for as long as you need to. Fortunately, attention can be strengthened like a muscle, and zazen practice is partly about exercising your attention muscle. Not only does this improve your daily life, it's also important for the cultivation of Zen insight. Once you have some ability to put your attention where you want it to be, you can focus on deeper questions that take some time to unlock.

Habitual Mind Is Monkey Mind

Most people, without some conscious attention training, suffer from what Zen calls monkey mind. This is a mind that leaps from object to object with a curious, greedy energy, but without an overall purpose. It's a short-term thinking mind that will let go of the banana it has in hand as soon as it spots a riper-looking piece of fruit. It gets so caught up in seizing on newly arising thoughts, emotions, sensations, and experiences that it rarely stays still long enough to thoroughly perceive or understand something.

Another aspect of habitual mind is your inability to control it. It may sound harsh to want to "control" your mind, but the reality of the situation is more like you are usually *controlled by* monkey mind and don't have any choice about it. Monkey mind is set on fantasizing about your vacation rather than focusing on the work you have to finish before you go. You struggle to concentrate but end up taking much longer to get your work done than you ordinarily would. Monkey mind might be obsessed with a mistake you made last week, so your mind is repeatedly filled with images of your humiliation. A friend tells you to let it go, but you can't.

> **CONSIDER THIS**
>
> When you're caught up in thinking, it's almost like being intoxicated. Your judgment is impaired because one thought leads to another, your mind is energized by all the activity, and at some level you become convinced all the thinking is of the utmost importance. It's only when you're able to let go of the thinking for a moment that you see how irrelevant most of it is, and how thinking all the time is just a habit, rather like an addiction.

It's possible, through regular meditation practice, to tame your monkey mind, at least a little. (And a little can make a big difference.) By making the effort to bring your mind back to the present over and over, you learn more about how to relate to your thoughts, feelings, sensations, and experiences in a new way. You figure out how to *choose* to be present, instead of struggling with your own mind. You notice how thoughts and feelings are not you, they are just experiences that come and go, so you are less identified with them—and therefore less concerned about them.

Three Levels of Mind

As you navigate your mind during zazen, it's useful to think about how there are three different levels of mind (referred to as the three *nen* in Japanese). The first level of mind is pure perception. A sound composed of vibrating air registers on the hearing apparatus in your ear, which then sends a signal to your brain. You become conscious of sound, and it has a particular quality—loudness, pitch, duration.

The second level of mind is naming and categorizing. You identify and name what the sound is most likely coming from. A whole host of knowledge, generalizations, and memories come along as a package with the act of naming.

The third level of mind is commentary, where your mind becomes active deciding whether the sound is pleasant or not, what the sound might mean to you and what you might need to do about it, and then on and on, making plans and arguments. Usually you start commenting on comments and most of your mind spins around at this third level indefinitely.

For example, you hear a dog barking during meditation. With the first level of mind you simply perceive the sound. You engage the second level of mind when you label the sound "dog barking," or perhaps go further and identify that it's your neighbor's dog that's barking. The third level of mind gets involved when you decide the barking is annoying, and wonder how your neighbor can be so insensitive about leaving his dog out in the yard, and then think about how you should join the neighborhood association and do something about it, except you're too busy with your job to do that, and come to think of it maybe you should get a new job ....

It's not that the third level of mind, commentary, is inherently bad or harmful. In fact, it's very useful. The problem is that you probably spend too much time spinning around in the third level of mind, rarely checking back into the first level of perception so you can get some new data on your life. Also, your mind gets overwhelmed and confused by too much commentary—judgments, plans, worries, analysis.

When you dip back into the first or second level of mind, your brain can relax a little because all you're trying to do is deal with what's in front of you, not analyze all your various problems and come up with solutions. In zazen you work on the ability to pull your mind out of its third-level obsessing and put your attention on first- and second-level input.

Staying present in the first or second level of mind doesn't require an absence of thinking. In the Buddhist view the mind is like another sense organ, and its object is thoughts. Whether or not this is a physiologically accurate description, it reflects a true aspect of your subjective experience. It's possible for a thought or feeling to arise more or less spontaneously, and then for you to refrain from commentary on it. You treat the perception of the thought or feeling as you would treat a perception of sound or warmth.

This doesn't mean that you hold yourself back from your experience with some kind of dissociation. What it means is that you include your thoughts and feelings in the wider landscape of your experience; you don't give thoughts or feelings any more weight than anything else. When you refrain from commentary on a thought or feeling, you're succeeding in your effort to remain present in the first or second level of mind, despite the arising of thoughts.

Attention Exercise Techniques

Zazen is not just attention exercise—it's much more profound than that—but daily practice does indeed involve working with your attention. There are various techniques to help you focus your attention, gain some independence from monkey mind, and let go of your mental commentary. All of them involve ways to bring your attention back to perceptions at the first or second levels of mind—pure perception, or simple naming.

The classic technique for bringing your attention back to the present is to pay attention to your breath. Your breath is always happening in the present, and there is a motion to it that provides something dynamic for you to pay attention to. You don't alter your breath in any way, you just try to remain aware of it. You can notice the rising and falling of your chest or abdomen, the feeling of coolness spreading from your throat into your lungs as you breathe in, or the sensation of air passing into your nose or mouth. Any aspect of the breath can be the object of your attention if it allows you to maintain your awareness of the breath.

Another method is to think to yourself, "breathing in I breathe a long breath ... breathing out I breathe a short breath," with these being observations of what is naturally occurring (not an effort to change the length of the breath). A more general, all-over body awareness of the breath may work better for you. Finally, you can count your breaths if that helps you stay focused or gives you useful feedback about whether you are remaining focused. The typical recommendation is to count exhalations 1 to 10, and then start over at 1.

When your attention has wandered from the breath, you simply notice that and turn your attention back to it. You may have to do this a hundred times in a 30-minute sitting. In fact, even if you can maintain a constant awareness of the breath, there are always subtle ways you can deepen your awareness (it's possible to more or less keep count of your breaths while the mind wanders in between the numbers). The more calmly you can do this, the better. Any frustration or agitation that arises when you realize your mind has wandered *again* only draws you up into the mind level of commentary and distracts you from your purpose.

Other techniques for returning your attention to the direct input from reality are paying attention to your general body sensations, what's in your visual field, or the sounds you can hear around you. In all these cases your attention should end up steady, as if you're paying attention to one thing, rather than jumping around.

For example, if you're paying attention to bodily sensations, don't let the attention wander around the body randomly: my toe hurts, there's a breeze on my cheek, my arm itches. Try to keep a sense of the body as a whole, or, if your attention is drawn to one area like your toe, then try to keep your attention there as long as you can. If you get too distracted naming all the different sensations or perceptions that are occurring, it defeats the purpose of zazen. You can just let input wash over you, without worrying about registering all of it.

Concentration and Expansion

There are two different ways to deepen or intensify your attentiveness in zazen: concentration and expansion. The word classically used to describe the state of deep meditation in Zen is *samadhi*, which is often translated as "one-pointed concentration." In ideal samadhi, your mind is completely alert, aware, and collected. Samadhi is the opposite of having a scattered mind, where you mentally grasp after, or push away, all the various thoughts, emotions, and sensations that arise in your experience. Although samadhi is often translated as concentration, this state can also be achieved through a diligent expansion of your awareness.

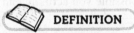 **DEFINITION**

> **Samadhi** is an ancient Pali and Sanskrit term for the experience of one-pointed concentration, alternatively translated as absorption or collectedness.

When you aim for concentration in your meditation, you focus your attention more and more sharply, until the object of your awareness fills up your experience. For example, if you're concentrating on the breath, you follow it more and more closely—noticing the beginning of the inhalation, the flow of air in the middle of the inhalation, the end of the inhalation, the pause before the exhalation, the beginning of the exhalation, and so on. You try very hard to keep the attention on the breath for longer and longer periods of time, and diligently return the attention to the breath whenever it has wandered.

It helps to think of this as an effort to become completely absorbed in or fascinated by the breath, rather than a struggle to subdue the active part of your mind. There's no limit to how absorbed you can become in your full experience, whether you are concentrating on the breath, on sound, or on a koan.

For some people the effort to concentrate the mind becomes a fruitless struggle, as if the decision to concentrate is itself agitating. If you try concentration but feel like there's a force field around your mental busyness that you can't pierce no matter how hard you work at it, you might try expansion instead. It requires a similar diligence of mind, but has a different flavor. The effort to expand your awareness rather than concentrate it can feel more like *not doing* than *doing*, and therefore can be a more conducive approach for people with very active or noncompliant minds.

 POTENTIAL PITFALL

Deep meditative states are not the point of zazen, but they are also not to be avoided. They are the natural result of intense zazen practice and can be very instructive. When you have experienced a new level of stillness, your appreciation of what is possible expands, and you have a new understanding of how to work with your mind. On the other hand, deep meditative states are generally very elusive, especially if you enjoy them and seek to attain them again. It's really best to forget about them, get back to your basic meditation practice, and let the states happen again at some point in the future.

In expansion meditation, you constantly make the effort to expand the edges of your awareness, without letting it shrink down and seize on any one sound, sensation, thought, etc. You become like a video camera, just receiving all the input in front of you without trying to do anything about it, and keeping the widest possible visual field rather than focusing close up on any particular. If you concentrate on any aspect of your experience, you compromise your awareness of everything else, so by trying to remain as open and receptive as possible you actually end up decreasing your mental activity.

There's no room for commentary, because that shuts down some of your perceptive channels. Still, it can be helpful to allow the breath to be at the center of your awareness, just to give you a reference point. If you do this, you don't allow your awareness to be pulled into the breath, you simply let the breath be a companion in your meditation.

Effort Versus Non-effort

Now you know how to do zazen. Or do you? This apparently simple practice can be very difficult. Or, even if you don't perceive it as difficult, you may not have a good sense of whether your zazen is as good as it could be, or how to improve it, or whether you should bother to improve it.

While on the one hand you're seeking absolutely nothing in zazen, it still requires great effort to fully understand how to take the physical and mental posture of Zen meditation. In particular you need to continually recognize and let go of your expectations about how meditation is going to be, refrain from judgments that may seem very justified and rational, and turn toward a mental spaciousness that may appear from afar to be too passive or even frighteningly empty.

Expectations About Meditation

You probably can't help having some ideas and hopes about how your meditation should be. After all, it's perfectly natural to prefer clarity over confusion, peacefulness over anxiety, and ease over pain. You probably wouldn't be practicing meditation at all if you didn't have some hope that it would provide some relief from stress, confusion, and suffering. It may not help that descriptions of the potential results of meditation—like the ones in the previous section—include lots of words like stillness and clarity.

Ideas and hopes about what "good" meditation feels like are not in themselves a problem, as long as you recognize them as simply ideas and hopes. They are not necessarily right or true. In zazen you make the effort to allow your expectations about your meditation to be, just as you allow everything else in your experience to arise and pass away, without being triggered into a volitional response. You don't believe your expectations, and you don't try to get rid of them.

Here's an example. Let's say you notice during meditation that your mind is very full of worries and plans. You try to let them go and return to the present, because when you experience some mental quiet in zazen it's very renewing and helps reduce your stress levels. And after all, zazen is about simply being present, and your thoughts are about things that are elsewhere in space and time. However, trying to let go of the thoughts doesn't seem to help—they just keep coming back! How annoying. Clearly you're too stressed to meditate, right?

Now consider this: your busy mind is part of your experience, as is your reaction to it and your disappointment about the state of your zazen. You may prefer mentally and emotionally quiet zazen, but that's not what's going on. You're annoyed by all the busyness in your mind and wish it would go away so you can have the zazen experience you want.

If you really want to do good zazen, you remain fully present with your experience exactly as it is. That's it. If you manage to stay present with zazen you don't like, you'll actually be strengthening your zazen. Ironically, you may also find a subtle relief from stress even though you were apparently unable to calm your mind during meditation—because, after all, you *were* doing zazen.

Some benefits of meditation are surprising, and suggest that the practice affects you at a subconscious, unconscious, or physical level. For example, I bit my nails from childhood onward, but when I started sitting zazen I stopped. You can't count on such results, but you might find that zazen practice ends up liberating you from some stubborn habits.

Resistance to Just Being

All kinds of resistance can come up when you try to just be present and let go of all volitional actions of body, speech, and mind other than your meditation itself. The resistance doesn't have to be based on a rational fear. You may find yourself concerned, at some subconscious level, about becoming stupid, vapid, passive, lazy, out of touch, vulnerable, or even so enlightened that your current life will lose all its meaning for you.

You may not think you have these kinds of fears, but if you experience some resistance to settling into very still meditation, you might look deeper and surprise yourself. I confess to having had, early in my meditation practice, a subtle but pervasive fear that if all of my volitional activity stopped, I would cease to exist. I wasn't sure whether I would just go unconscious and fall over, or whether I would blink out of existence entirely. Such a fear may seem far-fetched, but it doesn't have to make sense to impede your zazen practice.

"Zazen is not learning to do concentration. It is the dharma gate of great ease and joy. It is undefiled practice-enlightenment."

—Zen Master Dogen (1200-1253), from "Rules for Zazen," translated by Dan Welch and Kaz Tanahashi in *Moon in a Dewdrop*

The beautiful thing is that your very resistance can be an extremely fruitful thing to investigate, because it reveals your deeper fears and assumptions about life. There's a reason why so many people can't stand silence and solitude, or have to distract themselves constantly with music, reading, work, or entertainment. If they sat very still, what would happen? What would they see? Investigating your fears can be scary and needs to be done carefully and gently, but ultimately it's very liberating.

Instead of consciously investigating and facing the fears and assumptions behind your resistance, you can also simply work on gradually overcoming your resistance in meditation. Each time you're able to become a bit more still than you have before, you build up your trust in the process. You prove to yourself that the world doesn't fall apart, that your mind doesn't permanently turn to jelly, and that you don't cease to exist.

When you get up from your meditation seat, the world is waiting for you, and you're fully capable of engaging it. You gain the confidence to let go a little more, until you realize that your volitional activity does not keep the universe running. You can set aside volitional activity at will and pick it back up when it's appropriate. You become more able to just *be*.

Sitting When Things Aren't Okay

Finally, something needs to be said about sitting zazen when you feel terrible physically or emotionally, or when you're in the middle of some difficulty. These are the times when you're probably most likely to decide not to meditate, but they are also the times when zazen is most important. There are several reasons for this.

First, if you sit when you're upset or experiencing difficulty, you have a chance to notice how you're feeling and what you're thinking. Just acknowledging these things can help. Through zazen you also check back into those first and second levels of mind discussed earlier, and this relieves some stress. Your mind is better equipped to deal with what's right here, right now, so when you turn your attention to the present your mind can relax a little bit.

CONSIDER THIS

Sometimes you don't even know how you're feeling until you sit down to meditate. Your daily responsibilities and activities can be so demanding that you rarely get a chance to check in with yourself. When you finally take a few moments to simply be present in your life, you may find yourself realizing things like, "Oh! I'm really worried about ...." Whatever you realize, you'll be able to go about the rest of your life with more awareness and care.

Sitting when you're uncomfortable also cultivates your ability to endure discomfort without having to run away from it or distract yourself. When your preferences are no longer such imperatives, you have much more freedom of choice. At some point you'll need to stay present with a painful or difficult experience—like an illness, or an interaction with someone that's full of conflict—and any ability you've built up to stay present anyway will be extremely valuable.

Last but not least, sitting when things aren't okay strengthens your habit of zazen. You just do it, regardless of how you're feeling or how it makes you feel, because zazen is not about how you feel. It's about being present for your life, which is going to contain a whole range of feelings and experiences. Many Zen practitioners find zazen to be a touchstone that helps carry them through all kinds of difficulties and transitions, so establishing a steady zazen practice can serve you well.

The Least You Need to Know

- The best way to understand zazen is to do it.
- If you're making an effort to be present, you really can't do bad zazen.
- The habitual mind leaps from one thing to another like a monkey, while the mind of zazen is aware of things but doesn't grasp after them or push them away.
- In zazen you learn to be aware of whatever is going on without being pulled into endless mental loops of analyzing, planning, worrying, regretting, or fantasizing.
- Zazen is the practice of profoundly *not doing*, but ironically it still requires lots of effort.

Mindfulness: Awareness in Everyday Life

Sometimes life can seem to be whizzing by too quickly; before you know it, another year is gone. How much of your life do you actually notice? The cliché encourages you to "stop and smell the roses," but how often do you manage to do this, particularly in the midst of routine or stress? You may have a particular rose you enjoy smelling when you get home from work, but do you tend to miss much of what's going on before you get home?

If you end up being unaware of many of the moments of your daily life, you probably also miss many opportunities to do things like appreciate the presence of a loved one or make a choice to respond to a situation in a fresh, rather than habitual, way. Mindfulness is the practice of being more aware of, and present for, your life.

Zen offers tools for cultivating mindfulness, which is an essential part of Zen practice—and not just because you'd like to stop and smell the roses more often. Mindfulness is like the practice of zazen except it's done while engaging in your daily activities. Given the difference in mode, mindfulness feels and manifests differently than zazen, but it involves the cultivation of similar abilities: the ability to place and hold your attention where you want it, the ability to pull yourself out

In This Chapter

- The practice of mindfulness
- Mindfulness compared to meditation
- How to notice and appreciate things more
- Awareness exercises for everyday life
- Cultivating the ability to be careful and respectful

of commentary and return to the present, and the ability to perceive things, including your own thoughts and feelings, more clearly.

> **ZEN WISDOM**
>
> "You don't have to go to a month-long meditation retreat or move to a monastery to restore peace and balance to your life. They are already available to you. Bit by bit, daily mindfulness practice will help you uncover satisfaction and fulfillment in the very life you are living now."
>
> —Zen Teacher Jan Chozen Bays, MD, from *How to Train a Wild Elephant: And Other Adventures in Mindfulness*

The Effort to Be Mindful

Mindfulness takes work, and unlike meditation you can work on it all day long. First, you try to notice the ways you dismiss certain of your activities and experiences as unworthy of your attention or care, and work on valuing all parts of your life. Then, as in meditation, when you realize you're daydreaming, worrying, planning, analyzing, or fantasizing, you return your attention to your present experience. Finally, you work on strengthening your habit of mindfulness in order to be able to remember to pay attention more often. This is often the hardest part, but over time there can be a great increase in the number of times a day your awareness opens up to your present experience.

Nothing Is Beneath Your Attention

The first step in mindfulness practice is to generate a willingness to be present for activities or times in your life that you might normally consider boring, burdensome, useless, annoying, or even uncomfortable. It's easy to pay attention to something you like or something that interests you—a fascinating book, or a beautiful sunset. It's much more difficult to pay attention to driving your thousandth trip home from work, sitting through an overlong meeting, or going to the dentist.

Still, do you really want to "check out" from parts of your life when you only have so many hours left on this earth? And, if you only pay attention to the interesting and enjoyable stuff, what happens if the conditions of your life change and the boring and unpleasant parts start to outweigh the good parts? Then it can seem like you've lost your life.

When you start to pay closer attention to your life no matter what, you'll find that simple activities can be very pleasant and onerous ones are richer than you might think. For example, when you're mowing the lawn, you can feel the vibrations of the mower in your hands and the way the vibrations travel up your arms but don't quite make it to your shoulders. You can appreciate how the noise of the mower is loud but in a certain sense it's peaceful—no distractions from your task because you can't hear anything else. The fresh smell of cut grass fills your nostrils, and there's a strange level of satisfaction you get from making perfectly parallel and barely overlapping diagonals across the lawn.

In another example, while sitting in a long, inefficient meeting you can recognize that there's much more going on than a bad meeting. The rain outside is hitting the windows and cascading down the glass in a shimmering sheet. A friend makes you laugh inside because his eyelids are drooping despite how hard he's trying to pay attention. The attempts of the meeting facilitator to get things moving reveal a great deal about the group's dynamics. And through it all, miraculously, your body continues breathing. If you had simply decided to check out of the meeting mentally because it was a waste of your time, you would have been unlikely to have noticed any of these things.

 ZEN WISDOM

"If while washing dishes, we think only of the cup of tea that awaits us, thus hurrying to get the dishes out of the way as if they were a nuisance ... we are not alive during the time we are washing the dishes .... If we can't wash the dishes, the chances are we won't be able to drink our tea either. While drinking the cup of tea, we will only be thinking of other things, barely aware of the cup in our hands. Thus we are sucked away into the future—and we are incapable of actually living one minute of life."

—Zen Teacher Thich Nhat Hanh, from *The Miracle of Mindfulness*

If you're like most people, you pay attention when you're fully engrossed in a task or some kind of entertainment, but the rest of the time you let your mind wander. There's nothing inherently wrong with this; thinking can be very enjoyable, stimulating, and productive. It may be one of your life's pleasures to ponder deep questions, imagine creative solutions, or play in your mind with words and images.

However, when your mind is free to wander, how much of the time is it actually doing enjoyable or fruitful things? Most likely, much of the time your mind is engaged in semiconscious, pointless activity like delivering judgments on each thing you encounter, rehashing scenes from last night's TV show, or rehearsing speeches to your archenemy that you'll never actually deliver.

Many people are shocked when they start meditation and mindfulness practice because they suddenly realize how chaotic and busy their minds are. Once you recognize the low quality of most of your mind-stream content, just being present with whatever is going on starts to seem much more attractive than just letting the mind buzz all day long.

CONSIDER THIS

When trying to let go of habitual thinking and return to mindfulness of the present, try turning your attention to your thinking before setting up a struggle with your own mind. Rather than trying to cut off or brush away thoughts, take a moment to look at them and ask yourself whether the current content of your thinking is worth more of your attention than input from your surroundings. If your thoughts aren't worth it, you'll be inspired to let them go. If they *are* worth your energy and time, by all means go ahead and think—just do it with awareness.

Wholehearted Activity

Three levels of mind were described in detail in the previous chapter on zazen: pure perception, naming, and commentary. Just as in zazen, when you practice mindfulness you make the effort to let go of the commentary and return to the first and second levels of mind, which involve directly perceiving what's going on around and within you. Mindfulness can be even more challenging than meditation, though, because generally speaking the more active your body is, the more active your mind gets. As a result, when you're going about your daily activities, you're likely to get caught up in a long chain of comments on comments and rarely pay attention to the incoming data of your moment-to-moment reality.

As you continually turn your attention to what's actually going on around you, it's important to realize you are not trying to do zazen while you're walking around, driving, or working. Another name for zazen is *shikantaza*, or "just sitting." When you're doing zazen, this is all you're doing—just sitting there. Keeping your awareness focused on the present in zazen involves awareness of an extremely simple activity in which you can set aside almost all of your volition (all you have to do is stay awake and upright). Because there isn't much else going on, you can pay very close attention to what arises and falls in your own mind.

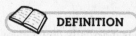

DEFINITION

Shikantaza means "only (*shikan*) precisely (*ta*) sitting (*za*)." This refers particularly to themeless zazen, as opposed to meditating with koans.

In contrast, mindfulness is cultivating awareness during activity; you don't do zazen while washing the dishes, you wash the dishes. The experience is going to be very different from your experience of meditation, although you might say that mindfulness is a kind of meditation in motion. Ideally, mindfulness feels more like wholeheartedness than an effort to realize a self-conscious state of hyperawareness while doing something. When you're wholehearted, your attentiveness and energy flow naturally into your effort.

At first your mindfulness practice might feel a bit like adding a level of self-conscious observation to your life, like "I am taking a walk, I am noticing the sensations from my feet as I walk." That's okay at first, but eventually you're aiming for an even more complete engagement in your walking. This allows you to engage in more complicated tasks and experiences with mindfulness. You can wholeheartedly construct a database or get your children off to school, but it will probably prove awkward to effectively do a complex, demanding activity while adding to it a more self-conscious practice like intense awareness of the breath.

Remembering to Be Mindful

How can you remember to do something like mindfulness when you're forgetting to do it—and thus, by definition, aren't paying much attention to things outside of the content of your thinking? You have to be mindful in order to realize you're not being mindful!

The hardest part about mindfulness can be simply remembering it. If your habit is to spend lots of time in the third level of mind (commentary), chances are good that you will get caught up in a train of thought before you even know it, and only later realize you've spent hours or even days rather oblivious to what's been going on around you. When you finally realize you haven't been practicing mindfulness, you might feel some frustration and wonder how on earth you can make yourself remember more often. There's no quick, easy solution to forgetfulness, but every time you return your attention to what's in front of you, you reinforce that action as a habit. Eventually you remember to pay attention more often, and for longer periods of time.

There are also tools you can use to support your mindfulness practice. The most important of these is the use of rituals, or patterns of behavior you can create around regular daily activities. Mindfulness rituals can be very simple, like making a habit of holding your coffee mug with two hands, taking a long breath before picking up the telephone, or spending the first five minutes of your morning commute in silence. Go ahead and get creative! Devise simple routines around mundane activities that remind you to be mindful and are conducive to the practice.

If you'd like some ideas, Jan Chozen Bays' book *How to Train a Wild Elephant* is full of mindfulness exercises you can try in the midst of your daily life, like taking one bite at a time while eating, or paying special attention to sensations of hot and cold. The use of verses as mindfulness tools dates back at least 2,000 years (mindfulness verses appear in the Buddhist *Avatamsaka Sutra*, which was compiled in the first or second century A.D.). The verses are tied to specific activities or experiences, and generally include some kind of generous intention. For example, "As I fall asleep, I wish for all beings to be safe and at ease."

There are ready-made verses available for your use in books like Thich Nhat Hanh's *Present Moment Wonderful Moment*, appropriate for times like brushing your teeth, throwing out the garbage, or drinking a cup of tea. You can even post your verses in the places where you're likely to use them.

Whether you're using a ritual or verse, doing it along with the activity to which it is attached will eventually help you remember to be mindful. Sooner or later it will feel strange to brush your teeth without saying your mindfulness verse, or to balance a cup in one hand while trying to do two tasks at once. The rituals encourage you to pay attention.

Awareness of the Body

Mindfulness practice generally begins with cultivating awareness of the body. The body is a subject for your attention that is always present, available, and relatively uncomplicated. Body awareness encourages simple attentiveness at the first or second level of mind, rather than commentary and analysis (although anything can inspire active thinking if you let it). For mindfulness practice it simplifies things even further to concentrate on a single aspect of your physical experience, such as the sensations and movements of your hands, the breath, or simple, repetitive movements.

Hands

You're almost always using your hands, so noticing what your hands are up to is a mindfulness practice you can do anywhere, anytime. You either watch your hands as they go about their task, or pay attention to the sensations in the hands, or both.

Even a moment or two of attentiveness to the hands each time you remember to do it means you can incorporate mindfulness into your day many times: when your hands rub your eyes in the morning, when they bring food to your mouth at breakfast, when they shift gears in your car, when they type on a computer keyboard, and when they pet your dog. There's usually plenty of sensory input around the activities of your hands to keep your mind occupied for at least 10 seconds or so, and maybe longer.

One of the fascinating things about being mindful of your hands is that they often seem to belong to someone else, or to be operating on their own. They go about their complicated tasks with very little input from you—or, at least, the self-conscious part of yourself with which you usually feel identified.

In fact, if you start to consciously think about what the hands are doing, they often slow down or falter in their task, as if you're getting in the way. This phenomenon in itself can be a useful subject for mindfulness practice, as it reminds you that your conscious self is only part of a larger flow, and you don't have to mentally orchestrate the whole world. It can be calming to gently attend to the hands and feel like part of something greater.

Breath

Breath is probably the original Buddhist mindfulness object. As long as you're alive the breath is with you, and it involves an intimate, complex sensation of repetitive movement that provides plenty of input to which you can pay attention. In addition, it's an automatic bodily process that occurs without your conscious effort, so even though it's a physical experience it's fairly easy to observe the breath as if it's entirely outside of your sphere of volition. This can make simple awareness of the breath—as opposed to analysis or control of the breath—easier.

POTENTIAL PITFALL

You may be tempted to think breath practice sounds too simple, or like it's just a beginner's exercise. In fact, breath awareness is a practice that can last a lifetime and has many levels of depth. One of the most ancient Buddhist texts, based on the teachings of Siddhartha Gautama (after he became Shakyamuni Buddha 2,500 years ago), is called *The Sutra on the Full Awareness of Breathing*, and proposes that full awareness of breathing can be a gateway to enlightenment.

There's nothing special about being mindful of your breath; you can turn your attention to it in an instant, and it can be a very simple, natural experience. You don't need to get absorbed in your breath, and you don't want awareness of it to shut out awareness of other things. Intense attention to the breath in meditation is different. In that case your whole awareness might be filled with the breath, and there's no limit to the level of detail you can notice in the sensations of the breath.

In mindfulness of the breath, you simply become aware of being a breathing organism in the midst of your conditions. Although the practice sounds simple, it can be extremely useful to be able to settle into awareness of the breath at difficult or stressful times; many people find it grounds them and helps them deal with their circumstances more effectively.

Movement

Another classic object for mindfulness is simple physical movement. Movement of any kind can be used for mindfulness practice, but slow, careful movements like stretching or very slow walking are the most conducive to calm, sustained attention. Generally, the faster your body is moving and the more complicated the movement, the faster your mind will be tempted to "move." However, an all-consuming physical activity like dancing or running can also be a good opportunity for mindfulness practice.

The classic Buddhist mindful movement exercise is slow walking meditation, which in Zen is called *kinhin*. (You can take the description of kinhin given here and apply it to other movements you would like to use as an object of mindfulness.) In kinhin you coordinate your walking with your breathing and take very small steps. Don't alter your breathing, and start with one foot about half a foot-length in front of the other.

At the beginning of your inhalation, start to shift the weight off your back foot. At the end of the inhalation, that foot will end up free to move forward about one foot-length (ending up half a foot-length in front of the other foot). As you exhale, gradually shift half of your weight onto the front foot. Then as you inhale, shift the weight off your back foot, as before. Repeat the process for as long as you would like to do walking meditation. Walk around the perimeter of a room, or choose two points and walk back and forth between them.

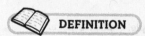

DEFINITION

Kinhin is walking meditation. It can be done slowly and timed with your breathing, as described in the text, or very quickly. In either case the goal is to keep the attention entirely on your movement. Kinhin is often done in Zen groups between periods of zazen.

If you practice mindfulness of faster movements, you'll need to pay more attention to flow and energy, but if you're doing something slow like walking meditation, the idea is to strive for your entire attention to be on the movement. In zazen you are just sitting, in kinhin you are just walking.

A similar intensity and continuity of attentiveness can be attained when practicing mindfulness of a slow movement. To do this you use the movement to anchor your attention in the same way breath can be used to anchor your zazen. Allow the movement to be either the object of your concentration, or the center of your expansive awareness (see Chapter 4 for more about this technique for cultivating attention).

Taking Care with Everything

Another way to think of mindfulness is taking care of each and every thing (or person, or situation) you encounter. While the effort to pay attention to activities and experiences increases the strength of your attention "muscle" in the same way seated meditation does, you can approach the practice with more feeling. If you're trying to take care of, or be with, something, you *have to* pay attention to it. At the same time, you have a chance to give up a bit of your self-centeredness and cultivate appreciation for each thing you encounter in your life.

Valuable, Not Valuable

If you think something is very valuable, you naturally handle it very carefully and mindfully. If I hand you an earthenware vessel from a museum and tell you it's worth five thousand dollars, you're going to be sure to clean your hands before you touch it, handle it with both hands, and pay close attention to it the whole time you have it so it doesn't accidentally fall and break. On the other hand, if you grab a cheap garage-sale bowl out of your cupboard for your cereal, you probably won't even think twice about where you set it except to make sure it doesn't spill cereal on your floor.

When you think something is unimportant or easy to come by, you tend to have an attitude of dismissiveness toward it. This dismissiveness is a thinly veiled rejection of part of your life, which you will subsequently miss because you aren't paying much attention to it. When you discriminate too much between valuable and cheap, rare and common, important and unimportant, beautiful and ugly, delicious and bland, you start to see everything in the whole world through a filter: how much does it matter to *you?*

Even if selflessness is not your goal, looking at everything through this filter of self-concern sets you up for lots of agitation and disappointment when you are deprived of the things (or people, or experiences) you value, and are instead surrounded by what you categorize as junk.

Respect and Attention

You can practice taking care with everything, regardless of how you might objectively value it. In a Zen Center you take your shoes off when you come in to spare the carpet, even if the carpet is kind of old and shabby. You place your shoes on a shelf, side by side, lined up in a row with everyone else's. Doing so, you take care of your shoes and show respect for the place of practice.

At home you can try to use only one paper towel to dry your hands, and then place it mindfully in the can for compost instead of the can for garbage. You can try not to slam doors, bang pots, or waste water. In this culture of care and respect, you quickly learn not to dismiss or be careless with anything. You end up paying close attention to each thing—voilà, mindfulness!

If you're in a room full of people—and mindful yourself—it quickly becomes obvious which people practice mindfulness and which do not. The unmindful person will accidentally drop a wrapper and not even notice. The mindful person next to them will quietly pick it up and throw it away. The unmindful person will stand smoking under a no-smoking sign, or neglect to pay attention while their dog leaves an unpleasant surprise on someone else's lawn. The mindful person will notice these things and behave more respectfully and carefully, but not because they're morally superior; the unmindful people would probably say, "Oops!" if they realized what they had done. It's just that mindful people are much more likely to perceive what's going on around them and be thoughtful about how they respond.

The Least You Need to Know

- Mindfulness is something you can work on all day, every day; everything in your life can be the object of your awareness.
- Mindfulness, like zazen, is exercise for your attention.
- Great mindfulness practices include awareness of your hands and breath, and slow physical movement.
- You can think of mindfulness as the cultivation of wholeheartedness or appreciation.
- Mindfulness allows you to be careful and respectful.

Precepts: The Zen Moral Code

The ideas about Zen in popular culture rarely include the important role moral behavior plays in Zen practice. In fact, many people are familiar with Zen only through fictional characters and the occasional story about an iconoclastic Zen master, and the impression they might get from this is that Zen is very individualistic and above petty concerns like moral behavior. Add to this the fact that there is no deity in Zen ready to reward or punish your deeds, and Zen can perhaps even seem antimoralistic.

In fact, morality is a central part of Zen practice. First, morality in Zen is about not causing suffering for oneself and others. The whole point of Zen practice is to alleviate suffering and increase happiness, so any deliberate behavior that increases the suffering in the world is antithetical to Zen practice. Moral conduct is also considered a prerequisite for the calm concentration that's necessary for spiritual insight, and the effort to follow a moral code is valued as a challenging practice in and of itself.

Both lay and ordained practitioners vow to follow the Zen precepts as part of the ceremony of becoming Zen Buddhists. They don't promise to meditate, or study Buddhist texts, or believe Buddhist teachings; they promise to keep the precepts.

In This Chapter

- The relationship between Zen and morality
- Reasons to be careful about your actions
- Practicing with a moral code
- The ten Zen precepts

This is an indication of how morality is seen as the starting point and minimum requirement for Zen practice.

Why Be Moral?

You probably agree that it's a good thing to try to be nice and generally trustworthy, but why go to the lengths of adopting a moral code and striving to keep it? There's no deity in Zen, so there's no God-given set of rules to follow because of their divine authority. In Buddhist cosmology the only thing you have to do to attain an afterlife is to mess this life up so you have to come back and continue living out the chain of causation you perpetuated. From the Zen point of view, why be so concerned about morality?

 ZEN WISDOM

"Without the precepts as guidelines, Zen Buddhism tends to become a hobby, made to fit the needs of the ego."

–Robert Aitken Roshi (1917-2010), from *The Mind of Clover: Essays in Zen Buddhist Ethics*

Not Causing Suffering

You may or may not see yourself as devoted to the cause of alleviating suffering and increasing happiness. If you relate to this effort, it's probably because you're aware of your own suffering or the suffering of others. If you don't relate to this effort, it might be because you're defining the term "suffering" too narrowly.

The Buddhist teachings about suffering will be described in more detail in a later chapter, but suffice it to say that when Buddhists talk about suffering they're referring to a wide range of human experiences. Suffering can be in response to extremely challenging things like acute physical or emotional pain, trauma, or injustice. This is dramatic suffering. Suffering can also be much more subtle—or even existential. This kind of suffering includes things like a sense of isolation, a lack of meaning in your life, or having to watch as you hurt others with a temper you can't control.

The basis of Zen practice is a recognition that suffering exists—in your life, and in the lives of others—and an intention to try to do something about it. This does not entail a frantic effort to eradicate every bit of discomfort in the world, but it does require an energetic devotion to do what you can. When you have a choice, you can opt for the path that causes the least amount of suffering and maximizes happiness for everyone. Doing so, you aspire to the path of the *bodhisattva*, a being that vows to work for the welfare of all living things. This is why the Zen precepts as I present them in this chapter are called the "bodhisattva precepts."

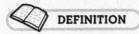 **DEFINITION**

> **Bodhisattva** refers to the Buddhist ideal of a being that diligently cultivates his or her own discipline and wisdom in order to attain enlightenment, but also has great compassion for all living beings and works for their happiness as well. In other words, the bodhisattva is not satisfied with his or her own attainment of peace and liberation.

Your Suffering and My Suffering

Of course, the irony is that when I refrain from causing you suffering, it also prevents or alleviates my suffering. In this complex and interdependent world, my happiness is not entirely separate from your happiness. This fact is not something Zen Buddhists seek to prove to you through philosophical arguments; it's something you are invited to prove to yourself by carefully observing the causes and effects of your own behavior. Interdependence in the moral sphere is not about the lack of real boundaries between things due to all the space inside our atoms, or an extension of ecology. There may be truth to these things and they probably are not unrelated, but interdependence in the Zen view is about direct, personal experience.

If I am able to take a Zen approach to the world, I am open and aware, and this results in *me* suffering when I see *you* suffering. You are familiar with this phenomenon at the very least when you witness the struggles of people you care deeply about, such as your child, parent, partner, or friend. You feel pain about their pain. In Zen practice you strive to make your circle of care as wide as possible because any limitations on it have to do with self-concern, and self-concern causes suffering. So more and more often you recognize that there is no clear separation between your suffering and that of others, or between your happiness and that of others.

What if someone isn't open and aware? What if they don't care if they cause someone else harm? Buddhism proposes that such a person suffers when they harm others, despite any outward appearances. The classic example is the person who seriously hurts someone, but is never connected to the crime. In a practical sense the attacker "gets away with it." He may go on to lead a life full of wealth, social status, and apparent success. He may even manage to block his past action out of his consciousness for the most part, or perhaps he rationalizes it into a minor transgression.

According to the moral law of the universe, as observable as any physical law, you can't cause harm to another without suffering negative repercussions yourself. In the case of our attacker, he has compromised his relationship with all people because he always has to worry about being found out. In order to live with his crime, he has to structure his mind such that some people are unworthy of respect, so his intimacy with life and others is necessarily limited. To whatever extent he manages to avoid thinking about his crime, the fact of it will cause stress that will emerge eventually in mental or physical health problems. The list of negative repercussions goes on.

CONSIDER THIS

Responding sympathetically to another's pain may be hard-wired into you! Doing so is the natural outcome of empathy, or the ability to know what someone else is feeling. Research has proven the existence of something scientists call "mirror neurons"; when you see me prick my finger, the same *ouch* areas of the brain light up in both of us. Citing examples like these in his book *Field Notes on the Compassionate Life*, Marc Barasch suggests that compassion may be more an integral aspect of humanity than merely a nice idea.

You can't see into other people's minds in order to verify the proposition that they can't hurt others without hurting themselves, but you *can* see into your own mind to verify it. You can carefully observe your behaviors and their repercussions outside and within you, and you can learn which kinds of actions tend to cause suffering and which do not. Generally speaking you are going to notice that if your motivation for an action is primarily self-concern, and you are aware that it may compromise the happiness of others, the action is quite likely to cause suffering to both self and other. You are also going to notice that any reward you obtain at the expense of others is likely to have unforeseen costs.

Actions That Disturb Your Zazen

If you want to be even more pragmatic about reasons to embrace moral behavior, consider that acting in ways that cause suffering creates disturbances in your environment that are counterproductive to your Zen practice. There you are, sitting on your meditation seat, trying to let go of commentary and analysis. You try to focus your volition on your meditation. How well are you going to be able to do this if your life is full of people who are angry at you because of your selfish actions?

It will be very difficult to rest in the present moment when you are worried that your boss is going to find out that you are stealing, or your spouse is going to find out that you are having an affair. One careless or harmful action often leads to another, so it's easy to overindulge in things like gambling, lying, promiscuity, and intoxicants and make a big mess of your life. It will be very difficult to concentrate on Zen practice if you're deep in debt or running from the law.

CONSIDER THIS

According to Shakyamuni Buddha (as quoted in a Pali Canon sutra), the reward and blessing of moral behavior is freedom from remorse, which in turn leads to joy; joy leads to states of peacefulness and happiness, and those states allow concentration, followed by insight, followed by detachment, and finally, liberation.

The Buddhist term for the disturbance created by certain actions is *karma*. The term originally meant an action or deed, but it has also come to refer to the chain of causation that deeds put into motion or perpetuate. It is certainly possible to generate positive karma (you help your friends move, they will probably be happy to help you in return), but it's part of the law of karma that a selfish or harmful action will always generate some negative karma. The karma generated is like a ripple sent through your life. Remember the image of letting your mind settle in zazen as if it were a turbid pond, so the sediment will fall out and you can see clearly? That's not going to happen if you keep stirring everything up.

It also helps calm and simplify your life (and therefore your zazen) to have a moral code. You don't necessarily have to adopt the Zen precepts, but deciding ahead of time how you would like to act means that you don't have to spend lots of time pondering certain kinds of choices. For example, you may still be tempted to ignore a rule or legal requirement in order to save some money or be able to do something you want, but if you've decided you won't lie if the authorities question you about it—well, as nice as it would be to cheat, you can't do it.

In another example, although you would love to tell off your arrogant co-worker in the middle of a meeting, you have a precept about not indulging anger, so you'll have to find another way to deal with your feelings. Having a moral code still leaves you with lots of moral ambiguity to consider as you decide how it applies in each circumstance, but it's a lot more conducive to Zen practice than always wondering how to get maximum advantage for yourself in every situation.

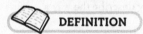

DEFINITION

> **Karma** means action or deed, but it also refers to the chain of causes and effects that result from that deed when effects in turn become causes.

How the Precepts Work

The Zen precepts are a description of enlightened activity rather than a list of rules. Equipped with a tool like the precepts, you have a reference point for all of your activities, but this reference point is not a standard against which you judge yourself as good or bad. Rather, it's a direction you want to go. You have chosen this direction because of your aspirations, such as decreasing suffering, increasing happiness, and achieving some of the wisdom and peace of a buddha. When you look at your actions in terms of the precepts, you can get a sense of whether you're headed in the right direction or not.

The Behavior of a Buddha

The Zen proposition is this: if you were completely enlightened and liberated, you wouldn't be motivated to act selfishly. If you really understood the true relationship between self and other, you would never intend to harm anyone or anything without an extremely good reason for doing so. You wouldn't be arrogant or defensive; you would be generous, patient, and kind. You would have a deep source of peace and stability inside you, so you wouldn't need to look out for "numero uno."

This proposition can be a useful thing to call to mind when you encounter difficult people; if they were truly at peace within themselves, they wouldn't be abusive, cruel, or disrespectful. It's also easy to verify for yourself: how do you act when you have everything you need and want? How do you act when you are in a familiar setting, where you feel secure in your role and confident in your ability to respond skillfully? How do you act when you are surrounded by people who love, respect, and support you? How do you act when you feel fortunate and like you have more than you need? In these situations you will most likely be generous, patient, and kind, because you have no reason to get angry, defensive, or worried about yourself.

ZEN WISDOM

"When you sit, you manifest the enlightenment of all Buddhas. You actualize wisdom and compassion in the sitting itself. The same can be said for the precepts —the precepts are the definition of the life of a Buddha. They describe the way a Buddha lives his or her life."

—John Daido Loori Roshi (1931-2009), from *The Heart of Being: Moral and Ethical Teachings of Zen Buddhism*

The only difference between you and a buddha—a completely enlightened being—is that the buddha doesn't have to depend on external circumstances like the ones described above in order to feel like she has everything she needs and wants. Through practice she has come to understand her relationship to the world in a very different way, one that doesn't depend on the ordinary concept of self. As you engage in a practice that is aimed at realizing something of what a buddha realizes, you can know something about your progress in practice by observing how well and how easily you keep the Zen precepts, because they describe how a buddha naturally acts.

Intention and Clarity

Your intention has a big effect on the results of your actions, but you don't escape negative repercussions because you didn't mean to do something, you didn't realize you were doing it, or you couldn't help yourself. Accidentally killing or stealing is very different from deliberately doing so, but the action obviously will have negative effects anyway. You may not realize you're being stingy, but the failure to be generous affects others, as well as encouraging selfishness in your own mind. Losing your temper despite yourself will have fewer negative effects than consciously unleashing your anger on someone with a sense that it's justified, but it may not make much difference to the victim of your anger.

To keep a moral code, you have to work not only on your conscious intention (which is hard enough), you also have to cultivate clarity in order to see what you're doing, how you can take better care of things so fewer accidents happen, and how you can work with your own body and mind to change your negative habits. It's not enough to say you don't mean to get angry, but you just can't help it. It's good that you don't intend to indulge anger, but it's clearly not that helpful if you stop there. Fortunately, the other aspects of Zen practice—zazen, mindfulness, and karma work, for example—are ways you can cultivate clarity and work on habits.

Compassion Is the Trump Card

It isn't helpful to get all caught up in the precepts as a list of absolutes you *must* follow legalistically. This is why the precepts are often described as "guidelines." Unfortunately the term "guideline" can imply that you're only meant to follow the precepts if you feel like it, and halfheartedness or sloppiness with respect to moral conduct is not the Zen intention. On the other hand, "guideline" acknowledges that you're ultimately free to make your own choices (although you get to deal with the results of those choices).

More importantly, the precepts function like guidelines because the spirit of the law is more important than the letter of the law, and the spirit of the law is compassion. The only legitimate excuse for breaking the precepts is compassion, and even then there is still karma from the action.

For example, you may euthanize an animal because it is suffering terribly and there is no possibility it will recover; this is an act of compassion. Some people may debate this point, but from your sincere point of view you would be turning away from compassion if you kept the precept of not killing instead. Nevertheless, the act of euthanasia will have negative effects, including your grief if you care about the animal. If you don't particularly care about the animal but are acting out of a more abstract sense of what's good, you risk becoming numb to the act of killing.

Given all this complexity, what should you do? You can do your best, break precepts only for very good reasons, be aware of the consequences, and accept those consequences with as much grace as possible.

CONSIDER THIS

Whether or not you believe in rebirth—the idea that something of you passes on to another life when you die—the Buddhist imagery around this concept can be useful. According to Buddhist wisdom, if you do something selfish or malicious, you will *inevitably* feel the negative effects of that action—but you may feel them in this life, maybe in the next life, or maybe in the life after next. This acknowledges how complex the chain of causation can be, but still holds that an action taken without regard to others will always have some kind of negative effect.

Daily Precept Practice

Paying attention to the morality of your behavior allows you to avoid causing suffering and making a mess of your life, but it also is a valuable practice in and of itself. When you are challenged to keep a precept, you are essentially being challenged to let go of self-concern, so keeping the precepts in mind gives you plenty of opportunities for working on yourself. This self-concern is one of the primary objects of study in Zen practice, along with all the delusions and attachments that go with it. Seeing clearly how you relate to the world as a "self" is a key to liberation.

As you go about your day, the precepts will come up constantly. When you're trying to do a practice like mindfulness you have to remember to do it, and it may be unclear at times how well you are doing it. The precepts, on the other hand, are difficult to forget or ignore once you've formed the intention to follow them. Challenges to keeping the precepts will arise as soon as you get out of bed in the morning, and continue until you return to bed at night.

There's no getting around the fact that you just have to try to keep the precepts. But when you notice a temptation to break one, or you give in to that temptation, there's no point in beating yourself up. It certainly doesn't help to give up trying to keep the precepts as a consequence.

Instead, you treat precept work like any of the other Zen practices: you first try to see clearly. Notice your behavior and take responsibility for it, apologize if necessary, and notice as much as you can about the circumstances that led to the precept challenge. What triggered it? What were you thinking and feeling? Where and when did you make a choice that you would rather not have made? In doing this kind of study, you can learn more about your self-concern, as well as how to better keep the precepts.

Precepts and Other People

The *law of karma* states that one cannot escape at least some negative consequences of selfish or harmful actions. If you are following the precepts because you are convinced of the law of karma, you are probably going to start looking around you for evidence that it's true. This will inevitably lead to frustration and confusion, because the unfolding of causes and conditions in the world is unimaginably complex.

Your neighbor may steal from work, cheat on his taxes, unleash his anger on his dog, and abuse intoxicants, but he may still insist he's *just fine*, thank you very much. Your partner may squash bugs and eat meat without a second thought, apparently immune to any consequences. Trying to figure out whether and how the law of karma applies to others can drive you crazy, because there is so much more going on than the one cause you are noticing, and because the repercussions of actions may be delayed in time.

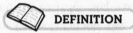

> **DEFINITION**
>
> The **law of karma** is the moral law of the universe, a natural law rather like the law of gravity, which states that selfish or harmful actions—especially ones that are intentionally so—always result in at least some negative results for the doer (as well as others).

The good thing is that your own moral practice need not depend on the law of karma being true in some universal sense. You only have to notice that it's true for you. You can be aware of your own intentions, conditions, and the way things affect you internally. At a certain level only you can know whether you are keeping a precept; an action of yours that appears to be stinginess to someone else may in fact be compassionately setting a boundary. In a certain situation you might indulge anger because you have tried other kinds of communication and you haven't been heard. In the end, your moral life is your own responsibility, and your neighbor's moral life is his responsibility.

In the same vein, if you start following moral guidelines like the Zen precepts, you are going to recognize how much suffering and confusion you prevent by doing so. It's natural to want to share this great discovery with others, but beware of alienating friends, family, and co-workers with moral suggestions. Try to keep your enthusiasm to yourself, and let others find their own way (your advice is very unlikely to help matters anyhow).

The Ten Zen Precepts

The Zen moral code begins with several precepts commonly referred to as the "three pure precepts." These are: cease from harmful action, do only good, and do good for others. These three are the essence of moral behavior, rather like admonitions in many religions to treat others as you would like others to treat you. If you were able to follow the three pure precepts perfectly, you wouldn't have any moral problem. On the other hand, human beings generally need things spelled out a little more specifically. The "ten grave precepts" explained in this section are what the three pure precepts look like in practical application.

Each Zen precept can be understood at multiple levels, and in the following explanations I will describe the function of each precept at each of these levels.

At their most concrete, the precepts are instructions for your observable behaviors. At this level, not dwelling on past mistakes means not elaborating on the shortcomings of others in your speech.

At a deeper level, the precepts are about your intention and the state of your mind, whether or not you act out your inclinations. At this level, not stealing would mean not spending lots of time longing for what other people have.

At an even deeper level, the precepts are about the state of your being—how separate do you still feel from the rest of the universe? When you use the precepts in this way, not being stingy means working on letting go of self-concern to the point that it is no longer the first thing that comes to your mind when someone needs something you might be able to give. It is impossible to keep the precepts perfectly at these deeper levels, so there is no end to precept practice.

Not Killing

At its most concrete, this precept is about not killing other human beings. Few people reading this book are going to have to fight that temptation, but the importance of this literal injunction is not to be underestimated. For one thing, while intention matters (there are more negative repercussions from killing someone deliberately than from killing someone accidentally), there is *always* karma from causing someone's death. This is part of the reason why war is so traumatic for soldiers.

This precept also recommends minimizing the killing of non-human beings. While you have to at least kill vegetables to live, the more you can avoid killing and still maintain your health, the better. The bottom line is that killing of any kind generates negative karma, so it's best to minimize it. This is why many Buddhists are vegetarians.

However, there are other things you can kill, and other ways of killing. You break this precept to some extent when you reject anyone or anything, in essence cutting it off from that which you value. You can kill someone's generosity by refusing to eat the meal they have lovingly prepared for you because they cooked meat and you are a vegetarian.

If you have to kill, you try to do so mindfully, acknowledging the value of that which you are killing. If you thoughtlessly step on a spider instead of taking a moment to put it outside, it breaks the spirit of this precept more than when someone hunting for food respectfully says a prayer of gratitude over the body of an animal they have just killed.

Not Stealing

Not stealing means not taking other people's stuff. However, this isn't about honoring ownership or capitalism as being part of the divine order of things. The precept of not stealing is about being respectful in your human relationships and refraining from indulging your selfish desires at the expense of others. Most of the time when people steal, they justify their actions by saying that they aren't really hurting anyone—the people they're stealing from have more than they need, or it's just money or stuff.

However, if you've ever been stolen from, you realize that's not all there is to it. You rely on a culture of mutual trust, and when someone steals from you, that trust is violated. Of course, when someone steals from a corporation, they may not care at all about whether that corporation trusts them, but what is the act of stealing or cheating doing to the thief or cheater? It's building up a habit in them to bend the rules to suit themselves.

You can steal in more subtle ways, of course. One of the translations of this precept is "do not covet." When you obsess over what you don't have and how you can obtain it, you neglect your current life. You are always chasing after things, and what you have is never enough. This is not to say that you can't try to improve your life or have ambitions, but that you can do these things without operating from a sense of lack or insufficiency.

 POTENTIAL PITFALL

> You might resist the precept against stealing because it seems to endorse secular material values or laws that may or may not be fair or just. However, this precept is about honoring your relationships with other people, and refraining from indulging selfish desires. You're welcome to try to change the culture and laws, but in the meantime your fellow citizens are counting on you to follow the rules.

Not Misusing Sexual Energy

The precept on not misusing sexual energy requires you to acknowledge the power of such energy and to use it thoughtfully, carefully, and respectfully. There is nothing inherently wrong with sexual energy, or beauty, or sensuality, but all of these things are tied up with human instincts that may run even deeper than the instinct to survive. In brief, this is potent stuff, and if you use sexual energy in selfish ways it can be very destructive and harmful.

You have to decide for yourself what it means for *you* to misuse sexual energy. This precept is about taking responsibility for yourself, and cultivating awareness of how you use and respond to sexuality. Most of the precepts involve being faithful in your relationships, and in the case of sex you can use this goal as a barometer to test the appropriateness of your actions.

Does your current indulgence in sex or playfulness with sexual energy honor your relationships or endanger them? If you really look at the person with whom you are engaging sexually, can you honestly say the engagement is good for them, or are you just using them? When you dress provocatively or flirt, are you doing so with full awareness of your actions and motivations, or might you be emphasizing your sexuality because you have become dependent on it as part of your identity? No one can answer these questions for you.

At the deepest level the precept on sexual energy is about intimacy, and your relationship to everyone and everything. When you have a sense of completeness and peace within yourself, intimacy follows naturally from openness and honesty and does not require seduction or pursuit.

Not Lying

There are all kinds of reasons people lie, and some are more harmful than others. This precept is about self-serving lies, half-truths, or omissions. When you look carefully, however, even small lies are often about trying to avoid having to do something generous or be held accountable. In short, they are self-serving and endanger the trust in your relationships.

For example, when your boss asks you whether you double-checked something on your last job and you didn't, it's much easier to just say, "Yes, I did," than it is to own up, face your superior's anger, and then have to go back to the job site and do what you forgot to do. Maybe you think, "So what? I don't really need to double-check anyway." You may be right, but is that what this lie is about? Not really. You can argue with your boss that you can do without a double-check, but the lie is really about your own convenience and the avoidance of unpleasantness.

The most subtle form of lying is hiding from the world. This happens when you're afraid of what might happen if you didn't keep up the charade: rejection, censure, a loss of respect? Bit by bit you can experiment with more honesty and see what happens, and eventually you will find that as long as you're doing your best there's nothing to fear. However, it's important to differentiate honesty from the expression of self-interest; self-interest is flavored with self-justification, while honesty feels humble and open.

POTENTIAL PITFALL

What about compassionate lies? Again, the trump card when it comes to the precepts is compassion; it's the only good reason to break a precept. However, just because a lie prevents hard feelings doesn't mean it's compassionate. When your friend asks if he offended you (and he did) but you say, "No," you avoid a difficult conversation, but maybe telling the truth and having that difficult conversation is the most compassionate thing to do. On the other hand, telling your aunt that the meal she made for you is delicious (when it's not) is probably more for her sake than for yours.

Not Abusing Intoxicants

Intoxication is about altering your experience of reality. The whole point of Zen is to be aware of, and present for, your life just as it is. Intoxicants generally dull or distort your awareness, encourage you to forget your aspirations, and allow you to escape from aspects of your life you don't like.

Of course, it's a matter of degree. Having a glass of wine to feel a little more relaxed after work is probably not a big deal, while getting drunk after work because otherwise you would be in anguish all evening is a problem. Zen practice is tough. It asks you to face that anguish while sober so you can understand it, work with it, and ultimately resolve it so you don't need to take refuge in intoxicants.

Drugs and alcohol are not the only intoxicants you can abuse. All kinds of other substances and activities allow you to alter your experience of reality so you can avoid difficult things like boredom, loneliness, or a sense of doubt about the direction of your life. Television, books, gambling, and even work can be used to escape. Of course, occasional escape is fine and can renew your energy. It's when these activities start to interfere with your cultivation of clarity that they become a problem.

Not Dwelling on Past Mistakes

First and foremost, not dwelling on past mistakes means not bad-mouthing others. It can be tricky deciding whether something you want to say is constructive criticism or just self-serving. Constructive criticism is generally something that has the potential to help others if it is heard, and therefore this precept does *not* prohibit constructive criticism. On the other hand, self-serving criticism of others is usually something you would rather the subject of the criticism never heard, or is expressed more harshly than you would ever express it to them face-to-face.

People bad-mouth others for many reasons: to vent troubling feelings, justify positions or actions, make themselves feel superior to an adversary, or decrease their sense of insecurity by getting others to agree with their opinions. All of these contain at least a little reward for the person doing the criticizing. If you break the precept on not dwelling on past mistakes in order to avail yourself of one of these rewards, it's okay to have some compassion for yourself and recognize you're feeling a little needy. That's a lot different from feeling righteous or justified.

It's also possible to break this precept by dwelling on your own past mistakes. You can beat yourself up inside with a tirade of inner criticism, and many people are more harsh with themselves than they are with others. Despite the fact that you're the object of the criticism and trying to get yourself to change, this is still not helpful. You will need the willing participation of every part of yourself to do Zen practice; inner violence is counterproductive. Instead, for yourself and for others, you try to cultivate patience and awareness so you will be able to do something truly conducive to change when the opportunity arises.

Not Being Attached to Praise or Blame

Not being attached to praise and blame means not getting caught up in the opinions of others, and not basing your sense of self-worth on comparisons. Like all the other precepts, this is addressing self-centeredness, so it's not in any way suggesting you should discount the feelings and opinions of others in order to just do it *your* way. What you want to avoid is seeking after the approval of others in order to build up your sense of self—or blaming others in order to feel superior to them.

There's no denying there are differences in this world. Some people are hardworking and some are lazy, some people are generous and some are stingy. However, impartially noting these differences has nothing to do with you personally, while expounding upon them in order to feel righteous, proud, or justified is all about you.

 CONSIDER THIS

> If you look for approval from others, even if it's just from a few others that you
> respect, it may be because you doubt yourself. If you try to overcome that doubt, it
> often doesn't help to evaluate yourself in terms of your likelihood of success or failure.
> There are no guarantees, and there's always someone more skilled than you are.
> Instead, try to reconcile yourself to doing your best, without apology for being who
> and what you are.

Keeping this precept ultimately requires you to thoroughly explore your sense of self, and to find a deeper frame of reference for your life than how you compare to others. The Buddhist phrase "leap beyond praise and blame" points you toward a way of being in the world where neither praise nor blame alters your true sense of self. When you can live like this, praise and blame are both useful sources of information about the reactions of others, which you can choose to respond to or not.

Not Being Stingy

Not being stingy is one of the hardest precepts to keep because you can be stingy with just about everything, including your money, your possessions, your time, your sympathy, and your attention. Stinginess is perhaps one of the two most basic manifestations of self-concern, along with anger.

Unfortunately there is no clear line between stinginess and taking reasonable care of your life and responsibilities. It's a moment-to-moment judgment call, but the basic idea is clear: be as generous as you can. Again, awareness is the key. If you decide not to give money to the panhandler on the street, make this a conscious decision that you take responsibility for, not a subconscious tightening of your grip on your purse.

While practicing Zen does not require you to give, give, give without discrimination, I actually think this precept *is* suggesting that you would suffer less if you did so. Few of us are going to choose to give away everything, but this precept suggests that negative karma is generated by holding on to something when someone else needs it. You may hold on to things for compassionate reasons—care of yourself and your family, or in order to support beneficial work in the world—but that twinge you feel when you see people in need is the karmic result of your decision.

Not Indulging Anger

Anger arises when you feel you, or something you care about, is under threat. It can be valuable information, because maybe there really is a threat to be dealt with. However, Buddhists hold that it would be better to let go of your anger before dealing with it, because anger distorts your perceptions. It narrows your field of vision down until you can only see the object of your anger.

While this phenomenon may have helped our ancestors fight off predators, it's maladaptive when it comes to negotiating the complex social environments of modern human life. If you act while your field of perception is narrowed by anger, you will lack a frame of reference for your actions in space and time, and you will probably regret your action. This is especially true because unleashed anger is destructive. Even if you achieve your aim by indulging your anger, there was probably a way to do it without the destruction.

 CONSIDER THIS

You may think you can't help being angry. After all, something caused your anger, and your reaction only makes sense. If you look at it another way, however, you might say that something happened and then you felt anger. This is not about blaming yourself, but about putting some space between events and your response to them and choosing the best way to respond.

Despite your intentions, anger will probably keep arising. You can learn how to avoid acting it out, but at a deeper level working with anger allows you to examine your sense of self and your ideas about the world. Often, your anger is based on a view you have about the world and the way it should be. Whether or not your views are righteous and justified, they are just views. If you feel anger, clearly reality is not conforming to your views. If you can loosen your grip on your views, anger loses some of its steam.

Not Disparaging Aspiration

This precept is actually "not disparaging the three treasures," which are buddha, dharma, and sangha. For readers of this book who may not be Buddhist, I have taken the liberty of translating this precept differently, in a way that I think gets at its most important aspects.

The three Buddhist treasures are about cultivating faith that (greater) liberation is possible for anyone, including you, and about having reverence and respect for those things that support your aspiration. The traditional translation of the precept is about not bad-mouthing Buddhism and the sangha, but you can substitute for these your own deepest aspiration. If you start disparaging or doubting God, or Truth, or Justice, you undermine your own and other people's source of strength and inspiration. This can be done through direct criticism or general cynicism.

When you break precepts you are acting out of self-concern—so how is the small self served by breaking this precept on not disparaging aspiration? It's a little like the fox in Aesop's fable who decides the grapes he can't reach must be sour. When you feel discouraged in your aspiration or you begin to doubt the existence or truth of something you value deeply, it can be easier to disparage what you formerly treasured than to face your frustration and disappointment.

The unfortunate thing about this disparagement is that it may keep you from realizing your aspiration after all. It may have been your limited patience, understanding, or diligence that kept you from getting the grapes. In fact, central to Zen is the idea that the grapes do indeed exist, and if you haven't tasted them yet it's because you haven't yet figured out how to reach them.

The Least You Need to Know

- Moral conduct is about preventing suffering, supporting happiness, and taking care of your life.
- Immorality is primarily about acting out of self-centeredness.
- A moral code gives you a frame of reference for your whole life.
- Precepts are great selfishness detectors, and provide countless practice opportunities in everyday life.
- It's not about rules, it's about awareness and compassion.

Karma Work: Habits of Body, Speech, and Mind

The ultimate Zen paradox is that your life is complete and precious just as it is, but in order to maintain a sense of that preciousness you have to work constantly to decrease the amount of suffering you cause yourself and others.

Chances are good that if you've tried some of the practices described in this book so far—meditation, mindfulness, and keeping the precepts—you will have run into some difficulty. Despite your intention to be present during meditation, perhaps your mind is filled with anxiety. You fully intend to be mindful throughout your day, but half the day goes by before you even remember your intention. Keeping the precepts sounds like a good idea, but criticism of others comes flying out of your mouth before you can stop it.

Your habits and tendencies of body, speech, and mind are collectively called your karma. Your karma is the result of all of your past actions and experiences—some of which you had control over, and some of which you did not. Regardless of how it came to be, your karma is the package of energy and momentum you have to work with in your life, and any lasting change requires that you develop an understanding of it and take responsibility for it. Then you can use the Zen tools of meditation, mindfulness, and the precepts to gradually change some of your less-than-helpful behaviors.

In This Chapter

- The Zen concept of karma
- What to do when you want to change your behavior
- Things that get in the way of change
- Using Zen tools to understand and change a habit
- How to set yourself up for success in change

About Karma

The way the concept of karma is used in Zen is different from the way it's used in some other religions, and varying uses of the concept lead to some ideas in popular culture that are misconceptions from a Zen perspective. An example of such a non-Zen concept about karma is the idea that there's someone or something keeping track of all bad deeds to ensure everyone receives payback eventually. Another example is the idea that karma is like a big game of chance, and if you're lucky you get some good karma but if you're unlucky you end up with some bad karma.

In Hinduism and some other forms of Buddhism, such as Vajrayana (from Tibet), karma, or the resulting sum of your past actions, is presented as the only explanation for your circumstances; the choices you made in past lives or in this one explain everything from your depression to your pimples to your financial situation. For some people this explanation is comforting, because it implies you have complete control over your future (it's all about your behavior). For other people this presentation of karma as the only causal factor in the world doesn't make sense, and it comes too close to blaming innocent victims for their suffering.

 CONSIDER THIS

In an ancient text, Shakyamuni Buddha is quoted as saying there are four topics about which it is pointless to conjecture, because they will only lead to madness and vexation. Two of the four are about spiritual powers, one is the origin of the world, and the fourth is the precise workings of karma. Understanding the precise workings of karma would involve identifying all the causes and conditions that led to a particular result, or exactly how one cause connects to all of its effects. This is impossible, because the web of causation is infinitely complex.

Alternatively, in Zen, karma is used to acknowledge the importance of your intention and choices in the shaping of your circumstances, especially the condition of your mind. Other factors affect your life, including genetics, the way you were raised, and your culture. However, although you can influence your conditions to some extent, you primarily have control over your own choices, so the concept of karma emphasizes how you can take responsibility for your life and shape it depending on what decisions you make. With your choices you primarily affect the state of your own mind, and because Zen considers the state of your mind to be of primary importance when it comes to your experience of the world, the role of karma in Zen is very significant.

Your Karmic Package

It's pretty natural to wonder, "Why me?" Why did you end up with such a short temper? Why did you end up with a serious illness? Why do you have such a shortage of self-discipline? If you can understand how it came to be, it seems like you will be better equipped to deal with the problem; but sometimes the answers can seem difficult to come by. It's often easier to see the main causes of *other people's* difficulties!

While you acknowledge that Joe probably had some genes and family-of-origin experiences that predisposed him to abuse intoxicants, you can clearly see that as long as he blames his circumstances and refuses to take responsibility for his actions, he won't break free of his addictions. Mary may wonder why she ended up with heart problems, but her friends don't wonder why at all because they're well aware of the fact that Mary doesn't exercise or eat well.

All of your habits and conditions of body, speech, and mind are due at least in some small part to choices you have made in the past (or continue to make). There is always some element of responsibility: some way you could have responded more constructively to the circumstances in which you ended up, or some way you added to the suffering because of your ideas or desires. The point of acknowledging this responsibility is not to blame yourself and dwell in a sense of guilt, but to start to see causes and effects more clearly and to take responsibility for the things you can change.

POTENTIAL PITFALL

Sometimes people feel unwilling to work on a problem until they can understand how it came to be. This kind of understanding has limited usefulness, however, as illustrated by the ancient Buddhist metaphor of a man who has been shot in the eye with an arrow, but who will not accept medical attention until he gets the answers to all kinds of questions: who shot the arrow, what clan the shooter was from, how the arrow was made, etc. The Buddha concludes that this man will die before he gets all the answers he wants, so he'd better get to work on his problem before they are all answered.

Delayed Effects Can Fool You

One of the trickiest things about understanding karma is that effects can be removed from their causes in space and time. Human beings seem to be very limited in their ability to pay attention to the chain of causation for very long or over much distance; we tend to concentrate on the most immediate effects and figure the chain ends there. This is why people engage in harmful behaviors that have terrible long-term consequences—or terrible consequences on the other side of the world—but have a positive immediate payoff.

Part of the study of karma involves learning to pay close attention to the chain of cause and effect over time and space, and learning to look more carefully at the connections between things. If you latch on to too simple an explanation for something, you may miss other possible contributing causes. Some of those other possible causes may be ones you can personally do something about, so it's well worth cultivating the habit of carefully studying the unfolding of karma in your life and in the world around you.

The Desire to Change

One of the central teachings of Zen, which will be discussed further in Chapter 11, is that suffering is caused by your desire for things to be other than what they are. So what about the desire to change yourself or your life? Doesn't that desire just cause suffering? Wouldn't the Zen way be to try to accept yourself exactly as you are?

Answering these questions is not so simple. One answer is that you have to work on change and acceptance simultaneously, which isn't easy (more on that later). Another answer is that a constructive wish for change can be wholesome and helpful as long as it isn't a selfish desire. In other words, it isn't about *you* and how *you* would rather be, it's about taking care of your life and compassionately trying to minimize suffering and maximize true happiness. To do this you first acknowledge your less-than-helpful behaviors. These can be anything from watching too much TV to unleashing your anger through violence, but chances are good that the behavior will break Zen precepts at some level or another. Then you decide to do what you can to change.

Sorry About That

It may alarm you to know that the traditional Zen path to working on your karma starts with an act called contrition, or confession. This may evoke images of the act of confession in which penitents are led to believe they are obliged to feel guilty for something, and that they must confess their faults to an authority figure.

This is not how Zen contrition works; it can be an entirely private affair and there is no expectation that you should feel constant contrition, that is, sorrow or remorse over your shortcomings. The point about contrition is that you recognize that an aspect of your behavior has been causing harm or confusion, and a sincere desire arises in you to act differently. This is another way of putting the old saying, "You can't change if you don't admit you have a problem."

The point where you feel some remorse or sorrow about something you have done, or continue to do, is a very crucial one. When you arrive here it can be painful and humbling. It's good not to move past this point too quickly, because the discomfort or regret that you feel serves as part of your inspiration to change. On the other hand, of course, dwelling here in despair or self-loathing isn't helpful at all. The main point of Zen is that you can do something about your life, so the next step involves some determination and hope that things won't always be this way.

CONSIDER THIS

There's a Zen confession verse that goes like this: "All my past and harmful karma, born from beginningless greed, hate, and delusion, through body, speech, and mind, I now fully avow." Greed, hate, and delusion are the motivations behind any harmful action, and behind these motivations you just find more harmful actions that led to them. You can't find any final place to lay the blame, so instead you avow the karma you ended up with. This means to take responsibility for it without shame, and go on from there.

Taking Responsibility

So, you've recognized and 'fessed up to a habit of body, speech, or mind that you'd really like to change. In order to take the next step and make a lasting change in your life, you first have to take full responsibility for making that change. There's no room for blame anymore. Even if the people who contributed to your problem were to apologize and offer to make amends (probably unlikely in any case), they can't change your behavior for you. The buck stops here.

When you're trying to take responsibility in an effective way, it's helpful to think of yourself as objectively as possible. You might even want to think of the "you" that does the problem behavior as a different person. What's called for is determination and a firm hand, but in order to get that "other" person to change, you're also going to need patience, compassion, and creativity.

Just judging and bad-mouthing your inner overeater, gossiper, or thief is unlikely to result in any change; after all, they're taking advantage of the same store of determination as you are! When you take responsibility you admit that no one else is going to be able to bring about the change you want, so you'd better use all your resources and intelligence to do it yourself, whatever it takes.

Obstacles to Change

Why *is* change so hard, and how can we deal with obstacles to change? The bad news is that the answers to these questions won't give you any quick and easy solutions. If they did, Zen teachers would be rich and everyone would be a Zen practitioner! The good news is that understanding the obstacles to change can help you start to break them down, slowly but surely. At the very least you can begin to appreciate why change can be so hard, and to not feel too discouraged if you aren't getting the results you would like.

Habit Energy

Habits can be thought of as having energy in and of themselves, rather like behavioral momentum. What at first takes effort or feels rather uncomfortable later becomes easy, and still later becomes something you find yourself doing before you even realize it. It's like the habit itself has energy that either sucks you in or is capable of just going on without you. No matter your intentions or how much insight you've gotten about your behavior, you keep getting caught in the habit energy and doing the same thing over and over.

One of my Zen teachers, Kyogen Carlson, told a simple but very helpful story to illustrate the power of habit energy. The screen door to his yard got replaced, and it ended up opening on the opposite side from where the old door had opened. This was the door his cat ran to when she wanted to go outside. For many days after the door had been changed, the cat ran eagerly to wait at the side of the door that used to open.

Kyogen, despite knowing that the door had been changed, despite having the intelligence to understand the laws of mechanics, *also* moved toward the side of the door that used to open. He and his cat finally got used to the new door, and moved toward the correct side, after about the same amount of time. Kyogen's understanding didn't help, but the repeated effort to move the right way eventually did.

 ZEN WISDOM

"Don't be pulled along by habit energies, or you will not be able to avoid adversity. When musicians are in harmony, the music is beautiful. When forms are upright, the shadows are clear. Everything comes into existence due to causes and conditions. Stand in awe of this teaching, and look at all situations globally, both in time and in space. Once an action has been performed, the result is already there, even if it takes a hundred thousand lifetimes to manifest."

—Zen Master Guishan (771–853), from his treatise "Encouraging Words," as translated by Thich Nhat Hanh in *Stepping Into Freedom*

It takes time and energy to change a habit. This is like Newton's third law of motion, which states that when you exert force on something, it exerts an equal and opposite amount of force on you. A habit is a behavioral object, and in order to move it—especially if you want it to go in the opposite direction—you will have to exert plenty of force.

In the case of a purely physical habit like the one above, moving toward a door in a particular way, the effort can also be purely physical. When it comes to more complex habits of body, speech, and mind, it can take some work just to find out where to exert force in order to change things. I'll discuss how to do this in the upcoming section on unraveling habits.

Conflicting Desires

You can also be your own obstacle to change because you have conflicting desires. One part of you wants to change, but another part of you doesn't. All of your habits formed, at some point, for a reason. For example, the behavior you would like to change may have originally been a way of protecting yourself in a difficult situation, and part of you is scared to give it up. Another behavior may result in temporary comfort or relief even though it has negative long-term consequences; when you feel the need for comfort, you're likely to forget about your aspiration to change.

The important thing when it comes to conflicting desires is to recognize them. If you're overly identified with the righteous part of you that wants to make healthy improvements to your life, chances are you'll blind yourself to the ways you undermine your own efforts to change. If you notice and acknowledge the motivations you have to keep up a habit, you may be able to negotiate with yourself.

In the examples above, you could try to recognize that the intense need to protect yourself has passed (assuming this is the case), so you can change your habitual behavior and still be safe. You can acknowledge your need to seek comfort at times, and try some alternative ways of meeting that need. You generally won't manage to make a change until all of the parts of you are on board.

Not Thinking Outside the Box

If you have a set idea about a problem and that problem isn't going away, it may be because you're looking at the problem incorrectly or incompletely. For example, say your tongue gets tied when you face conflict, so you end up unable to express your viewpoint when you need to. You decide this must happen because you lack self-esteem due to a difficult childhood. You get some therapy and spend time doing things you're good at to give you confidence, but the problem doesn't change much.

Then you step back and observe the pattern again, letting go of your preconceived ideas about what's happening, and realize something quite different is going on. You actually have plenty of self-esteem, but you're biting your tongue when faced with conflict because you don't want to indulge anger and make a mess of things. While angry, you can't think of anything constructive to say. Now the problem looks very different, and you can try entirely different ways to approach it. You might take a communication course that helps you express your needs without anger, as well as carefully examine the nature of your anger during meditation and mindfulness.

When trying to change habits, think outside the box. Get creative, like an artist, scientist, or engineer. Don't limit yourself to a certain set of tools, even Zen ones. You never know what will tip the balance and let you change the direction of your habit energy.

> **POTENTIAL PITFALL**
>
> Some people refuse to consider certain tools when it comes to working on their karma, such as the support of other people, the competitive spirit, or even medication. Sometimes it's easy to get caught up in an idea that if you don't "go it alone" or "without a crutch," your success won't count. It's better to be open to using any tool that doesn't break the precepts; change is hard enough without making an extra standard for yourself.

Unraveling a Habit

Habits of body, speech, and mind can be complex and influenced by all kinds of things—like assumptions, beliefs, memories, fears, and triggers. While the habit has a kind of blind momentum, it also manifests in particular kinds of circumstances, in particular ways. Unraveling a habit so you can see where to exert the force of change involves paying close attention to conditions and events that encourage the habit to manifest. The more familiar you get with watching the habit unfold, the sooner in the process of manifestation you will be able to become aware of it.

Watching How Things Unfold

Mindfulness practice will help you cultivate the ability to pay close, sustained attention to the events of your life and watch as karma shows itself in the form of your habit. Just as in zazen and mindfulness, you try to observe what happens while maintaining a mind-body posture of alertness, uprightness, and openness.

Often the first sign that something is happening to which you should pay attention is the "yuck" feeling you get from breaking a precept. After you do something carelessly or selfishly, there's usually a physical reaction of some kind, such as a feeling of tightness in your chest or slight nausea in your stomach. Clueing into these phenomena can be your mindfulness reminder when it comes to karma work: pay attention!

At first, you're not trying to change your behavior. This is important, because your clarity and stillness will be compromised by the desire to change things, or by a negative judgment of your own actions. You just watch. Or, more accurately, you stay present for the unfolding of the habit instead of letting yourself get distracted.

A great example to illustrate the process of unraveling (and then stopping) a karmic pattern is working with a habit of speech. As you begin working on a tendency to bad-mouth others, you'll probably catch the habit well after your conversation is over, when you notice a slightly unpleasant feeling. "Oh, I did it again," you think. Instead of letting judgment derail you, however, you just pay attention to how you currently feel, and see if you can recall any of the circumstances that led to your harmful speech. You might be able to recall what you were thinking when you spoke and how caught up in the habit you were. Then you let the whole episode go and live your life until the next time you catch your habit—again, probably after the whole behavior pattern has played itself out.

Catching It Sooner

Eventually, if you keep up the practice of paying mindful attention to your habit, you will catch it sooner and sooner. In the example of harmful speech, after a while you realize you have acted out your habit right after your conversation ends. Then you start noticing the habit in the middle of your conversation but you're powerless to stop it. (This can be particularly frustrating.) Then you become aware earlier in your conversation and might have a few points where you can act a little differently.

Eventually you approach conversations with an awareness of your habitual tendencies and are able to carry a consciousness of them with you, throughout the entire interaction. Due to your attentiveness, it ends up feeling like there's more space (or time) between a stimulus you can react to and your response. In that space you can make a choice, rather than simply be carried along by your habit energy.

Making a Change

When you have sufficiently unraveled a habit so you can find the space to make a different choice, what do you do? How do you learn to act in a new way? The problem is, you are only familiar with your habitual way. Even when you notice the space between stimulus and reaction, it's easy for habit energy to suck you down the same old road. The Zen recommendation is to emphasize stopping your old pattern before you worry about establishing a new one.

First Just Stop

The first pure, or essential, Zen precept is to "cease from harmful actions." Cessation is the starting point for change, and it can be the toughest part. *Just stopping* can sound negative, but it's being done for compassionate reasons. The point is not to stop forever, in order to become a passive zombie that can't take action. The point is to stop long enough to break a pattern. How long will you have to just stop? It's difficult to say. But don't get waylaid on your path to change by concern about what you'll do with yourself once your habit is gone. Just stop indulging your anger, abusing intoxicants, or lying. What comes next will take care of itself in time.

ZEN WISDOM

"Sometimes deluded impulses arise so quickly and powerfully that we are barely able to acknowledge them and recognize their unwholesome quality. When we feel overwhelmed by selfish impulses, we may have to temporarily disqualify ourselves from any kind of action in order to prevent harm. We may need to take a 'time out.'"

—Zen Teacher Reb Anderson, from *Being Upright: Zen Meditation and the Bodhisattva Precepts*

Cessation is where "the rubber hits the road," as the saying goes. No matter how much clarity you've gotten about your behavior, if you are ultimately unwilling to give it up, you won't end up with the change that at least part of you wants to see. This is where the motivations behind your habit often become clear.

In the example we've been using about harmful speech, when the time comes for you to simply refrain from saying *anything* rather than engage in bad-mouthing someone, it feels quite awkward. You want to keep up a social connection with the person you're with, you have a really legitimate point to make, and you're afraid you'll seem boring or stupid if you just say, "Hmmm …" rather than respond with a witty criticism. You want to say something so badly, you have to literally bite your tongue to keep from doing so.

Then Try Something New

Once you've changed your habit to the point that you're no longer acting the way you used to, you're ready to try something new. It's best to take your time and be open-minded about what that new way will look like. This is your chance to pay close attention to what's going on around you, so you can respond in the wisest, most compassionate way you can.

Our example about harmful speech is one I can appreciate, because it's an example from my own practice. I tended to criticize people and things in conversation in a way that I thought displayed my wit and intelligence. When I was finally able to stop engaging in this behavior, I went through a rather awkward social time. I wasn't sure how to talk to people anymore. Some of my friendships lapsed because I had changed, and I kind of dreaded conversations.

Eventually, I began to notice that people weren't spending time with me to hear me pronounce my judgments on people and things. They wanted to know how I was doing, and they had things they wanted to share with me. A whole new field of possibilities opened up for me in conversation. Although I still get caught up in my habit of criticism from time to time, I know a better way and can easily shift my behavior to more healthy forms of speech.

Support for Karma Work

There are several things you can do to support your effort to make changes in your life. If you have any difficulty at all changing habits you've identified as being harmful or unhealthy, it would be good to keep these suggestions in mind.

The first way to support your karma work is to choose your goals wisely. The thing you're determined to change may not be the most important thing to work on right now, or you may not be able to address it until you've worked on some other things first. Examine carefully your reasons for wanting to change. If your reasons have mostly to do with the opinions of others, you probably don't have sufficient motivation to see the process of change through to the end.

Your goals also need to be reasonable, and by this I mean they should be achievable. By *you*, in the near future. A goal such as "I will not get angry" probably needs to be broken into smaller goals, with the first goal being something like, "I will try to notice my anger three times each day." Achievable goals often seem ridiculously small, but making them any bigger makes them unachievable, which doesn't make any sense.

 CONSIDER THIS

> In case you resist the idea of needing support from other people in your practice, you should know that Shakyamuni Buddha is said to have corrected his senior monk when the monk made the statement, "Having good spiritual friends amounts to half of the holy life" (meaning, it is extremely important). The Buddha said, "No, Ananda, having good spiritual friends is the whole of the holy life." In a tradition where you have to take responsibility for yourself and do your own practice, this is a remarkable comment on the importance of your connections with other human beings.

The next thing you can do to support your efforts to change is to seek the support of others. Being surrounded by nice, positive people who understand and appreciate what you're trying to do helps immensely. It's even better if they're trying to do the same thing you are. If you can find people who have achieved something you would like to achieve, ask them how they did it. The support of others even extends to a kind of positive peer pressure; when you know others are making progress, it's a little harder to accept your own excuses.

Finally, even as you work on your karma, it's good to keep working on your Zen wisdom, especially on your personal experience of how you're empty of an inherent, enduring self-nature. There is no fixed "you" that is flawed; you're just part of a karmic stream that has some unhealthy elements. You still have to take responsibility for that karmic stream, but a growing conviction about emptiness helps make the burden of change feel lighter. Instead of living in a mire of self-criticism and guilt, it's possible to know you're fundamentally okay. As long as you're fundamentally okay, you have nothing to get really upset about, so you might as well try to improve your life!

The Least You Need to Know

- The Zen concept of karma is about emphasizing how important your behavior and choices are to your happiness.
- Change begins with an acknowledgment that your behavior has been causing suffering or confusion, and this can be a difficult thing to face.
- Every part of you has to be willing to change in order for the change to actually happen.
- If you pay careful attention to a habit, you can create enough space between stimulus and response to make a different choice.
- Get creative and clever about making change happen in yourself. Use all the tools at your disposal.

Cultivating Insight: Seeking the Truth

In Zen there is much discussion of *practice* and *enlightenment*. The typical way of understanding practice involves the kinds of things that have already been covered in this book: zazen, mindfulness, moral behavior, and working to improve your habits of body, speech, and mind. Enlightenment is an elusive concept, but generally speaking it is about a transformative or liberating understanding of something, whether that understanding is about universal principles or your personal life. Another word for this understanding is insight, or seeing into the inner nature of things or situations.

Over the centuries Zen practitioners have disagreed about whether the most important aspect of Zen is practice or insight, or whether the two can be separated at all. The most simplistic view is that you practice in order to attain insight. At a more subtle level, you might look at practice as embodying enlightenment; so at some point you might add understanding to the picture, which is nice, but it doesn't change what you do.

Others argue that insight is what is ultimately liberating, so if you only practice without working on your deeper understanding, you are missing the main point of Zen. Most Zen

In This Chapter

- The role of insight in Zen
- How you go about seeking the truth
- What zazen has to do with insight
- Samatha and vipassana aspects of meditation
- Preparing for and inviting understanding

practitioners would agree that doing the daily work of Zen is essential, but comprehending the truth of your reality is what truly sets you free.

The Importance of Insight

From the beginning of Buddhism, insight has been emphasized as essential to the goal of liberation. This is true no matter how you want to conceive of liberation—mastering the art of living, manifesting dignity and readiness in all conditions, attaining freedom from suffering, waking up to your life, or embodying generosity and compassion. Whatever your aspiration, according to Buddhism you won't be able to fully achieve it without an experiential understanding of the nature of reality—including both universal truths and truths about your unique life.

The Truth Sets You Free

In the story of Shakyamuni Buddha, the pivotal moment came when he *saw* the nature of human suffering, how it arises, and how it can be dealt with. He had spent six years doing rigorous spiritual practices in the Indian wilderness, but resolution of his spiritual quest came only when he understood something in a new way. Given this understanding, his entire way of relating to the world changed. Since then, the Buddhist ideal has been to strive not just to improve your life and behavior, but also to seek an understanding of the truth.

CONSIDER THIS

> You probably already understand how the truth can set you free. Think of a time when the way you related to a situation completely changed because of one new piece of information. Perhaps a co-worker is being difficult, but you learn that her child is very ill. Like magic you are free of your resentment! You still have to deal with your co-worker, but your understanding of the situation is transformed.

What truth will set you free depends on the question you are asking or the problem you are facing. In the Buddha's case, he desperately needed to understand the truth about human suffering so he could decide how best to live his life. He had been born into circumstances where he could have been a king, and subsequently could have benefitted many people by generosity and wise leadership. Given what he realized about the inevitability of illness, old age, and death, however, being a king seemed meaningless to him. In the same circumstances, someone other than the Buddha may not have felt this quandary. They might have been seized by some equally compelling question, such as how to maintain a strong state while minimizing harm.

Not all questions or problems that you really need to answer or resolve are grand or universal. What you may really need to understand are the dynamics of your relationship to your children, or how to ascertain what you truly want to do with your life. In any case, when you achieve enough clarity to see what is really going on within you and around you, you gain the insight to relate to the subject of your concern in a new, more effective way. This way will be more effective because it is based on reality, rather than on your misconceptions, fears, or desires.

Stuff You Ignore

Insight is also important because if you neglect it, it can be like living with a blindfold on. In some cases understanding is not a special benefit of spiritual practice that you can opt out of working for because you don't have the interest or the time. Ignoring certain aspects of your reality limits your ability to live fully, compassionately, and wisely.

At the very least, you want to see the truths in your personal life. For example, you want to perceive your patterns of behavior, and the connections between causes and effects in your relationships. It's also important to recognize that the more universal questions—like questions about finding meaning in life, or how to relate to death—also affect you.

Even if you don't consider yourself philosophical or inclined to ponder deep spiritual questions, the great human concerns like life and death, or love and loss, are yours as much as they are any-one's. Your life is greatly influenced by the assumptions or fears that you subconsciously carry around due to the way you answer or avoid "deep" questions. It is better to deliberately explore difficult issues than it is to let your life be controlled by unexamined views.

The Zen Approach to Insight

You can definitely develop a certain kind of understanding through your usual means, such as reading, intellectual analysis, or simple observation. The thing is, these typical methods don't work so well when it comes to resolving problems with which you are personally very involved; your self-concern gets in the way of arriving at clear, lasting answers.

Typical approaches also don't generally lead to a transformative personal relationship to the answers to profound questions. You can understand intellectually that everything is connected, but that understanding doesn't necessarily result in any fundamental changes in how you relate to the world. Fortunately, for effective and transformative insight, all you have to do is use Zen tools to work on your ability to see things clearly.

The Truth Is Right in Front of You

The "seeing clearly" benefit of Zen practice depends on a fundamental Buddhist truth that has been personally verified by Zen practitioners over and over: the truth of anything you need to understand is right in front of you, available for your perception as soon as you can see clearly enough. Note that I said the truth of anything *you need to understand.* Zen is not going to let you see answers to questions like how the universe was created or whether there is life after death. These are issues that, at least according to Buddhism, are irrelevant to the real matter at hand: how can you best live your life, right now?

> **POTENTIAL PITFALL**
>
> Pondering big questions about the universe can be fascinating. How did the universe as we know it come to be? What happens to us after our physical body dies? In Buddhism these kinds of inquiries are called "questions that do not tend to edification," meaning that their answers to do not lead to better moral or spiritual understanding or behavior. Investigating such "non-edifying" questions may be interesting and beneficial to the world in other ways, but the point is to not make your spiritual development dependent on their answers.

You *can* directly perceive answers to questions that are about you: Why am I feeling this grief? Why do I react with anger to so-and-so? What am I afraid of? What is the true nature of my self? The truth of these matters is right in front of you because you are intimately connected to the questions. All truths about yourself and the ways you perceive, view, and react to the world are in your own body-mind, like a book waiting to be read. It's not always easy to read it, but the information is there and actually can't be anywhere else.

It may seem limiting to only be able to answer questions that are about you, but it's not. This is because your body-mind reflects a lot of universal truths and is not actually separate from everything and everyone else. You might be surprised by how much you can find out about the nature of the world and sentient beings just by getting to know yourself. Don't expect any grand insights into the laws of physics at an atomic level, or intuitions about whether there is other intelligent life in the universe. However, you might very well get an insight into the way compassion functions that seems to apply at a scale far beyond your one human life.

Different Kinds of Knowing

Limitations in language confuse the significant differences between types of knowing. You can say you know something because you read it in a book, and you can say you know something because you have spent a lifetime intimately working with it. Transformative or liberating insight always falls toward the personal, intimate knowledge end of the spectrum.

An analogy may be helpful here. Let's say the subject you want to understand is New York City. Knowing that the city exists and where it is on a map is legitimate knowledge, but obviously still quite limited. In your effort to understand New York better, you read about it, look at pictures of it, and watch movies about it. Now you're really learning a lot about New York, right? But when you start to interview people who have lived in New York, you realize there's a whole dimension to the city you were never able to catch a glimpse of from your previous study.

POTENTIAL PITFALL

If you are interested at all in gaining insight into something, it can be easy to get discouraged when the problem or teaching seems to resist your understanding. It can be helpful to realize there is no clear line between knowing and not-knowing something. Rather, there is a spectrum of knowledge from the merely intellectual to the intimately personal, and there are many ways to work toward greater familiarity with your subject of interest.

Eventually you decide to take a trip to New York yourself, and after spending a week there your understanding of the city is taking on some real depth. You start to have insights about how the city functions. Still, your sense of New York after one trip is going to be incredibly limited compared to someone who has lived in the city all of his or her life.

Directly perceiving something leads to the kind of knowing that deeply affects you on many different levels, and can change the whole way you view the world. It's what's referred to again and again in Zen as knowing for yourself, a direct experience, or personal verification. The more personal, involved, and prolonged your exposure to something, the better you know it, and the more transformative and liberating your understanding can be. Still, there's no hard-and-fast line between shallow and deep knowing, and there's no illegitimate knowing. Who can claim to *really* understand something as complex as New York City, anyway?

Insight and Zazen

The primary Zen tool for cultivating insight is zazen, but this presents a very challenging paradox. You've been working hard on zazen: trying to let go of all active thinking, just noticing whatever arises and passes away without grasping after anything or pushing anything away, and returning your attention to the first and second levels of mind (pure perception and simple naming). Given all of your habits, concerns, and responsibilities, settling the mind can be very difficult. Now you're supposed to study something in zazen? Isn't that exactly opposed to the effort you've been making?

Doing or Not-Doing

Some Zen teachers will indeed discourage any volitional activity in zazen. Kodo Sawaki Roshi, a fiery Japanese Zen teacher, emphatically taught, "Zazen is useless!" Generally from the Soto school of Zen, such teachers will maintain that doing Zen practice without any "gaining idea" at all *is* enlightenment itself. Conceiving of some insight you would like to obtain is creating a separation between you and enlightenment, while the whole point is that enlightenment is nowhere other than right here.

When you think deeply about this, you realize that doing Zen or zazen with absolutely no gaining idea at all—no concern for yourself or whether you are going to get anything out of your effort—is extremely difficult. If you can train rigorously in a monastery for 20 years, sitting for 8 hours a day, with no effort to attain anything, ironically you will face great struggle and end up actually attaining something. It's not that this form of Zen discourages insight, it just refuses to let you conceptualize it in any way and demands that you demonstrate your insight through your everyday behavior.

 CONSIDER THIS

Zen Master Hongzhi (1091–1157) was a Chinese teacher who taught "silent illumination" as opposed to striving for insight by concentrating on teaching stories. However, according to Taigen Leighton in *Cultivating the Empty Field,* even Hongzhi acknowledged the importance of insight:

"… in his important poem 'Guidepost of Silent Illumination,' Hongzhi clearly stresses the indispensability and interdependence of both serenity (or calm) and illumination (or insight): 'if illumination neglects serenity then aggressiveness appears … if serenity neglects illumination, murkiness leads to wasted dharma' (useless teaching)."

The other Zen way, exemplified by but not limited to the Rinzai school of Zen, makes a good counterargument that being free of concepts like attaining insight doesn't mean avoiding them, but developing the ability to pick them up and put them down at will. In this form of Zen you are encouraged to constantly push the edges of your understanding, attain new insight … and then let it go and move on.

The funny thing is, this tension between seeking or non-seeking has been present in Zen since it first arose as Ch'an in ancient China. There have always been arguments between proponents of sudden versus gradual enlightenment, insight work with koans versus silent illumination, and later, Rinzai versus Soto Zen. This tension actually informs and enlivens Zen, as each side challenges the other and can serve as a corrective measure for the other's excesses. Zen really wouldn't be complete without both.

Samatha and Vipassana

There's another way to look at the relationship between stillness and insight in zazen. Buddhist meditation has been described as having two aspects since early Buddhism. One is *samatha*, which is alternatively translated as "tranquility" or "calm abiding." Samatha is quite consistent with the form of zazen introduced in this book so far, although I will go into more depth about it in this chapter. The other aspect of meditation is *vipassana*, or "insight." This type of meditation is not actually separate from samatha, but in fact depends on it; first you settle into samatha, and then you make very judicious use of volitional thinking to examine a teaching or question.

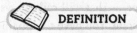 **DEFINITION**

> **Samatha**, meaning tranquility or calm abiding, is the aspect of meditation that involves letting go of any volitional engagement with thinking in order to experience reality as a whole. **Vipassana** (or vipasyana), meaning insight or wisdom, is meditation in which you begin from a state of tranquility and then judiciously employ volitional thinking to contemplate teachings or questions.

Just to be clear, it is not traditional in Zen to break zazen up into samatha and vipassana. Zazen is generally presented as a whole practice that is approached the same way whether you are a beginner or a master, and regardless of whether you desire calm or wisdom. Some good Zen teachers may not even know the terms.

However, these two ways of looking at meditation are thoroughly Buddhist, and are very helpful when discussing the cultivation of insight. In using them I follow the example of Zen Teacher Reb Anderson, who is thoroughly Zen but who has used the teachings on samatha and vipassana with his students for over a decade. (He's written a book that includes a discussion of these concepts titled *The Third Turning of the Wheel: Wisdom of the Samdhinirmocana Sutra*.) It's optional whether you want to conceptually divide your zazen into two aspects. Both samatha and vipassana will make their appearance at different times in your meditation even if you don't consciously differentiate them.

Samatha: Working on Stillness

Before you can see clearly, you need to cultivate stillness. This is the samatha aspect of zazen. Many people assume this stillness means the absence of thoughts or feelings, but this is not the case. What you hold still in zazen is something other than your mind in the ordinary sense of the word. Samatha zazen requires you to give things up—especially your self-concern and your judgments. Rather than devote any mental activity to pursuing your self-interest, you just sit.

Clear Versus Turbid

Think of your mind as a pond that has, as most ponds do, a thick layer of mud on the bottom. Our ordinary activities churn up the water in the pond until it's turbid and opaque. Sitting very still allows the sediment to settle gradually out of the water, and sitting very still for a prolonged period can let the water become crystal clear. You can see everything in the pond perfectly clearly—the bottom, the plants and fish, any garbage that may have fallen in.

The process of letting turbid water clear cannot be rushed; there's nothing active you can do to make it happen. You can't brush the sediment aside in impatience; you'll only make things worse. You just have to hold still and wait. However, in the case of the mind—as opposed to a pond—this waiting is not passive. You can't just let your mind wander, as that will roil the water. You can't even fall asleep, because dreaming is a very active mental state. You have to remain alert so you can take advantage of the clarity when it occurs.

 ZEN WISDOM

"If there is a lot of excitement, you first use concentration to conform to noumenon [objects in and of themselves] and rein in the scattered mind; by not going along with mental objects, you merge with original silence. If there is a lot of oblivion, then next you use insight to analyze things and contemplate emptiness; when consciousness is free from confusion, you merge with original awareness. You quell random imagination by concentration, and quell insensibility by insight ... Only when you spontaneously practice both together are you considered free."

–Korean Son (Zen) Master Pojo Chinul (1158–1210), from "Secrets of Cultivating the Mind," as translated by Thomas Cleary in *Classics of Buddhism and Zen*

It's Your Volition That Remains Still

What is it that remains still in the samatha aspect of zazen? Thoughts and feelings may continue to arise and pass away, so it's not that brain activity is necessarily still. There may be occasions when thoughts and feelings subside and there's a nice sense of spacious possibility, but this is like a break in the clouds and not something you should strive for. You create the conditions for that break in the clouds by doing your zazen, and sometimes you are rewarded for your efforts.

If it's not your brain activity that you seek to hold still, what is it? Your volition. You keep your willful activity focused on keeping the physical and mental posture of zazen: staying alert, aware, and open, and refraining from analyzing, judging, grasping after things, or pushing things away. This is the one-pointed concentration of samadhi; your volition is concentrated one-pointedly in the act of meditation.

Whatever happens during meditation—whatever physical sensations you have, whatever you hear, whatever thoughts arise, whatever emotions you feel, whatever insights you have, whatever plans or regrets occur to you—you keep your volition still, fixed to the act of meditation. You don't let anything that happens force you to react and give up your meditation seat. You refuse to further stir the waters, no matter how tempting or provocative your experiences.

You hold still in samatha zazen not because you are setting yourself apart from all that stuff *out there* that's trying to upset you; you hold still because you want to see clearly. You want to let the turbidity in the mind settle out, so you can perceive and understand things better. In a way, you refrain from reacting to things in meditation precisely because you care so much about them.

Judgment Prevents Clarity

When you judge something that you perceive in meditation, it disturbs the water in your mind-pond (to continue using the pond metaphor introduced earlier) and results in more turbidity and less clarity. However, it can be very hard not to indulge your judgments about things, especially when you notice, remember, or realize things in meditation that you don't like, and especially if they affect you personally. You may not be able to help a judgment appearing in your mind, but you don't have to believe it has inherent truth, and you don't have to jump on its bandwagon.

It's especially important to be able to avoid indulging in judgments in your meditation if you want to move on to the vipassana aspect of zazen. Any judgment—or even potential judgment—can chase away insight.

As an example, let's say you're trying to gain a deeper understanding of some of your harmful habits. Part of you is seeking clarity and insight and is willing to face the naked truth in order to relieve suffering. Another part knows it has been a little lazy, selfish, or deluded, and plans to hide out as long as it can.

The lazy, selfish, or deluded part may feel ashamed, unwilling to give up its habits, or afraid of the harsh judgments your wisdom-seeking part is going to unleash on it. Unless your wisdom-seeking part cultivates a nonthreatening, nonjudgmental stance, it's going to keep chasing away the part you need to see. In samatha you are cultivating unconditional restraint from judgment.

 POTENTIAL PITFALL

> It may feel like giving up judgments, especially ones about other people and the world, is giving up the fight against suffering and injustice. However, giving up judgment in zazen does not in any way impede your efforts to make positive changes in your life or in the world. In fact, being able to set aside the judgment and see more clearly can only help your efforts to effect change. This is because the judgment you are giving up is just the self-centered commentary on the world, "This is not what *I* believe is right." When you give up that extra judgment, your powers of discernment are left perfectly intact, and lots of energy is freed up to devote to your cause.

Vipassana: Inviting Insight

When your samatha is still enough, you can introduce a teaching or a question that you want to gain some insight into. This is the vipassana aspect of zazen. How still is still enough? There's no clear guideline here, except that you can watch the state of your mind as you introduce a concept and arouse volitional thinking. If you start losing focus or getting agitated, you return to samatha. The mind should remain in samadhi (one-pointed concentration) even during vipassana meditation. That is, all of your volition should stay focused on the subject of your meditation and not get sidetracked by something else.

Focusing on a Question

Generally speaking, you want to focus on a question in vipassana zazen. If you contemplate a teaching, ask a question about it and contemplate the question. Questions give your volition a place to focus and apply some mental pressure. The best questions are those about which you have intense personal interest, because then you're naturally drawn to them and motivated to resolve them. You invite the question into your zazen and observe it without reacting to anything you see except to examine the subject more and more closely. If you do anything, you ask additional questions to gently push the inquiry toward insight.

 ZEN WISDOM

"Bodhisattvas generate pliancy and ease by attending to the uninterrupted mind. Then abiding in that samatha, that tranquillity, they turn to analyze, investigate, and inwardly consider the doctrines again. In other words, first they give up discursive thought until the dawning of the tranquil state. Then, either because of previous intention or because of the teacher's instructions, their mind pivots and starts looking at the teachings again. But now they are looking at the teachings in a state of Samadhi ... They thoroughly differentiate, they thoroughly investigate, they thoroughly analyze these objects as they appear in the state of tranquillity."

—Zen Teacher Reb Anderson, from *The Third Turning of the Wheel: Wisdom of the Samdhinirmocana Sutra*

The process of investigating a question in zazen is probably best illustrated by an example. Let's say you want insight into your depression. You start from the tranquility of samatha, and then bring to mind your troubling emotional state. Where is it right now? Where can you feel it? What thoughts are connected to your depression? This is not abstract analysis, or any kind of attempt to use the past to explain why you feel the way you are feeling. This is a direct inquiry into the depression that you are carrying.

Perhaps you notice a thought that life isn't worth the effort. You keep your attention on this thought without judging it, arguing with it, or agreeing with it. Then you ask a clarifying question that makes you examine this thought more deeply, like, "What would make life worth the effort?" You then see what arises. Maybe nothing, and you return to other aspects of your study, but maybe a thought arises that more of a sense of intimacy with others would make life worth it. Then you focus on that thought, and see where it leads. You might ask, "What does it mean to be intimate with another?" Or, "What is getting in the way of the intimacy I want?"

Remember early in the chapter, where I talked about how you can only reliably find answers to questions that are about *you?* Well, the answers have to be about you, too. It wouldn't be helpful if you were to answer the last question above by placing the reason outside of yourself, like, "I haven't met the right person yet." There's only so much you can do about meeting the right person. You can try, but in the meantime what can you do to improve your life? How might you understand intimacy differently, so that you didn't have to rely on a romantic relationship to meet your needs? Is there a different way of looking at your life, so you can find it rewarding just as it is?

Vipassana isn't a simple process of sitting down to figure out an answer in one meditation session. It's a long process of diligently getting to know your subject inside and out. Eventually you may happen upon the pivotal question that unlocks the whole puzzle.

Experiencing the Answer

There's a big difference between how you usually try to answer questions and resolve problems, and how you perceive the answers in vipassana. When you come to truly know something in zazen (or outside of it, if you've cultivated enough clarity), you *experience it*. You don't just understand it intellectually; you recognize the truth as part of yourself. You feel its edges; its flavor; the way it affects your gut, your emotions, and your thinking.

For example, let's say you're investigating the Buddhist teaching of no-self. As described previously, you start asking yourself questions about this teaching that bring the issue alive for you personally. You might start by searching for your sense of self, and perhaps you're lucky enough to have some lingering anger as you sit on the meditation cushion. Letting yourself feel the anger, you ask, "Where is my sense of self?" It occurs to you that in this moment your anger *is* your sense of self, that your sense of self is nothing other than your effort to protect yourself from the world.

Then you might ask, "What happens if I drop this anger?" You may or may not be able to do it, but if you can, for a moment you *experience* no-self. One minute there's clearly a self, the next minute there's ... what? There's your breath, and the floor, and the bird singing outside. Where did you go? You get a personal inkling that the self is an illusion conjured up by your own mind. This inkling is very different from an intellectual understanding of the Buddhist theory that the self doesn't really exist. No matter how much sense a teaching makes to you, you won't really understand it until you experience it for yourself.

The Least You Need to Know

- Gaining direct insight into things both personal and universal can transform the way you relate to the world.
- The truth of anything you really need to understand is right in front of you. All you have to do is get clear enough to perceive it.

- With the stillness of zazen comes clarity, as if you are allowing turbid water to become clear.
- Zen meditation has two aspects, calm abiding and insight. The relationship between the two has been debated for centuries.
- If you want to cultivate insight in your meditation, you start with calm abiding and then focus on a question within the space of tranquility.

Sangha: Practicing with Others

In this chapter you'll find the Zen methods that generally involve practicing Zen with other people. I present them together because I think you can have a valuable Zen practice without them. That is, you can practice alone, and without engaging with Zen teachers, going to meditation retreats, taking advantage of Zen ritual, or making formal vows.

Many Zen students and teachers find these practices essential and inseparable from the rest of Zen, and they'll have good arguments for why you can't do without them. However, I think it would be a shame if you steered clear of Zen because you aren't interested in participating in a group or embracing aspects of the tradition that appear religious.

Consider this the "optional but recommended" chapter of the book. You might want to give the things described here a try and see if they work for you. At the very least it will be useful to you to know these practices are a part of the Zen tradition. Be aware that there is great variation between Zen lineages in the roles teachers and ordained people play, the emphasis on meditation retreats, and the use of ritual and vow.

In This Chapter

- What sangha means and reasons to practice with one
- Various benefits of working with a Zen teacher
- The experience of meditation retreats
- Rituals and other religious elements in Zen
- Formally becoming a Zen Buddhist

Communities of Zen Practitioners

There are many reasons why sangha, a community of Zen practitioners, is considered one of the *three treasures* of Buddhism. Sangha makes Zen a living tradition rather than a philosophy that exists primarily in books or history. You may be deeply inspired by the writings of Henry David Thoreau or Seneca the Stoic philosopher, or by the actions of someone like Gandhi, but what can you do with your inspiration? You can certainly study, contemplate, and try to live your life in accordance with what you believe to be true, but there's a limit to how actively you can make Thoreau or Gandhi part of your life.

Contrast this with the Zen tradition, which, for better or worse, has created so much for you to practice, study, and participate in that you could "do" Zen 24/7 for the rest of your life! Of course, this level of involvement probably doesn't interest you, but it's an indication of how much richness has been generated by the sangha over a couple thousand years.

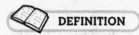 **DEFINITION**

> The **three treasures** of Buddhism are buddha, dharma, and sangha. These three things have been considered central and essential to Buddhist practice for over 2,500 years.

Sanghas Together

For many thousands of years, the typical form of a Buddhist sangha was a monastery full of monks or nuns, practicing full time, who were supported and visited by lay (non-ordained) Buddhists. In modern-day Zen there are some sanghas that live together in a monastery and devote their entire time to Zen practices, but in most cases those practitioners don't stay in the monastery forever.

There are also usually lay people practicing in any given monastery or residential practice center. Lay people have more freedom and leisure than they did in past centuries and they want to do Zen practice themselves, not just support monks and nuns who are doing it. Also, in the West men and women usually practice in the same communities.

The vast majority of Western Zen sanghas are lay-centered. There may be one or a few monks or priests present (more about Zen ordination later), but they are there to support the Zen practice of a largely lay sangha. Lay Zen practitioners have jobs and families and participate fully in the world outside the sangha. They come together to sit zazen, study and discuss Zen teachings and practice, and share activities like work and meals with a community of like-minded people who are trying to be mindful and ethical.

Benefits of Sangha

The benefits of sangha are many and varied, so I'll cover just a few of them here. Perhaps the most obvious is the collective wisdom and experience of the group. It's common in Zen to work on a practice or study a teaching for a long time, but not really be able to master or understand it until you hear it described by a particular individual at a particular time.

Revered Zen master so-and-so may have tried to explain a concept to you, but it wasn't until Bill gave you his point of view that it all fell into place. In this case, you and Bill may have something in common, like ethnic background, personality, or life circumstances. But actually, anyone can be your teacher if they help you understand something, and practicing in sangha gives you the chance to have many teachers, most of them unaware that they are teaching you anything.

Sangha members also provide positive peer pressure for one another. This may sound creepy, but it's not. Positive peer pressure is just social support, and doesn't require anyone to deliberately try to influence anyone else. In fact, the culture of most Zen sanghas encourages you to concentrate on your own practice and not keep track of what other people do—how often they attend, how profound their comments, etc.

The positive peer pressure happens naturally when you notice what other people are willing to do, or what they are capable of. For example, most people find they can sit zazen much longer and remain much more still (at least physically) when they sit with others. When everyone else is seated silent and motionless for a whole 30 minutes, you're probably going to try your very best to stay still for that whole 30 minutes, too!

 ZEN WISDOM

"Taking refuge in the Sangha means putting your trust in a community of solid members who practice mindfulness together. You do not have to practice intensively—just being in a Sangha where people are happy, living deeply the moments of their days, is enough. Each person's way of sitting, walking, eating, working and smiling is a source of inspiration; and transformation takes place without effort. If someone who is troubled is placed in a good Sangha, just being there is enough to bring about a transformation."

—Zen Teacher Thich Nhat Hanh, from *Cultivating the Mind of Love*

Perhaps the most valuable part of sangha is that it becomes a positive, supportive community in which you and your practice are visible and known. This rather mysteriously ends up making you more fully aware of yourself and your practice, which of course is one of the goals of Zen. One of my Zen teachers is fond of saying, "Sangha is a mirror." You come to know yourself more fully through relationship, and especially through relationship with people who are also taking responsibility for their own actions and reactions and trying to be mindful of each thing that happens.

For example, if you have a habit of being overbearing in conversation, outside the sangha people will probably either avoid you or confront you. When you are confronted, you'll usually feel defensive and think uncharitable thoughts about the other person. In sangha, people are more likely to take responsibility for their own reactions and just put up with you—neither avoiding you nor confronting you. In the context of sangha, how a conversation goes is not the important thing; mindfulness and the precepts are important.

After a while of doing your overbearing thing without people reacting, all that's left for you to notice is your own habit. There you'll be, enacting it all by yourself, with nothing distracting you from having to see it in all its glory. Through the quiet generosity of sangha, you'll be much closer to breaking free of a habit that probably causes you grief in other parts of your life.

Working with a Zen Teacher

The Zen literature says a great deal about teachers. Enlightenment stories almost always involve a teacher and student, and in many places it's stated clearly that you need a teacher in order to truly fulfill the Zen way. However, whether you want to work with a teacher, and in what way, depends on what you want to do with your Zen practice. Plenty of people practice Zen with only books, their own insight, and perhaps a sangha to help guide them.

Zen teachers can help at many different levels, though, so it's worth seeing what working with a teacher can be like. Also, every teacher is unique, and teachers operate very differently in the various Zen lineages. One teacher might be next to useless for you, while another might open up Zen for you in a whole new way.

Guidance and Encouragement

At the most basic level, a Zen teacher is just someone who is a few steps ahead of you on the path of practice, and who is very familiar with Zen methods and teachings. A teacher can give you personal instruction on Zen practices and suggest things to study or try that might never have occurred to you otherwise.

In addition, over their many years of practice a teacher will usually have witnessed the struggles of Zen students of all different kinds—men and women, young and old, devout and skeptical, athletic and physically handicapped, you name it. Because of this they have an appreciation for how unique each person's engagement with Zen is. Something that proves extremely beneficial for one person might actually be frustrating and discouraging to another. This is precisely why Zen and Buddhist teachings are so vast in quantity and variety; over the centuries teachers have looked for ways to reach and help different kinds of students.

A teacher is also useful for encouragement when you aren't sure whether you are doing Zen correctly or what results you should be looking for. One of my teachers explained that she doesn't know ahead of time where a student's path is going to lead, or what their practice will end up looking like, but she can recognize authentic and fruitful practice when she sees it.

Going back to our bread baking analogy, consulting with a teacher can be like asking an experienced baker to take a look in your oven to see whether your bread seems to be progressing the way it's supposed to. Later, when you take the bread out of the oven and rap on the bottom, you know you're supposed to hear a hollow sound, but is what you're hearing a hollow sound? It helps to be able to ask someone who knows. Over the years many of my consultations with my Zen teacher simply involved me asking her whether what I was experiencing looked like practice, or whether I was just fooling myself. When she reassured me that I seemed to be doing fine, it gave me the confidence to go on.

Personal guidance from the teacher happens differently depending on the Zen lineage. In some pure Soto Zen lineages, instruction from the teacher happens informally, as teacher and student interact at the Zen center, temple, or monastery while working, eating, or having tea. In Zen lineages that use koans, there is strong emphasis on short, formal one-to-one interviews with the teacher, called *dokusan* or *sanzen*, particularly during meditation retreats. Most lineages have blended these practices, and teachers will offer one-on-one interviews regularly, as well as make themselves available for longer, informal meetings.

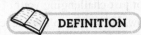 **DEFINITION**

> **Dokusan**, also called **sanzen**, is a formal, one-on-one meeting between a Zen student and an authorized Zen teacher. The student presents his or her practice by asking a question or sharing his or her experience, and the teacher responds in such a way as to encourage or deepen the student's Zen. Dokusan or sanzen is usually brief, about 5 to 10 minutes or less, and focused on one pivotal issue.

Witness and Challenge

The Zen literature most often features teachers fulfilling their witnessing or challenging functions. It's not that ancient teachers didn't instruct or encourage their students, it's just that verifying or testing a student's understanding makes for more dramatic stories. In this capacity Zen teachers function as a sort of gateway through which a student needs to pass as they master Zen.

Of course, if mastering Zen doesn't sound inspiring to you, you don't need a teacher-gateway. You also may be able to master Zen on your own, but then no one but you will know that you've done so. To become part of the Zen lineage, your understanding and practice need to be recognized by another human being. It's the ultimate test, like slicing open your baked loaf of bread and letting someone taste it, rather than leaving the loaf to sit on your shelf and look good.

Ideally a teacher witnesses your practice over time and comes to understand you and your karma intimately. When this has happened, the teacher will have the perspective to appreciate your challenges and successes in a way few other people can. For example, if you've been working for a long time on your anger and have just managed to have the first civil conversation with your mother in years, your Zen teacher will understand how significant this is for you.

 ZEN WISDOM

"The roshi [teacher] *gives* private instruction, the student *receives* it, but the latter gets nothing he or she did not already have. The disciple cannot boast of increased knowledge as a result of contact with the roshi, for nothing at all has been gained. Rather, much has been lost—chesty opinions, sticky notions of how things should or should not be, rash judgments, evaluations, deluded ideas, preconceptions—in short, all manner of mental hindrances. In general, then, Zen training can be described as an emptying or cleansing process ...."

—Roshi Philip Kapleau (1912–2004), from *Awakening to Zen*

Of course, the teacher will also see the areas you still need to work on and be able to point those out to you if you get too complacent or sure of yourself. Especially if you aspire to teach Zen to others, a teacher will be obliged to test you. This includes not just challenging your understanding, but also making sure you can manifest what you know. Do you keep the precepts? How do you react when someone insults or confronts you? Are you attached to a fixed idea of your competence or incompetence, or do you meet each moment with humility and willingness?

Behind every crazy-sounding Zen story of a teacher rapping a student on the head or answering a question with an apparent non sequitur about a tree, there is a history of interaction between teacher and student. This history resulted in the teacher knowing just how to challenge the student so the student could get past any obstructions.

Meditation Retreats

Some Zen lineages did not historically emphasize meditation retreats, but in other lineages they are considered essential. In the West most Zen sanghas deeply value them. Meditation retreats can last anywhere from one to ten days or more, and ones lasting at least three days are often referred to by the Japanese term *sesshin* (pronounced seh-sheen). The traditional retreat form is sometimes adapted in order to allow participation by busy lay students who can't leave their responsibilities, but classically a retreat involves a 24-hour schedule. This means that all of your activities—sleeping, eating, and bathing, as well as meditation and study—occur at a prescribed time. Most things are done as a community, and here's the clincher for many people: they are done in complete silence.

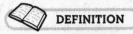

DEFINITION

Sesshin are intensive, communal, silent meditation retreats, usually lasting at least three days and involving a 24-hour schedule. The schedule includes formal Zen practices like zazen, chanting, and study, but also all of the basic activities of daily life like eating, working, and sleeping.

To many people a silent meditation retreat sounds very daunting. Not only do retreats typically involve five or more hours of zazen each day, you have to give up your usual comforts (TV, alcohol, sleeping in), and follow a communal schedule. You also have to maintain silence except for very basic exchanges of practical information that are absolutely necessary, such as during a work period. This silence is not just about speech, it's about communication, so other ways people usually communicate—through eye contact or gestures—are also discouraged.

Why on earth would people submit to such a regimen? It boils down to two basic reasons: one, to turn up the heat on their practice, particularly their zazen; and two, to perform a grand experiment on the self and watch carefully what happens in a setting that's supremely conducive to mindfulness.

Sesshin is like intensifying your practice, because you have to concentrate on Zen with very few distractions. In order to attend sesshin you will have had to plan carefully and set aside all of your usual activities, responsibilities, and relationships. The whole point of the retreat is practice, so even eating, sleeping, and work are done entirely within that context. At a retreat you don't work to get something done, you work to practice mindfulness. In addition, simply doing many hours of zazen every day is going to have an effect. No matter how busy your mind usually is, it will eventually tire itself out and settle down to a greater extent than you may have ever experienced before.

ZEN WISDOM

"*Sesshin* means to directly encounter one's mind, to touch one's mind; the word also expresses the gathering together of mind. This is not something we can do in our day-to-day lives. During sesshin, we must separate ourselves from all daily routine; we must touch directly, encounter directly, that very place from which the mind comes forth."

—Shodo Harada Roshi in *The Path to Bodhidharma*

A retreat amounts to an experiment on yourself in that it subjects you to unusual conditions and then lets you observe the effects, because you're in a setting so conducive to mindfulness you can scarcely avoid it. Who are you without your home, your partner, your self-expression, your dog, your yoga class, your independence, your entertainment, and access to your favorite snacks? You get to notice all of your thoughts, feelings, and judgments because there's really not much else going on. Your state of mind and the state of your life can become very clear.

The thing is, this clarity isn't always pleasant. In fact, at times sesshin can be grueling, boring, and emotionally painful. Almost anyone who tries it finds it rewarding in some way, however, in the end. Still, it can be pretty funny when you return to work after a retreat and a co-worker remarks on how nice it must have been. You probably won't bother to explain, though, as he or she will think you were crazy for spending your vacation time doing such a thing.

Ritual and Religion

If you visit a Zen center or monastery, you may be surprised at how "religious" it feels. Some Zen lineages use more ceremony and ritual than others, but chances are good that at a Zen practice place you will encounter altars, incense, chanting, ceremony, ritual objects, titles, and special clothing. Perhaps you'll enjoy these things, but they may trouble you. If so, you may decide not to practice with a sangha, or you may look for a sangha that minimizes the use of religious tools or techniques by consulting the Secular Buddhist Association.

Like the other things in this chapter, however, it's worth engaging religious aspects of Zen that might at first make you uncomfortable, to see if they're useful. You may at least find you can live with them, which is good because completely secular sanghas can be hard to find.

If You're Turned Off

The critical thing to keep in mind is that you are not expected to feel or think any particular way about the religious aspects of Zen. Like everything else, you're expected to try it out for yourself and come to your own conclusions. As long as you're respectful of the practice of others, you can participate skeptically or even find ways to engage certain parts of Zen and avoid others. At most practice centers no one is going to think twice if you attend zazen but leave before the chanting starts.

 CONSIDER THIS

Zen as a religious tradition can be challenging because it will inevitably contain elements you don't like or find useful. However, when an ancient tradition is preserved and presented in its entirety, it is generally much richer than a new creation that is designed to be palatable and easily accessible. The elements you don't like may later prove to hold pivotal lessons for you, and even if they don't, they benefit someone else in a diverse Zen community.

A good Zen center or teacher will also be open to questions. Go ahead and ask for the reasons why certain things are done or why things are a certain way. You may or may not appreciate the answers, but you might also realize that you were making assumptions about things that were incorrect.

For example, at most Zen centers there will be some bowing. This involves people going down into a kneeling position on the floor and then leaning down and touching their forehead to the floor. If you're not used to this, it can seem very strange. There's no god in Zen, so who are you bowing to? Are you worshipping graven idols, or groveling? Ask a teacher or senior practitioner why they do it, and they'll probably explain that for them, bowing is a gesture of deep respect for their own aspiration toward wisdom and compassion. This aspiration is usually represented on the altar in the form a statue. This may or may not make you feel like bowing, but it might allay some of your discomfort.

The Good of Ritual

Ritual and ceremony can be very useful tools. On a regular basis in a Zen setting, these include the regular chanting of important Zen texts and verses, bowing, and offering incense, water, and food at altars. There are also occasional ceremonies celebrating things like the Shakyamuni Buddha's birthday, or commemorating the passing of an important Zen ancestor.

Ritual and ceremony always involve some kind of physical action, and this engagement of Zen with your body affects you in a different way than when you engage it only with your mind. Actually, you could look at the physical posture of zazen as a kind of ritual. It results in more profound and substantial effects than you would achieve by simply attempting to meditate in your mind as you go about other activities.

Ritual can be especially important for people who tend to hold their emotions in check, or who prefer intellectual analysis to getting personally involved. From the beginning of human civilization, people have been creating rituals to facilitate transitions and celebrate significant relationships, precisely because the act of ceremony accesses a part of us that can end up getting neglected. The beautiful thing is that a good communal ritual doesn't require you to try to feel anything special. Just by going through it you are affected by it in some way, even if you are skeptical.

For example, at the ceremony celebrating the birth of Shakyamuni Buddha, the sangha processes around the room so that each person ends up passing in front of a statue of the baby buddha. The buddha is standing in a bowl of sweetened tea, underneath a bower covered with flowers. As you pass the statue, you take a ladleful of tea and pour it over the baby's head in accordance with the myth that sweet rain fell from the sky when the buddha was born.

Whatever you think of the ceremony before and after the moment when you make this gesture of gratitude and respect, it's hard not to feel touched. After all, this is about your gratitude for encountering wise, compassionate people and learning about things that relieve your suffering.

Buddhas and Bodhisattvas

Although Zen is a non-theistic tradition, it is populated with quite a few archetypal images of buddhas and bodhisattvas. Buddhas represent complete mastery and enlightenment, while bodhisattvas represent the diligent and selfless effort to awaken. In Zen, there are more buddhas spoken of than just Shakyamuni from 2,500 years ago. This is a symbolic acknowledgment that awakening is a possibility for all human beings, and that there were undoubtedly other awakened beings before (and after) Shakyamuni (although he is credited with teaching it in a way that people can understand and practice). Bodhisattvas tend to represent the perfection of a particular aspect of practice, like compassion, wisdom, loving kindness, or diligent effort.

CONSIDER THIS

The second-most recognizable Buddhist image, after Shakyamuni Buddha, is Kanzeon, the bodhisattva of compassion. In many images or statues she is reminiscent of the Christian Virgin Mary. In India the bodhisattva of compassion was portrayed as male and called Avalokiteshvara, in China she become female and was called Kuan Yin, and in Japan she is Kanzeon or Kannon. The idea of Kanzeon has captivated and inspired the devotion of countless people over the millennia, because according to the archetype her compassion compels her to hear the cries of the world and respond to them.

With the exception of Shakyamuni, buddhas and bodhisattvas are not people who are supposed to have existed in the past (or present). Instead, they function as archetypes, personifying aspirations. However, because they are personified, these characters can take on mystical or supernatural aspects in some people's minds. In fact, some of the most revered Zen masters in the tradition have prayed to the bodhisattva of compassion, Kuan Yin or Kanzeon, for deliverance from difficulty. This kind of devotion is generally neither encouraged nor discouraged in Zen; each individual is allowed to develop his or her own relationship to buddhas and bodhisattvas. If you prefer a purely rational perspective, you might, for example, think of how compassion actually can deliver you from difficulty in a certain way. Compassion is very powerful, and its power to affect your own mind and even the actions of others has been demonstrated by people like Nelson Mandela and Gandhi.

Vows to Become a Zen Buddhist

You take vows to formally become a Zen Buddhist within a sangha, and an authorized Zen teacher performs the ceremony. It isn't necessary to formally become a Zen Buddhist to practice Zen, of course, or even to consider yourself a Zen Buddhist. The vows and formality function in two ways: first, to indicate your commitment to sangha; and second, to up the ante on your practice by making a clear statement of your intentions.

Once you've made a vow, it's difficult to fool yourself when you're failing to honor your own aspiration. For example, if you've never promised to stay with your partner, when you feel like leaving them you can always remind yourself you never promised to stay. A past promise to stay with them, of course, may not keep you from leaving, but if you leave you'll have to admit to yourself that you're also departing from an aspiration you once had. Vows give shape to your intentions and increase the likelihood that you'll follow through.

Lay Zen Buddhists

The ceremony to become a Zen Buddhist is called *Jukai*, and it involves vowing to keep the Zen precepts. At Jukai, new Zen Buddhists receive a small article of clothing to wear around their neck. In some lineages this is a *wagessa*, or a narrow strip of cloth with a decorative knot connecting the two ends of the cloth. In other lineages they receive a *rakusu*, which looks like a rectangular bib pieced together out of smaller pieces of cloth. A student taking Jukai may also receive a Buddhist name that is chosen by the teacher, although in some lineages this step, along with the rakusu, occurs when someone becomes a formal student in a subsequent ceremony.

What it means to become or be a lay Zen Buddhist is pretty much up to you. You might think of the lay Buddhist's relationship to Zen as Protestant Christians think of their relationship with God—personal, and not requiring any intermediaries. Some lay Buddhists, even after Jukai, practice mostly on their own, in the context of their lay life. Others feel that the vows prioritize and change their life. Still others make a big commitment to sangha, regularly attending practice events including retreats, and volunteering their time and money to support the Zen community.

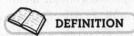 **DEFINITION**

> **Jukai** is the ceremony at which people take vows to follow the Zen precepts and formally become a Zen Buddhist. The precepts have to be given by an authorized Zen teacher. A **wagessa** is a narrow strip of cloth with the two ends united by a decorative knot, which is sometimes received during the Jukai ceremony and subsequently worn during sangha practice events. A **rakusu** is a biblike cloth garment, also worn during practice events, which may be received during Jukai or a formal student ceremony, along with a Buddhist name.

Formal Students

Some Zen students choose to establish a formal relationship with a teacher. This is not at all required, and many people practice indefinitely having only undergone the Jukai ceremony. In some lineages the Jukai ceremony implies something of a relationship with the teacher who gives you the precepts, but in this case there is great variation in how the subsequent teacher-student relationship will look. In other lineages the formal relationship with a teacher is marked by another ceremony, and this clearly indicates the student's intention to work closely with the teacher over a long period of time, and the teacher's intention to be available to guide and support the student.

Formal students will generally have a Buddhist name, also called a dharma name, although they might not use it. In many sanghas people use their dharma name when they are with sangha, but very few people use the name outside of that context unless they are ordained (see the next section).

Dharma names are usually of Japanese or Chinese origin, and when you first encounter their use they may seem strange. However, the tradition of receiving another name once you've reached maturity appears in many cultures throughout the world, and many Zen students end up treasuring their dharma name. Every name has a specific meaning, and a teacher chooses a name for a student that simultaneously highlights that student's strengths as well as what they need to work on.

Monks, Priests, and Teachers

Finally, something should be said about ordination in Zen. Throughout much of Zen and Buddhist history, ordained practitioners held center stage, with lay people playing a supporting role or occasionally making special appearances. The tide has completely turned in modern times, however, such that in a book like this a discussion of ordination can be limited to a small section out of hundreds of pages.

The change in the lay versus ordained composition of the Zen sangha is due in large part to changes in the economic circumstances of the average person. A lay person a couple hundred years ago typically worked hard for most of the daylight hours, almost every day of the week. If someone wanted to sit meditation and study Buddhism, they needed to become a monk and receive material support from lay people. Modern lay people have more time and resources to devote to practicing Zen, so they now make up the vast majority of Zen students.

In addition, Western culture doesn't have the tradition of supporting full-time monastics; and in fact the culture has a work ethic that questions the value of someone whose only job is to meditate and ponder spiritual questions. Therefore, many ordained Zen people have to work to support themselves. Add to this the fact that the Japanese government waived the celibacy requirement for Zen priests in the nineteenth century and many Zen priests are married, and the distinctions between ordained and lay in Zen can get pretty confusing.

Someone who receives ordination in Zen is generally referred to as a monk or a priest, although those terms tend to be associated with Christian traditions, and an ordained Zen person is unlike either a Christian monk or a priest. Traditionally the Zen ordination ceremony marks the *beginning* of a particular kind of Zen training. Unlike in Christianity, ordination doesn't indicate an intention to permanently live a cloistered life, or the completion of training that enables someone to serve as a pastor or minister.

The newly ordained Zen person, at this stage often called a monk, generally goes through a period of five years or longer during which he or she devotes him- or herself as fully as possible to Zen training. This training usually occurs in a monastery, a residential practice center, or at least in close association with a teacher and Zen center. If a student shows interest in, and aptitude for, serving sangha (such as leading practice events or classes, or maintaining a practice center), he or she may end up being referred to as a priest. At this point the term priest indicates a vocation, rather than a qualification.

When a formal Zen student, ordained or lay, has worked with a teacher for a long time—often as long as 10 to 20 years—the teacher may acknowledge the strength of the student's understanding and practice with a ceremony or some other kind of formal recognition. The forms of recognition differ by lineage, particularly between Soto Zen and the koan lineages, but within each lineage the traditions are established and clear.

Recognition, often called transmission or inka, empowers the student to become a Zen teacher in his or her own right and to operate independently of his or her teacher. Becoming a Zen teacher is not in any way a general goal of Zen students; someone may manifest perfect Zen as a parent, doctor, or carpenter and not be the slightest bit inclined to explicitly teach Zen or take formal Zen students.

The Least You Need to Know

- The Zen tradition is full of practices and teachings that you can decide not to engage in, but which may enrich and challenge your experience of Zen.
- Sangha is a community of Buddhist or Zen practitioners. Sangha is considered one of the three central components of Buddhism, along with buddha and dharma.
- Work with a Zen teacher can look many different ways, but may provide guidance, encouragement, and challenge.
- Meditation retreats, or sesshin, are a great way to intensify your practice, particularly your zazen.

- Zen contains religious imagery and practices you may find very useful. If you don't, try not to let them turn you away from Zen practice entirely; there are ways to relate to them that you may be able to live with.

- Your Zen practice is your own business, but if you want to you can formally become a Zen Buddhist, a formal student, or perhaps after a long time in practice even consider ordination.

Essential Zen Teachings

There are enough Zen and Buddhist teachings to fill a very large library, so where do you begin? In Part 3 I offer some of the most fundamental Zen teachings, and a few of the Buddhist (pre-Zen) teachings they are based on. These include the Four Noble Truths, the concepts of dukkha and impermanence, and the teachings of no-self, emptiness, and buddha-nature.

Teachings are statements about the way things are. They can be very useful if you use them to guide your investigation of your own mind and experience. Zen teachings are not meant to simply be accepted or believed, even though they may seem like statements about reality that seem to leave no room for discussion. It's better to think of them as hypotheses to be tested. You still need to achieve the results in your own body-mind lab in order to verify the truth of each teaching and really know it for yourself.

The Path to Liberation

The very first Buddhist teachings are foundational to almost all forms of Buddhism and subsequent teachings. They amount to what, according to the story, Siddhartha Gautama realized 2,500 years ago when he awakened to reality. He had been on a spiritual quest to discover what people can do about suffering. Were they merely subject to changing conditions, blessed with happiness in times of fortune, but doomed to suffer in times of misfortune or when inevitably faced with disease, old age, and death?

What the Buddha realized was in what way human beings contribute to their own suffering, and what they can do about it. Buddhism is sometimes criticized for being pessimistic because it begins with the discussion of things like pain and dissatisfaction, but Buddhism is actually quite optimistic. For one thing, the Buddha did not say all of life is suffering, just that no one seemed to be able to avoid it entirely. For another thing, the Buddha saw, and subsequently taught, a way for people to alleviate the worst of their suffering.

In This Chapter

- Things to keep in mind about Buddhist teachings
- The original teaching of the Buddha
- What Buddhists mean by "suffering"
- The way you cause some of your own dissatisfaction
- How to get relief from stress

How to Use Zen Teachings

Before launching into a discussion of essential Zen and Buddhist teachings, it might be helpful to say something about how to relate to and use them. Given Zen's emphasis on discovering your own truth and direct experience, it may seem strange to encounter so many statements telling you how things really are. Teachings are very important, but they are not meant to be believed or accepted. They are meant to be studied and tested, somewhat like hypotheses.

Even more accurate might be the analogy of learning a martial art, because Zen is not about learning something with your mind, it's about embodying something in your life. Your martial arts instructor may drill into you the philosophy of his martial arts school and explain how to move in order to be successful in the art, but *you* still have to learn how to enact and know it yourself. In Zen, you don't have to start from scratch in learning about reality, but until you personally experience how a teaching works, it hasn't actually been very helpful to you.

Another important aspect of relating to Zen and Buddhist teachings is this: teachings are like medicine. Each one has been formulated to address a particular misunderstanding, harmful behavior, or habit. Some concepts and imagery are going to be useful to you while others are not, and some will be useful at certain times but not at others. For example, if you are depressed, the teaching that all things are empty of inherent self-nature may be difficult to explore without feeding your depression, while a practice like chanting or mindful activity might help.

Someone who has a habit of lashing out at others can benefit from special attention to the precept of not indulging anger, while someone coming out of an abusive relationship may need to work on compassion for themselves, even if that means indulging anger for a while. A Zen teacher can be useful in helping you identify the aspects of Zen with which it will be most fruitful for you to engage, given your personality, history, and circumstances.

The Four Noble Truths

The first teaching of Shakyamuni Buddha consisted of the *Four Noble Truths*. You probably won't hear the Four Noble Truths discussed explicitly in Zen very often, but they are a root teaching from which almost all kinds of Buddhism evolved. You might say that Buddhists have found countless ways of restating the Four Noble Truths over the centuries, changing the language and imagery to suit the audience. The subsequent concepts and texts are so vast and approach the truth from so many different perspectives, it can be difficult to know where to start when introducing them.

In essence, though, almost all Buddhist teachings are pointing toward the same fundamental truths. One of my teachers, Kyogen Carlson, likened the truth to a familiar red fruit, and then admitted, "There are many ways to slice a tomato." Despite all the wonderful ways Zen has sliced the tomato, when it comes to introducing Zen teachings it seems most straightforward to start with the root of all subsequent Buddhist concepts, the Four Noble Truths.

The Four Noble Truths as presented in this chapter are stated somewhat differently than you often find them translated. They are usually listed as four facts about the world, something like this: life is suffering, suffering is caused by desire, you can be free from suffering if you end desire, and the Buddhist path is how you end desire.

Many scholars have argued over the best translations of this first Buddhist lesson, but most agree that the list as just stated here does a bad job of portraying what the Buddha intended. Instead, it's more accurate to think of four things that, explored and comprehended, result in liberation, rather than four truisms to be accepted. Here the Four Noble Truths are presented as 1) recognize *dukkha*; 2) see what causes dukkha; 3) let go of what causes dukkha; 4) practice what supports liberation from dukkha.

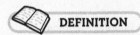

DEFINITION

The **Four Noble Truths** were Shakyamuni Buddha's first teaching and summarize the essence of Buddhist thought. Translations differ, but they can be expressed like this: 1) recognize the existence of dukkha in your life; 2) learn the causes of that dukkha; 3) let go of the causes of that dukkha; and 4) in all areas of your life, do what supports your ability to take the other three steps. **Dukkha** is alternatively translated as suffering, stress, dissatisfaction, or unease, and refers to the full spectrum of human unhappiness from acute suffering to a subtle sense of things not being quite right.

One: Recognize Dukkha

The first Noble Truth is "recognize dukkha." I'm using the term dukkha because it's impossible to find an English translation of the word that does the term justice. The word is most often translated as suffering, but is a much more complex and subtle experience than that one word can communicate. In fact, the whole next chapter is devoted to further unpacking the many different manifestations of dukkha and how you deal with them. Understanding dukkha is the key to understanding almost all Zen teaching, because it's the source of your motivation to practice Zen to begin with. Here I will introduce the concept and how it relates to the Noble Truths.

Admitting Life Isn't Perfect

It can be a bit of a downer to examine how life can be a bummer, and in what ways. It also takes courage and humility. Common sense tells you to keep yourself too busy with enjoyable and rewarding things to think about the uncomfortable or painful aspects of life. If you are forced to deal with those painful aspects, you are supposed to keep yourself busy getting rid of them as soon as possible. When you face difficulties you can't get rid of, well … you still try to avoid thinking about them as much as possible.

Buddhism suggests a different approach. Instead of avoiding the inevitable pain of life, you face it head on. You examine your feelings and thoughts about difficulty, and prepare yourself to meet it with as much equanimity as possible. There is a traditional Buddhist list of the eight kinds of hardship you are going to have to face at one point or another: birth (the initial discomfort that comes with change), aging, death, pain (emotional and physical), association with what you do not love, separation from what you love, and not getting what you want.

Contrary to popular belief, the Buddha did not teach that life is suffering. He simply observed that people endured these eight kinds of hardships pretty much constantly, to some degree or another, and wondered whether they were doomed to lose their happiness in the face of them.

 CONSIDER THIS

Stephen Batchelor describes encountering dukkha in his book *Buddhism Without Beliefs*:

"No matter how expertly we manage our lives, how convincing an image of well-being we project, we still find ourselves involved with what we hate and torn apart from what we love. We still don't get what we want and still get what we don't want. True, we experience joy, success, love, bliss. But in the end we find ourselves once more prone to anguish .... We may know this, but do we understand it? We see it, are even awed by it, but habit impels us to forget it. To cover it over and flee again to the lure of the tantalizing world. For were we to understand it, even in a glimpse, it might change everything."

When great difficulty seems far off, the question of how you are going to meet it may not seem important. Day-to-day discomfort, while annoying, is often not enough to call your attention to the issue, but the question becomes paramount when you're the one who is living in the nursing home, or the one who has just lost the dearest person to you in the world. Somehow, you never really think *you* are going to end up in such situations.

When you're taken by surprise and suddenly you're one of the ones facing great difficulty, it may not be easy to work on yourself spiritually with meditation, karma work, or insight. Your time, energy, and attention are likely to be swallowed up by other things (although a kind of natural mindfulness often arises in you when things are really tough). That's why Buddhists believe it's worth spending your good times preparing for your bad times. This may seem negative, but that's not all there is to it.

For one thing, the Buddha pointed out that even when everything is going great, there's part of you that knows things are eventually going to change and therefore feels ill at ease. This unease can be very subtle, or it can cause significant stress and anxiety. For another thing, the practices recommended for relieving dukkha are the same ones that help you be more aware and appreciative of your life, so your effort doesn't have to be about the future.

What Dukkha Is

Dukkha usually arises in you when you meet one of the eight human difficulties listed previously. It's the opposite of what you feel when everything is going splendidly, when all seems right with the world and you are at ease, contented, and comfortable. When faced with difficulty, everything suddenly feels off-kilter. You feel unease and stress. You may be suffering, but that may be overstating the matter. Dukkha is basically just the sense that *things aren't right*.

The most important thing to realize about dukkha is that it is not synonymous with painful feelings. You can experience dukkha alongside a whole range of emotions, such as anguish, depression, despair, grief, regret, angst, boredom, disappointment, or a sense of meaninglessness. However, you can also experience the sense that *things aren't right* when you are feeling pleasant emotions but you are aware that they won't last.

Dukkha is usually so tightly entwined with other emotions and experiences that you don't recognize it as something in and of itself, but it's the conviction deep down in your being that *this* is not the way things are supposed to be. This sense can be powerful, such as when you are the victim of injustice. It can also be subtle, such as a pervasive sense that the worthwhile events of your life haven't happened yet. The less dramatic, existential forms of dukkha may not sound like a big deal, but they are. They can be at the root of someone's depression or despair, and they may even make life seem not worth living.

When you examine your own experience, you realize dukkha itself causes pain and trouble. It adds a significant layer of stress or suffering to whatever adversity you are experiencing. For example, consider how terrible you would feel if your house burned down. Now consider how much worse you would feel if you had spent lots of time and energy carefully building a fire-resistant house, and then someone deliberately burned it down. In the latter situation you would not only face the hardship of the loss of your house, you would struggle with an overwhelming sense that *this should not have happened*.

The grief, shock, and worry you naturally feel in response to a challenge like losing a home are not actually a spiritual problem. You can be in a great deal of emotional or physical pain and still feel fundamentally okay. It's the dukkha that twists you up inside. It's a pervasive resistance to what is happening that tends to make the pain feel worse and often triggers anger, resentment, depression, and despair. Even when things are going well, the sense that things aren't quite right gets in the way of your enjoyment of life.

Two: See What Causes Dukkha

The next step, after you have recognized the existence of dukkha in your life, is to learn what causes it. You may think the answer is obvious: life causes dukkha. Human difficulties and their associated emotional and physical pain cause your sense that things aren't right (because, after all, things *aren't* right, right?).

Fortunately, the Buddha didn't stop there. He was like a scientist searching for a cure to a disease that everyone else thinks is incurable. He observed how people seemed to be entirely at the mercy of their conditions, enjoying fortune when they had it, and miserable when they met with misfortune. One image stuck with him as he contemplated whether this was all life had to offer: a monk he once saw, who was seated calmly in meditation. The monk seemed to have accessed some other way of being that was not so dependent on conditions. This inspired the Buddha to look more deeply at the issue of suffering.

 ZEN WISDOM

"If people do not meet with sadness or suffering, they will never seek for the true way of life. When they are driven into a tight corner where they can move neither forward nor backward, then they finally begin to reflect on themselves, harbor doubts about their lives, and ask themselves the question: What is the true way to live?"

—Shundo Aoyama Roshi, from *Zen Seeds: Reflections of a Female Zen Priest*

Desire Versus Grasping

The Buddha realized it was grasping and aversion that cause dukkha. It isn't desire that causes dukkha, as some translations of Buddhist teachings suggest. It's perfectly natural, and probably unavoidable, to have a preference that things go well. You don't like pain and difficulty, while there are many pleasant and rewarding things you like. There's a big difference, however, between an objective acknowledgment of your desire, and giving your preference the status of an imperative and subsequently grasping after it.

For example, you can desire to get to work on time as opposed to getting stuck in traffic. You cause problems when "I hope I get to work on time" becomes "I *have to* get to work on time, or else!" Then you stew in impotent rage as you creep along slowly in a long line of cars. The first of these statements is recognizing a desire you have, while the second is grasping after that desire.

When you grasp, it's like you lean off your spiritual center to reach for something. The opposite of grasping is aversion, or leaning away from something you don't want, but it's really the same activity. Either way, when you lean you give up your equanimity and move away from the upright, dignified, ready posture that is Zen practice.

Grasping Doesn't Help

Despite all appearances to the contrary, grasping and aversion don't bring you lasting satisfaction and happiness. In situations where you are able to act in order to bring the world more into line with your preferences, you generally do so anticipating greater reward and comfort. If you are successful in your efforts, you may feel gratified, and dukkha may seem like an adaptive experience that impels you to make the world a better place. Grasping and aversion may seem like useful human endeavors.

Unfortunately, you never reach satisfaction for long using this method because things are constantly changing. Just when you've gotten everything the way you like it, something else needs to be dealt with. Alternatively, if you are *not* successful in your efforts to bring the world more into line with your preferences, you have a real problem. You are stuck with dukkha, and all of your grasping or aversion is useless. This can cause real suffering.

 POTENTIAL PITFALL

Beware of thinking that Zen requires you to get rid of your desires. Not only is it extremely difficult to do so, it may require you to deny or suppress your needs, or turn away from ways you can benefit the world. The goal is to change the way you relate to your desires. When you see them as potential options rather than imperatives, you're able to act on them with more wisdom and compassion.

If grasping and aversion were the only ways to make changes in the world, of course, you'd have to use them in order to live a full human life. The amazing thing is they are completely unnecessary. It's possible to take effective action without giving up your spiritual center, by simply being present and responding with as much wisdom and compassion as you can muster.

To go back to our traffic example, you do not have to be simmering with impatience (grasping) in order to take the next exit off the freeway and find a better route to work. Calmly recognizing your preference to get to work on time, you avoid the traffic. Not grasping does not in any way entail passivity or stupidity, it just means doing without the extra "Noooooo!" in response to the way things are.

Three: Let Go of What Causes Dukkha

How do you let go of what causes dukkha, the troubling sense that *this is not the way things should be?* Dukkha arises when you let your simple desire turn into an imperative, leading to grasping and aversion. How, then, do you avoid allowing this process to unfold? It can be extremely difficult to convince yourself that what you are feeling is a "simple desire," not an absolute requirement.

In our traffic example, you *do* have to get to work on time, or else, right? If you're late you'll face all kinds of additional difficulties, and maybe even lose your job! At some level you know that your impatience in the midst of traffic is useless and probably even counterproductive, but it may still prove impossible to let it go. Even if you've got a certain philosophy about traffic that allows you to keep your cool when dealing with it, there's going to be another kind of situation in your life where it's not so easy.

This brings us to what is arguably the most radical discovery of the Buddha: it is possible to *just let go* of grasping and aversion. This "just" is not about the process being easy, it's about the fact that ultimately the process is incredibly simple.

You might think that to let go of grasping and aversion you need to adopt a whole new philosophy, or argue yourself into no longer chasing after your desires, or go through a lengthy process of behavioral reconditioning. After all, the impulse to get what you want (or avoid what you don't want) is *so* powerful! In the end, however, it's more like you search and search until you finally find the "off switch" in your own mind, so one moment you can be grasping and filled with dukkha, and the next moment you can be calm and relieved.

 CONSIDER THIS

In his book *Wings to Awakening*, Ajahn Thanissaro describes the process that the Buddha went through when he discovered how to attain the cessation of dukkha. Thanissaro calls the Buddha's process "this/that conditionality," which means that the Buddha employed a method of observing his own mind. This method can be applied to anything you experience. It involves noticing that when this is present, that is present; when this arises, that arises; when this is not present, that is not present; when this is ended, that is ended. It's like using the scientific method on your subjective experience in order to discover causal connections.

To cultivate the ability to just let go, you use the tools of meditation and mindfulness to carefully observe your own mind. It can take a long time to be able to concentrate well enough to watch your mind as it goes through the whole process of generating dukkha. A desire arises, the desire is interpreted as an imperative, grasping ensues, all your effort gets focused on changing things according to your preference, and dukkha is born.

As described in Chapter 7, after observing this process over and over, more space appears between the steps. Eventually you have room to make a conscious choice between one step and another, rather than all of it occurring on autopilot. Then one day you try something different. Instead of jumping from desire to imperative, you ask yourself, "What if I just left it there?"

Now the chain of cause and effect is broken, and you don't end up grasping or experiencing the resulting stress, dissatisfaction, or suffering. You've found the "off switch" for dukkha. It's not always easy to find the switch or to make yourself use it (resistance to letting go is discussed in Chapter 11), but after you've consciously turned it off even once, things are never the same.

Four: Practice What Supports Liberation

Another radical aspect of Buddhist teaching is that it doesn't just tell you *what* you need to do, it tells you *how* to do it. Given the first three Noble Truths you can recognize dukkha and its cause, and try to let go of the cause, but there is a very compelling reason not to let go of the cause of dukkha: self-interest. The subject of the fourth Noble Truth is the question of how to transcend your self-interest and learn to let go of grasping and aversion. The fourth truth is the path of practice. In ancient Buddhism this was called the *Noble Eightfold Path*, and consisted of two types of practices: those dealing with ethical behavior, and those dealing with the cultivation of insight.

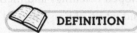

DEFINITION

The **Noble Eightfold Path** is the fourth Noble Truth, and it outlines the essential components of Buddhist practice: right speech, right action, right livelihood, right concentration, right mindfulness, right effort, right view, and right intention.

The ethical aspects of the Eightfold Path are right speech, right action, and right livelihood, each of which overlap with the various Zen precepts discussed in Chapter 6. Each aspect of the Eightfold Path begins with the word "right," but this is not meant to imply a narrow, prescribed course of action that results in moral superiority. In this case "right" means true, genuine, suitable or appropriate.

In a Buddhist context, something you did or said would not be right if it involved indulging self-interest at the expense of another, or any of the obvious harmful actions like killing or stealing. The basic idea is that, unless you live your life in a healthy way that minimizes harm, you will be unable to let go of grasping and aversion. Instead, you will be strengthening your habits based in self-interest and making a mess of your life, and therefore will be unable to liberate yourself from dukkha.

The remaining aspects of the Eightfold Path are devoted to the cultivation of the insight that's necessary for fully transcending your self-interest. Three of the practices are about developing concentration, or the ability to perceive reality clearly. These are right effort, right mindfulness, and right concentration. Concentration (in meditation) and mindfulness have already been discussed in Chapters 4 and 5. Right effort can be compared to the karma work discussed in Chapter 7, which is long-term and careful work to change habits so they are wholesome instead of harmful. Right effort refers particularly to habits of mind (habits of body and speech would be covered under right action and right speech).

Two of the Eightfold practices specifically address the cultivation of insight that leads to transcending self-interest. The first of these is right view, which amounts to a deep, firsthand knowledge of the way things really are. This is often phrased in terms of understanding the Buddhist teachings, including the law of karma and the Four Noble Truths. However, these teachings are there to be tested, so when you work on right view you are essentially trying to see reality, which at some point you may recognize is described accurately by Buddhist teachings.

The second insight-related aspect of the Eightfold Path is right intention, which is essentially transcendence of your self-interest. When you have mastered right intention, selfishness and immorality do not occur to you, because—through right view—you have come to understand that the true nature of your being is empty of any inherent, enduring self-nature (more on this in the next chapter).

Most types of Buddhism, including Zen, can be seen as unique elaborations on this fourth Noble Truth, the path of practice. Each kind of Buddhism has developed teachings and methods that address the *how* of practice—how you transcend self-interest and let go of grasping and aversion—that are well-suited to particular cultures, times, and types of people.

For example, the founders of Pure Land Buddhism believed that encouraging people to seek enlightenment actually just stimulated self-interest, so they advocated the cultivation of a deep devotion and self-surrender to Amida Buddha. In Nichiren Buddhism, the Lotus Sutra is viewed as being the pinnacle of Buddhist teaching, so effective that wholehearted focus on the recitation of a verse that pays homage to it is sufficient practice (*namu myoho renge kyo*). Zen advocates meditation and a personal experience of what the Buddha himself realized, arguing that this stays true to the original Buddhist practices and teachings.

The Least You Need to Know

- Zen and Buddhist teachings are meant to be investigated, not simply accepted.
- The first and fundamental Buddhist teaching centers on the question of how people can feel more or less okay despite the difficulties they face.
- The Buddhist term dukkha refers to a conviction that things aren't the way they should be. This idea can arise in the midst of all kinds of experiences, from great physical and emotional pain to a vague dissatisfaction with life.
- You experience dukkha when you let your natural desires turn into imperatives ("I would like it if …" turns into "Things have to … or else").
- You can let go of the thinking that causes dukkha, but it's difficult because of your natural self-interest. Buddhist practice is aimed at helping you transcend that self-interest.

The Fundamental Misunderstanding

As discussed in the previous chapter, you are not completely at the mercy of the changing fortunes of your life. While you may experience difficulty and consequently feel grief or pain, you can choose to let go of the grasping or aversion that leads to the additional suffering called dukkha, or the conviction that things are not as they should be.

The irony is that the ability to just let go is always available to you. You don't need to do Zen practice to access it. However, chances are good that you will find letting go quite difficult, even if you can convince yourself to try it. This is because, naturally, you want to protect and take care of yourself. When you're trying to look out for yourself, it doesn't make sense to let go of reaching for what you want or to stop pushing away what you don't want.

However, according to Zen, your efforts to protect and take care of yourself are likely to cause stress and suffering until you correct your fundamental misunderstanding about the nature of self. Once the true nature of self—and subsequently all things—is understood, it becomes much easier to transcend self-interest and let go. This is why Zen Master Dogen said that to study the buddha way is to study the self.

In This Chapter

- How your self-concept came to be
- The assumption of inherent, enduring self-nature
- The true nature of self
- Problems caused by a self-concept
- How understanding brings relief

Your Self-Concept

The fundamental reason you don't let go of grasping and aversion is because you believe you have an inherently existing, enduring self-nature. The first time you felt hungry or cold as a newborn baby and you weren't fed or warmed immediately, the idea started to form in your mind that it was *you* versus the world. Over time you learned that "you" consisted of certain elements that were in some way separate from the rest of the world: your body (separate from other bodies and objects), your experiences (which no one else exactly shared), your ideas (which others didn't automatically know or understand), and your desires (which the world didn't always cooperate in fulfilling).

Most importantly, your self included the element of consciousness—the awareness of continuity in the existence of all of your self elements. Along with memory, this consciousness resulted in a unique narrative about your life that was all your own. In Buddhism these self elements are called the *five aggregates*.

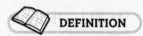 **DEFINITION**

The **five aggregates**, or five skandhas, are the elements that compose the self: physical form, sensations (or feelings, particularly sensing things as pleasant, unpleasant, or neutral), perceptions (or cognition, naming and identifying things), formations (volition and associated conceptions and mental habits), and consciousness (awareness of all of the elements and the world).

Given all of these self elements, you made the assumption—along with all of the human beings before you—that somewhere in the middle of all of these elements there was an enduring essence that tied them together over time. If it changed, your existence wouldn't make any sense. You'd be a different person at age 16 than you were at age 6. Obviously, some things change over time, but if *everything* changes over time, what does it mean to be a person? This self-essence also had to be inherent, or independent of the existence of other things or beings, and fundamentally unaffected by changing conditions. After all, that's the whole nature of a self—an individual, unique and separate from other individuals.

Subsequently, almost your entire life has been spent in the service of the inherent, enduring self-nature you presume you have. From day one you have sought to keep it happy, maintain its boundaries, and monitor its territory. When you were 5, you cried because you wanted an ice cream cone but didn't get one. As you got older you defined who you were by your preferences, then by your friends, then by your opinions, and later by your accomplishments, talents, skills, and possessions.

With more maturity, perhaps you identified more with your sense of being generous, kind, or possessed of common sense. Through it all, there has been your body and a sense of consciousness, so chances are you have never doubted you exist. You may have wondered about the nature of existence, but never doubted there was a *you* to ponder it.

The Real Nature of Self

There is a wonderful analogy that illustrates the Zen view of the real nature of self. In an ancient Buddhist text titled *The Questions of King Milinda*, a sage named Nagasena addresses the king's question of whether or not Nagasena can be said to exist. Nagasena asks the king whether he had arrived that day in a chariot. The king says yes. The sage then asks him if the axle is the chariot, or the wheels, the framework, the yoke, or the reins. To each of these propositions the king answers no, because none of them taken in isolation can be called a chariot.

Then Nagasena asks whether the mere combination of all of these pieces (picture them piled up in a heap) can be called a chariot. Again the answer is no, although the king also agrees that no chariot can be found apart from the pieces. Nagasena suggests that no chariot can ultimately be found, although in a sense it clearly exists because it was able to convey the king to the site of the teaching. Therefore, "chariot" is merely a useful designation, not something that can be said to truly exist in and of itself, and the same can be said of "Nagasena."

Empty of Inherent Self-Nature

You may react to this analogy by thinking that the self can be said to truly exist when all of its pieces are assembled correctly, in a way that they can perform their function. All the pieces together, in a particular configuration, result in a real, emergent phenomenon called the self. However, this means the existence of the self is dependent on the pieces. Remove one of the pieces and you no longer have a self. Perhaps some of the pieces can be removed—a limb, or a particular sense, or consciousness—while the remaining collection of elements retains its self-ness. But if too many pieces are removed (say, brain function), then there is no self anymore. There is no clear line between self and no-longer-self when you look at the matter in terms of a collection of elements.

 ZEN WISDOM

"Is there a real basis [for the notion of self] inside or outside your body now? Your body with hair and skin is just inherited from your father and mother. From beginning to end a drop of blood or lymph is empty. So none of these are the self. What about mind, thought, awareness, and knowledge? Or the breath going in and out, which ties a lifetime together: what is it after all? None of these are the self either. How could you be attached to any of them?"

—Zen Master Dogen (1200-1253), from his essay "Guidelines for Studying the Way," as translated by Ed Brown and Kaz Tanahashi in *Moon in a Dewdrop*

The idea of your self-nature being an emergent phenomenon due to a particular configuration of elements is also unlikely to be what you really had in mind when you developed your self-concept, anyway. Do you really think of your very existence as being dependent on your sensations, or thoughts, or consciousness? Probably not. Instead, you tend to think, "I have sensations," or, "I temporarily lost consciousness." The pieces of your self appear to be in the service of an inherent, enduring self-nature.

The Zen teaching of emptiness simply points out that you are *empty* of inherent, enduring self-nature—that is, your self-concept is just an idea. If you look diligently for it, as Nagasena and King Milinda looked for the self-nature of the chariot, you can't find it. Even more significantly (because you can't prove a negative), when you drop the idea of having an inherent, enduring self-nature, you can easily recognize through your own experience that living without the concept is more in harmony with reality than holding on to it. You think you need your self-concept to survive, or even simply to be alive, but you don't. The self as emergent phenomenon keeps on functioning without your favorite idea, and in fact it functions much, much better.

The Way You Really Exist

No one blames you for forming a self-concept; everyone does it, if they are mentally healthy, and it's a useful concept for navigating the world. However, there is a big difference between recognizing something as a useful tool, which can be picked up and put down, and the way you usually hold on to your self-concept. When you personally understand emptiness, you can make use of your sense of self and its accompanying narrative in order to take responsibility for your life, but you don't believe in all of it the same way you used to.

In fact, you *have* to make use of your self-concept, because while your self is empty, it's part of a flow of causes and effects. To think you don't exist at all—that everything is a mere collection of elements, there is no *you* that moves from moment to moment, so nothing really matters—is another fundamental misunderstanding of your self-nature. You do exist, just not in the way you think you do. You exist as a flow of causes and effects operating on and through your body and all the other elements of self. You are not the same person you were 10 years ago, or even yesterday, but you are related to that person, and you are the result of that person.

Zen teacher Shohaku Okumura compares this to a river: it makes sense to call the Mississippi the Mississippi, even though the water running through it is constantly changing. You are different from a river, however, in that your choices are going to form and affect your future flow and experience. When you look at things this way, you act carefully out of compassion for your future self.

You also exist as an emergent phenomenon arising in mutual dependence with everything around you. You would not be you without your relationship to everything else. You cannot be a mother without a daughter, you cannot be tall without things that are short, you cannot be a hermit without a society to withdraw from. You can't even be Doug Smith without Doug Smith's parents, all of the conditions that made Doug Smith who he is, people who recognize Doug Smith, and the air that Doug Smith breathes. In fact, change one tiny element in the world and you are no longer quite the same as you used to be.

ZEN WISDOM

"To speak about changes in our lives and communicate in a meaningful way, we must speak as if we assumed that there is an unchanging 'I' that has been experiencing the changes; otherwise, the word 'change' has no meaning. But according to Buddhist philosophy, self-identity, the 'I,' is a creation of the mind; we create self-identity because it's convenient and useful in certain ways. We must use self-identity to live responsibly in society, but we should realize that it is merely a tool, a symbol, a sign, or a concept."

—Zen Teacher Shohaku Okumura, from *Realizing Genjokoan*

Understanding No-self

In Zen, understanding the true nature of self is not an extra, optional endeavor. This is because holding on to the idea that you have an inherent, enduring self-nature is one of the primary causes of suffering. Remember the Four Noble Truths, and how liberation from dukkha could be achieved by refusing to let your preferences become imperatives?

As long as you haven't recognized your self-concept as merely being a useful tool, as long as you think you really exist, you will feel compelled to act on your preferences with grasping and aversion. As discussed in the previous chapter, these activities lead to stress, dissatisfaction, and suffering. You can try very hard to make your behavior less self-centered before you understand the true nature of self, but it will be a little bit like trying to act sober while still intoxicated. Your self-concept will impede your efforts every step of the way.

According to Zen, your true self is no-self. This may not sound comforting, but the actual experience of no-self is quite a relief. As mentioned earlier, you don't need to believe you have an inherent, enduring self-nature in order to live. In fact, that belief just gets in the way of living. Living with an appreciation of no-self also means that you can face both small and great difficulties with equanimity.

But wait a second, you might think—is Zen proposing that as long as you don't believe your self-concept, you won't care about pain, change, death, loss, or having a meaningful existence? Is the goal to become indifferent to everything that happens to you? Fortunately, the answer is, "No, definitely not!"

It can be quite surprising to drop your self-concept and realize how much remains behind. Your desires and preferences remain, as do your ideas, your passions, your talents, your memories—in short, *everything* except your delusion about self-nature. This means that you can engage with life and participate fully in the world without worrying about some inherently existing *you*. You care for your self elements, and take responsibility for the causal flow of your life, but you do it as a moment-by-moment dance with life, not because you are obliged to pit self against the world. With the realization of no-self, the perennial problems of humanity are not solved, the problems themselves are turned upside down.

CONSIDER THIS

Even when you have corrected your fundamental misunderstanding about the nature of self, most of the time you will still have a sense that you inherently exist. This is rather like one of those optical illusions where one line appears longer than the other; even when you measure the lines and realize they are the same length, one still appears longer. However, now you're not going to bet money that it really is!

Medicine for All Suffering

In Zen, "the medicine for all suffering" is a personal understanding of how all things, including your self, are empty of inherent, enduring self-nature. It might not be immediately obvious why this would be the case. Here I present three different kinds of suffering that are caused (or made significantly worse) by holding on to your self-concept, and how an appreciation of no-self can help.

The Misery of I, Me, and Mine

The first way your self-concept makes your life difficult is that it requires you to interpret everything you encounter in terms of your self. How am I doing? Do I have what I need? Is this a threat or an opportunity for me? What does this person think of me? Am I enjoying this? Why is this happening to me? Almost every moment of your day is spent evaluating how each thing you experience—sensations, ideas, people, situations—relates to *you*. This obsession probably gets tiresome even to you, and means that it's difficult to appreciate things in and of themselves, without reference to numero uno.

According to the Buddhist view, this way of relating to the world is a perfect setup for never-ending agitation and dissatisfaction. Everything that exists is constantly changing, so there's no end to the worries about your self. The misery of I, me, and mine is the endless work you do on behalf of self: protecting, maintaining, competing, defining, strengthening, and identifying threats. You do this work not only for your body, but also for all of the things that the self identifies with, or feels ownership of, including opinions, possessions, status, and relationships.

Because everything changes, you can never reach a place of perfect happiness. Even if you achieve everything you desire—the perfect home, the perfect job, the perfect spouse, the perfect spiritual state—you know things are going to change, so you can never be completely at ease.

Fortunately, if you understand the true nature of self, worry can be transformed into gratitude. From the point of view of no-self, the stuff of your life simply comes and goes. When you're enjoying health, or clarity, or fortune, you appreciate it. When these things change, you can let the self change with them. You may not like what's going on, but you don't hold on to an idea that your self must be protected from the experience of dislike. Efforts to improve your circumstances are simply a wholehearted response to conditions, not an imperative because your self is under threat.

Because of this wholeheartedness and lack of anxiety, you operate more effectively and learn to trust that your intelligence, determination, and ingenuity will take care of you without directions from your self-concept. You meet situations and people directly, not through the filter of your concern about how they are going to affect you.

Illness, Old Age, and Death

The second major drawback of a belief that you have an inherent, enduring self-nature is that it makes you dread illness, old age, and death. These are called the three divine messengers in Buddhism, because they remind you so acutely of impermanence. Buddhism freely acknowledges that the three messengers bring discomfort and pain, but discomfort and pain in themselves can't account for the anguish that illness, old age, and death usually cause in people. It's what the three messengers mean to your self-concept that's so frightening.

There's a sense in which old age and illness are also a kind of death—the end of a particular configuration of self elements. With ill health you lose some of the vitality, energy, abilities, and appearance you have previously identified as integral parts of your self. With illness this loss may or may not be temporary, but with old age it definitely becomes permanent.

It's natural for such loss to cause some grief and a period of adjustment, but you may feel additional suffering as your self-concept undergoes a radical shift. Who are you, now that you can't do what you used to do? How can you know who you are when you don't even recognize the person you see in the mirror? How can you maintain your sense of self when time seems to be whittling away at the edges of everything you have identified yourself with?

Finally, knowing that you will die someday puts you in a very difficult place. You can avoid thinking about it, which only works for so long. You can figure that after death there's only annihilation, as far as you're concerned, which is likely to be depressing. You can conceive of some kind of existence after death, but for many people it's difficult to cultivate unshakeable faith in such a thing. No matter which of these routes you take, there are potential difficulties.

In an ancient Buddhist text, the Nakulapita Sutta, the Buddha told a student who was experiencing physical pain and difficulty that while the student couldn't do anything about being afflicted in body, he could train himself to be unafflicted in mind. One of Buddha's disciples then explained that such training required the student to refrain from identifying his body, perceptions, feelings, thoughts, or consciousness as "self."

Understanding the true nature of self allows you to have a very different relationship to the three divine messengers. When you approach them from the point of view of no-self, they're just change. Because you recognize how your self is a causal flow and exists in relationship to everything else, you get used to it changing and shifting.

This is a bit like learning to surf the wave of change rather than struggle against it. You still want to be healthy and live as long as possible, but when illness and old age come, you watch in fascination while this self you have gotten so familiar with changes before your eyes like the view in a kaleidoscope. When death becomes inevitable, you *become* dying and then you become death. There is no *you* separate from the process, so it can be embraced with curiosity and willingness.

Existential Angst

Some people aren't possessed by a search for meaning; their lives feel rewarding enough that the painful parts seem worth it, or they have a philosophy of life that lets them put difficulty in perspective. If you *are* searching for meaning, however, this can be an all-consuming issue. Your success or failure in finding meaning can mean the difference between wholehearted enthusiasm and despair.

Whether you're searching for meaning in your own life, or looking for the meaning of human life in general, you're most likely starting from that same old assumption that you have an inherent, enduring self-nature. When you examine possible meanings, you relate to them the same way you relate to everything else: what does this meaning do for *you?*

Even when your concern is about the suffering in the rest of the world, ultimately it comes back to questions about you: what should you do? What can you do? How can you possibly enjoy your life when the world is like this? It's not even that such questions are selfish in the ordinary sense of the word, just that they use the self-concept as their main reference point. Since this self-concept is empty, any system of meaning or purpose that uses it will ultimately be unsatisfying or unstable.

Existential angst also arises because you have an intuition about emptiness but still don't understand the truth of it. Every moment you get clues that nothing in the world is permanent, and that your self-nature is also constantly changing and cannot be grasped. This seems like really bad news for your inherent, enduring self-nature! As discussed earlier, your life is spent pro-tecting and maintaining that self, and emptiness can seem like an awfully big threat. Daily experience ends up being unnerving because you can't locate your self-essence, your self is dependent on conditions, and you can't stake out any permanent territory. This leads to the ultimate dukkha: the sense that *things aren't right* with *me.* Who or what are you, really? The answer can be frustratingly elusive.

A self-concept is always relative, existing at a certain place and time, with a past and a future, and defined by being separate from everything else. Therefore, meaning for the self-concept will always involve comparisons, and sometimes things will look good and sometimes they won't. This kind of meaning does not provide the inherent, enduring thing to rely on that you are look-ing for. Ironically, the one thing that *is* inherent and enduring is your ability to just be, this very moment. When you do this completely, without comparing your experience to anything, you are embracing the truth of no-self.

When you understand no-self and contemplate existential matters, the question of who you really are is answered by the fact that you are asking the question, and meaning is revealed in the way you draw your next breath. Without comparison to anything else, without any reference to a self-concept, life is unfolding through you. This experience is full and precious without any need for meaning conferred from outside. It becomes more than enough to meet each moment of your life as best you can, because it's no longer about *you.*

Although not a Zen practitioner, Viktor Frankl beautifully describes this approach to life in his book *Man's Search for Meaning.* He writes about his experience of being in a concentration camp during World War II, and how he and others avoided despair: "What was really needed was a fundamental change in our attitude toward life. We had to learn ourselves and, furthermore, we had to teach the despairing men that *it did not really matter what we expected from life, but rather what life expected from us.*"

The Least You Need to Know

- Everyone ends up with a concept of self that's based on the assumption they have an inherent, enduring self-nature.
- Your concept of self as being inherent and enduring is a useful tool for living your everyday life, but it doesn't reflect the way you really exist.
- In reality, you contain no unchanging, independent self-essence. Instead, you are a causal flow that arises in relationship to everything else.

- Understanding the true nature of self helps relieve dukkha, or the pervasive extra suffering you add to your experience when you think, *"This is not the way things should be."*

- It may seem negative that Buddhists talk so much about suffering, but it's not. Facing, examining, and working through your suffering leads to wisdom, compassion, and joy.

The Way Things Really Are

In the last chapter I discussed the way *you* really are, and in this chapter I expand on that theme and talk about how the world looks when you understand the true nature of the self. In a sense, this is the enlightened worldview. In another sense, this is what the world looks like when you have *dropped* all of your views.

Hopefully, a description of the enlightened worldview will be inspiring. According to Zen, the universe has wisdom and compassion built right into it, and life is precious just as it is. However, the things described in this chapter, like all Zen teachings, are meant to be questioned and tested. It might help to adopt a philosophy based on what is presented here, but until you have proven things for yourself you might just find yourself struggling with intellectual arguments in support of your philosophy. Unfortunately, this will probably be frustrating. Zen teachings are arrived at through direct human experience, not through intellectual reasoning. It's not that they aren't rational, just that engaging only the intellect is insufficient to understand them.

In This Chapter

- How to gain an enlightened view
- What it's like to see the world as empty
- Your true nature is buddha-nature
- Why people don't act like buddhas
- Enlightened view and everyday life

Waking Up to Reality

The premise of Zen is that all you really have to do in order to access wisdom and compassion is wake up to reality. It's only when you don't see reality that you have to work yourself into a particular state of mind, or maintain an elaborate philosophy, or force yourself to see everything in a positive light. It's only when you're operating under delusion that you have to be careful to act with generosity and kindness. There's a time and place for just doing your best to minimize harm and seek happiness for self and others, of course. You don't wait until you're enlightened to act in an enlightened way. Still, seeing the truth of how things are makes gratitude, selflessness, and compassion seem like common sense.

CONSIDER THIS

In China, Ch'an (Zen) masters sometimes referred to their school of Buddhism as a "tradition outside the scriptures." By this they meant that the essence of Ch'an was a personal experience that could be guided or even caused by studying the teachings, but that studying the teachings alone couldn't give you truth. This also meant that while teachings were helpful, they were ultimately unnecessary for enlightenment. One of the most famous Zen masters, Hui Neng, is supposed to have been an illiterate woodcutter who awakened to the truth without having studied Zen at all (he later did, which is why he is counted as a Zen ancestor).

This means that an enlightened worldview is not something you attain. Instead, it's something you uncover by dropping all of your ideas, particularly the idea that you and all things possess inherent, enduring self-nature. The fact that enlightenment is just seeing the truth means you don't have to understand Zen teachings to awaken. You *do* have to understand what those teachings are pointing to, but you don't have to carry around concepts to have an enlightened view. A teaching may help guide you toward a particular realization, but then you can let it go. When you lose touch with the enlightened view, you don't have to recall your past wisdom. You simply pay attention to the present, and try to wake up to reality again.

The Empty World

So what does the world look like with an enlightened view? I talked a little bit about this in the previous chapter, particularly how the difficulties of life don't look as daunting when you don't assume you have an inherent, enduring self-nature to protect. You can allow the stuff of your life to come and go; face illness, old age, and death as part of the continuing process of change; and find meaning in life that has nothing to do with *you*. Here I describe more about your experience of the wider world when you are awake to reality.

One Big Reality

One of the first things you realize once you get a good look at reality is that a lot of the things you previously thought were real were simply your concepts about the world. It's kind of like you've been wearing a pair of glasses all your life that gave everything a certain hue and were covered with little stars. Naturally, you thought the world *was* that color, and you probably built your worldview around the constant presence of stars. And now they're gone!

When you view reality without the filters of your preferences, expectations, and concepts, you notice that it's your mind that creates the differentiation between things. All along you've believed that your mind was doing you a big favor by pointing out distinctions that actually existed, but now you see how conceptual distinctions are just an overlay on reality. Things are complete just as they are, without reference to one another. By its very nature this observation is difficult to explain using words and concepts, but suffice it to say things are not actually separate from each other. You create the separation in your own mind.

Now, obviously the world is populated with things that don't overlap in space and time: people and objects, places and actions. Zen is not denying any of that, which would be silly. The point is that those objects don't require any conceptual differentiation to keep them apart. The world does not depend on your mind! This may sound ridiculously obvious, but at some level you think it does.

There's no reason for there to be a *you* separate from *me* unless we need to engage in a practical interaction where such a distinction is useful, such as when we conduct a business transaction (it matters that you are the one paying me). When we pass each other on the street and exchange a smile, there is no need for *you* versus *me*. We are simply part of one big reality that manifests in many ways.

Because we are all part of one big reality, you can also say that all beings and things are interdependent. Whatever you do affects my reality, and vice versa. My unique position in the universe is in part characterized by your presence, and because we share a big reality anything each of us does affects the other. This accounts for the fact that at a certain level, your suffering is my suffering, as discussed in the chapter on the precepts.

However, in Zen, interdependence is not a philosophical theory to account for how morality functions, it's a direct experience you can have. Although when you have it, it's likely to feel surprisingly familiar. After all, you are part of the big reality whether you feel like it or not.

Bright and Precious

Viewed without the filters of conceptualization, the one big reality you're part of appears bright, luminous, and precious. There's no accounting for why this is, it's just been proven again and again through the personal experiences of people from all kinds of spiritual traditions (as well as people without an identified spiritual practice). The filters with which you habitually view the world darken and limit it, while reality itself, even the ugly parts, is starkly beautiful in a strange, surprising way.

Sometimes you'll hear this Zen teaching phrased as "things are perfect just as they are," but to me perfection invites too much comparison, and anything you compare will fall short. I prefer the word "precious" because whether something is seen as precious is entirely up to the beholder, and you can hold something as precious that appears ugly, useless, or meaningless to someone else. Preciousness is about the viewer, not the inherent characteristics of that which is viewed.

I know a man who managed to drop his conceptual filters completely for the first time while looking at a can of tomatoes. Tears ran down his face as he suddenly appreciated how amazing and beautiful this tomato can was. Now, by regular standards there is nothing remarkable about a container of vegetables, but if you let go of any comparisons, any expectations whatsoever, the situation is very different. The entire universe in all its wonder and benevolence manifests right there in whatever is in front of you.

This may sound far-out, but imagine you live on another planet where life is very different from Earth, and a can of tomatoes falls from the sky. Without any earthly context or comparisons, it's likely to be an object of wonder to you. What are these markings on the outside of the can? Why are there ridges along its sides? How do you open it? Who thought to put mushy red things inside a metal shell?

Eventually this ability to see things in such a direct, fresh way occurs not just in momentary peak experiences, but every day. The shape of a glass, the color of leaves on a tree, the sound of your child's voice—any of these can suddenly appear to you without a filter, complete and luminous phenomena in and of themselves. From time to time they probably do, you just may not appreciate why.

 ZEN WISDOM

"The field of boundless emptiness is what exists from the very beginning. You must purify, cure, grind down, or brush away all the tendencies you have fabricated into apparent habits. Then you can reside in the clear circle of brightness. Utter emptiness has no image, upright independence does not rely on anything."

—Zen Master Hongzhi (1091-1157), from *Cultivating the Empty Field*, translated by Taigen Dan Leighton

Your True Nature

In the previous chapter I talked about the real nature of the self as being a causal flow that happens in mutual dependence with everything around you. Understanding this is liberating, but there is actually more to the question of self than this. According to Zen, what is revealed when you drop your self-concept is your *buddha-nature.* The empty world, including no-self, has *characteristics,* and buddha-nature (awakened nature) refers to how those characteristics manifest in living beings (including you).

Wise and Compassionate

Before explaining, I offer a disclaimer: writing about buddha-nature is extremely tricky because any discussion of it encourages you to conceive of it as a *thing* that (once again) has an inherent, enduring self-nature. It's very easy to begin to think of it as something you have or don't have, or some core of good character underneath everyone's personality. Because of how difficult it is to misunderstand buddha-nature and subsequently try to concretize it, it has been a subject of much debate over the history of Buddhism. Many schools, including Theravada Buddhism, deny the existence of buddha-nature. However, it is widely discussed in Zen because it points to an essential aspect of the experience of awakening.

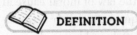 **DEFINITION**

> **Buddha-nature** is an elusive but important concept in Zen that refers to the innate potential of all beings to awaken to reality, the buddha-like characteristics that naturally manifest in awakened beings (such as wisdom and compassion), and/or the underlying completeness and preciousness of all existence.

Just what *is* buddha-nature? It can be difficult to find the answer, because almost all Zen discussions of this are about how to investigate or realize this teaching without conceptually placing the buddha-nature outside you, or within you—or, come to think of it, anywhere. For the most part Zen is a tradition that points you toward something by telling you all the things it is *not.*

However, the basic idea is that you have a nature that is not dependent in any way on the details of your existence. When you've dropped all of your conceptualizations, preferences, and expectations, and let go of trying to define the self in any way, you still exist. Just as the universe still exists when you drop all concepts, as discussed in the previous section, *you* still exist. *You* can't be located or grasped, but you are very, very much alive. You are aware, awake, and full of potential.

This "you" has access to the wisdom of the buddhas, or awakened beings, but this "you"—and here's the clincher—is not yours. It doesn't depend on any characteristics, remember? This nature is the same for everyone, and in a sense it's the same for everything. You can experience it, tap into it, but not contain it or own it. Because of this, buddha-nature can also be said to be unbounded in time or space; it's simply a just-is-ness that obviously has always been and can never not be. (Don't worry if all of this talk makes you crazy, you're not alone!)

What are the characteristics of buddha-nature? They are the characteristics of a buddha, or awakened being: clarity, selflessness, peacefulness, compassion, morality, dignity, stability, and freedom from grasping and delusion, just to name a few. The discovery of buddha-nature is quite amazing. Rather than being morally neutral, arbitrary, or mechanistic, your true nature is wise, calm, and generous. This amounts to a discovery that wisdom and compassion are part of the structure of the universe. When you drop your self-concept and flow with what is, your natural functioning conforms to this deeper truth.

Ignorance Gets in the Way

It makes perfect sense to ask the question, "If everyone's true nature is wise and compassionate, why does the opposite appear to be the case most of the time?" The Zen answer is that most of the time people are acting out of ignorance. That is, in one way or another they're not awake to reality. People get caught up in their self-concept, fail to appreciate the law of moral cause and effect, and at the most basic level aren't even aware of the full consequences of their actions. They erroneously think they can find ultimate happiness in the material world, that they can cause harm without feeling any ill effects themselves, or that they are inherently flawed and unworthy of respect and love. The list of potential human misunderstandings is infinite.

Given the overwhelming amount of ignorance in the world, isn't the prospect for humanity pretty bleak from a Zen point of view? The Zen answer to this is typically "yes and no." Yes, the likelihood that the world will be transformed into a land of buddhas anytime soon is very small, because people spend a great deal of time out of touch with reality, and it takes lots of work to break through all the layers of your misunderstanding. No, the prospect for humanity is *not* bleak, because there is a clear and effective remedy for suffering: work to dispel your ignorance.

It's not the job of Zen to make predictions about whether the sum of all suffering in the world is going to increase or decrease, but it sure seems like the tide will eventually have to turn when every day a new individual decides to work on their wisdom.

ZEN WISDOM

"The words the Buddha uttered involuntarily at [the moment of his enlightenment were]: 'Wonder of wonders! Intrinsically all living beings are Buddhas, endowed with wisdom and virtue, but because people's minds have become inverted through delusive thinking they fail to perceive this.'... That is to say, the nature of every being is inherently without a flaw, perfect, no different from that of Amida or any other Buddha .... We need therefore to return to our original perfection, to see through the false image of ourselves as incomplete and sinful, and to wake up to our inherent purity and wholeness."

—Hakuun Yasutani Roshi (1885-1973), from *The Three Pillars of Zen: Teaching, Practice, and Enlightenment* by Roshi Philip Kapleau

The Absolute and the Relative

When you first start to understand the true nature of reality, life can seem like it's occurring at two different levels that have very little to do with each other. At one level there is this wonderful sense of no separation, moment-to-moment clarity and freedom, and gratitude for everything just as it is. At another level there are your bills to be paid, mean people to deal with, and day-to-day life to be endured. Over time you can develop a deep conviction that your experience of a luminous, empty world is true, but it can take quite a while to see what on earth that experience has to do with your daily life.

In Zen these two levels of experience are called the absolute and the relative. They are discussed in Buddhism using many pairs of opposites: light and dark, differentiation and oneness, form and emptiness, worldly and ultimate, or ordinary being and buddha. These terms recognize the apparent tension between the transcendent spiritual view and the mundane experience of being in a human body. The use of these paired terms, however, also points out how the absolute and relative are not actually separate, because you can't have light without dark, for example, or differentiation without oneness to compare it to.

Absolute and relative are often said to be two sides of the same coin. You couldn't have a transcendent view of no separation if there were no beings and things to see as not separate from one another. There is no emptiness without a form (a thing) to be empty. It doesn't make any sense to talk about a buddha, an awakened being, if there aren't any sleepy beings who need to wake up. Still, for all this talk about absolute and relative being mutually dependent and intimately related, how you experience this in everyday life requires some further explanation.

Big Self and Small Self

Even once you have some understanding of reality, you can easily find yourself pulled back into acting in petty, selfish ways. When this happens, it can be useful to think of having a big self and a small self. Your big self is the one that knows better. It's the part of you that is informed by insight and can take a wide perspective. For example, your big self has an intuition that the angry person in front of you will respond best if you restrain your desire to react in kind. Your small self probably unleashes your angry reaction on them anyway, because from its point of view you are under threat.

This is somewhat analogous to the Freudian psychological view that the human psyche contains a superego (that moralizes and critiques) and an id (instinctual, self-centered drives). However, in the Buddhist view the only difference between your big self and small self is the extent of their viewpoints. They aren't opposing forces within you, they are just different ways you act depending on how self-centered you are at any given time.

It's good to try to act from your big self rather than your small self, but you don't do this by subjugating or suppressing your small self. Rejection is not constructive, whether you are rejecting something from outside or within (see the first precept). Instead, you develop an appropriate relationship between small self and big self. This is one in which the big self takes a role like that of an adult relating to a child. Big self patiently looks after the small self. Big self is in charge because, like an adult, it has much broader experience, knowledge, and perspective than small self. Big self doesn't try to get rid of small self or expect it to act differently. However, small self *can* learn to respect the wisdom of big self and recognize that following big self's advice will probably be the best course.

 CONSIDER THIS

A classic image put on the altar in Zen meditation halls is one of Manjushri, the bodhisattva of wisdom, portrayed as a monk sitting on top of a beast. The beast represents your unruly small self and has wild-looking eyes, huge claws, and fangs that stick out of its mouth. The beast looks very strong and full of energy (just like your small self), but Manjushri is sitting calmly in cross-legged meditation on top of it. The bodhisattva uses no reins to control the beast because he has developed a relationship with it; the beast is alive and well, but wisdom is the master.

Nirvana Is Not Elsewhere

From the beginning of Buddhism, students have wondered how to achieve a state of spiritual transcendence despite being stuck in a troubling world. The state of transcendence or liberation was called *nirvana*, while the troubling world was called *samsara*. Samsara refers to the cyclic nature of existence, particularly the constant change that means everyone will eventually face painful difficulties like illness, death, and loss.

Again, as discussed in Chapter 10, it is not the Buddhist view that all of life is suffering, just that suffering is unavoidable at some point, and maintaining your worldly happiness takes a lot of work. Nirvana, in comparison, is being able to step out of the rat race and dwell in peace. Alternatively, it's seen as liberation from the constant push and pull of life. The original Buddhist idea was to renounce samsara in order to enter nirvana.

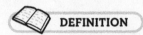 **DEFINITION**

> **Samsara** is an ancient pre-Buddhist term that refers to the endless cycle of birth and death, happiness and suffering, good fortune and bad fortune experienced by living beings. **Nirvana** is another ancient term meaning liberation from samsara, achieved by putting an end to the grasping and aversion that keep you bound to the cycle.

From the beginning of Zen, teachers have been telling their students that as long as they believed nirvana was somewhere else, separate from samsara, they would never find it. Samsara viewed with enlightened eyes *is* nirvana. As long as you reject samsara and look for some state, place, or experience apart from it, you will miss what you are looking for. Wanting nirvana to be a wonderful place for *you* to escape the rat race keeps you stuck in a limited view that will prevent you from clearly seeing reality. Ironically, when you give up your rejection of samsara and your self-interested desire for peace, you can view samsara as the bright, luminous, precious, empty world described earlier in this chapter.

On a day-to-day basis, not rejecting samsara or seeking nirvana means not rejecting your daily life. At first, liberating spiritual insights may seem separate from your job, family, and dirty house. You may imagine that Zen masters of the past lived different kinds of lives, ones that weren't as mundane and bothersome as yours. Surely something as lofty as nirvana can't be found in your laundry! And yet, as long as it seems to be somewhere else, you don't yet understand nirvana.

The Least You Need to Know

- To access an enlightened view, you don't have to use any concepts or teachings or remember any past experiences, you just have to wake up to reality.
- The world seen without the filters of your concepts, preferences, or expectations is one big reality that appears bright, amazing, and precious.

- You have a nature that is not dependent on any of the details of your existence. You share this "just is-ness" with everything, so it's not *your* nature, but it has the wisdom and compassion of a buddha.

- When you've experienced some insight, it can seem like there's a big gap between the world seen with enlightened eyes and the world of everyday life. This is okay, but if you further your understanding, you can see there's no gap—it's just that sometimes you're stuck in a smaller view.

The Zen Path

Now you have learned about Zen tools, and have been introduced to Zen teachings that can point you toward important aspects of life to investigate. In this part I will walk you through using Zen tools to make your living more Zen. A recurring theme throughout the book so far is the problem of self-centeredness, so it's probably not surprising that much of the work you do in Zen is aimed at curing this problem.

In this part I cover how Zen addresses the problem of self-centeredness by approaching it at different levels, all of which are important. You work on your attachment to things, because attachment refers to how you have inadvertently incorporated things and people into your self-concept, or made them a possession of self. You use Zen tools to gain a personal experience of no-self. You constantly challenge the limits of your own understanding, and if something that feels like enlightenment comes, you work extra hard not to make it just another possession of self.

Letting Go of Attachment

One way of applying Zen methods and teachings to your life is to examine and let go of your attachments, which results in a decrease in your self-centeredness. I've written quite a lot in this book so far about various aspects of self-centeredness and why it's a problem.

In Chapter 6 I discussed how selfish behavior always results in some kind of negative effect, and how a moral code can help you avoid causing harm and difficulty for yourself and others. In Chapter 10 I introduced the Buddhist teaching on how grasping—trying to force the world to conform to your preferences—leads to stress, dissatisfaction, and suffering. In Chapter 11 I explained how your self-concept causes you great worry about your well-being, but in reality it's this self-concept that is an illusion. If you recognize it as an illusion, you're much better off.

In this chapter I'll talk in greater depth about how you become attached to things (your body, objects, people, roles, ideas, etc.), what happens because of those attachments, and how to loosen your grip on your attachments.

In This Chapter

- What it means to be attached to something
- Problems with identifying things as *you* or *yours*
- The relief and intimacy of non-attachment
- How to let go of attachments of self
- A few popular attachments

The Nature of Attachment

To attach means to connect. In Zen, being attached to something in a way that's going to cause trouble means you have connected it to your self-concept. You have either identified yourself with it (identify can mean "think of as being united") or made it a possession of self. Subsequently, you feel motivated to protect and hold on to the things you are attached to in this way. When they're lost, are negatively impacted, or even just change, *you* are threatened. At least you think you are. In any case, you're probably going to respond by trying to make the world conform to your preferences, and cause yourself problems anywhere from stress to suffering.

CONSIDER THIS

Albert Einstein wrote, "The true value of a human being is determined primarily by the measure and the sense in which he has attained to liberation from the self."

From *The World As I See It*

Good Versus Problematic Attachment

Unfortunately, in English the word attachment can also mean "affectionate regard." If you interpret the word this way, and you hear Zen encouraging you to "give up your attachments," it can seem like Zen is asking you give up emotional warmth and caring. Nothing can be further from the truth. Caring is good, and can be experienced without any concern for self. As a matter of fact, if you try to avoid caring in order to avoid suffering, you're actually being quite selfish.

Try to think of affectionate regard as "good attachment" and commandeering things for the self as "problematic attachment." In most Zen discussions you will only hear the word attachment, but just translate it for yourself and add the modifier "problematic."

You started forming problematic attachments in childhood, as soon as you started forming the idea that you have an unchanging self-essence that persists through time, as discussed in Chapter 11. Because you believed in your inherent, enduring self-nature, you felt the need to take care of that self's existence—to protect it, watch out for its interests, maintain its boundaries, even expand its territory.

About certain things you came to think, "This is me," and about other things, "This is mine." Your self identified with, or saw itself in possession of, all kinds of things: physical manifestations like your body or your house; people such as your partner or children; relational things like your job; ideas or points of view; or attributes like strength or beauty. These were generally things you liked or that served you in some way, but not always.

For example, perhaps you ended up (probably with the help of others) identifying yourself as lazy. This isn't a flattering part of your self-image, but if you see it as part of who you are, there's a strange way in which at least part of you will be invested in the persistence of the idea, "I am lazy." At the very least it will become a familiar excuse or explanation.

Holding On

You know you are attached to something when you feel dukkha as it is going away or changing. Dukkha, again, is the sense that *things are not right*. You think, "This shouldn't be happening," or you just feel like yelling, "Nooooooo!" What follows feels like an imperative to resist the way things are going.

For example, you may be attached to being able to drive, but you are elderly and your ability to do so safely is coming into question. The disappointment and anxiety you probably feel as you contemplate giving up such an important aspect of your independence are not so much of a problem. What will be more painful is if you've identified as part of your self the freedom and self-reliance that driving provides. Then the loss of the ability to drive will not just be an inconvenience, it will be a threat to who you are, and you're likely to feel angry and bewildered on top of everything else. Subsequently, you may resist giving up your driver's license, discussing the possibility, or even thinking about it—until you get in an accident that forces the issue.

 POTENTIAL PITFALL

Beware of giving other people advice about their attachments. Letting go is a challenging process, and even thinking about letting go can be scary. Pointing out when someone is holding on to something, before they're ready to face that fact, is almost never helpful. Also, it's generally a whole lot easier to see other people's attachments than it is to see your own.

Another meaning of the word attachment is "a supplementary piece added to the main body of something," like the attachment on a vacuum cleaner or the attachment to an email. In a way, because the true nature of the self is empty and ungraspable, *everything* you identify as self or a possession of self is actually an attachment—an extra piece appended to the real thing. As discussed in Chapter 11, everything you think about as "I, me, and mine" will inevitably change, requiring you to constantly worry about yourself and the stuff of your life. The more you're holding on to, the more you have to worry about.

Non-attachment

What is non-attachment? Assuming that you maintain your good attachment (affection and regard) and take care of your life, what does it mean to be unattached to your body, attributes, relationships, and so on? Basically, you refrain from identifying things as part of your self, or from making them a possession of self. You can appreciate them and even try to keep them, but you feel grateful for their presence in your life rather than entitled to them.

When things change or go, you may feel sad or temporarily lost as you learn to live without them, but you don't feel angry, bitter, or resentful. It isn't at all that you don't care about things or about yourself, or that you're unaffected by loss or change. In fact, when you're not attached to things, you can be even more deeply touched and affected by them, because you are not so worried about yourself. A life lived with a minimum of the bad kind of attachment is full and rich, just not so self-centered.

Non-attachment allows you to experience real intimacy with people and experiences, while problematic attachment gets in the way of intimacy. Looking at people and things as part of your self-concept, or as a possession of self, results in a sense that you should be able to control them, at least to some extent. At the very least your attachments owe you consideration, because your well-being depends on them. You interpret any change in an object of your attachment in terms of how it affects you.

All of these ways of relating—the effort to control, a sense of being owed, and seeing everything in terms of self-interest—are obvious barriers to real intimacy. What person is going to want to respond to you with sincere openness and consideration when they sense you expect them to do so, or else? Intimacy is about a deep experience of contact with an *other*—a person or experience that exists and moves independently of your self, but is very close. When you let go of attaching things to your self, you give things the freedom to respond to you in a way that tells you that you aren't alone in the world.

 ZEN WISDOM

"Ordinary sentient beings identify the five skandhas as their 'self' and strongly cling to it. Not only do they cling to this as an 'I,' they also attach to the five skandhas as belonging to the 'I,' and because of this, all kinds of clinging, grasping, vexation, opposition, and finally anguish flourish. Buddhas refer to themselves as 'I' ... but the 'I' they refer to is only a conventional name, an expedient means to relate to sentient beings. Buddhas do not identify with the body and mind as self; they just manifest in the world to deliver sentient beings."

—Chan Master Sheng Yen (1930–2009), from *The Method of No-Method: The Chan Practice of Silent Illumination*

Letting Go

Moving from attached to unattached requires diligent practice and involves all of your Zen tools. However, keep in mind that the very intention to even *try* letting go of something is significant. Many of your attachments are so near and dear, it has never even occurred to you that they are *not* actually part of you, or that you could survive without them. Arriving at a realization that you'd be better off in a non-attached relationship to someone or something is precious, so pat yourself on the back if you've even gotten that far.

Getting to Know Your Attachments

You start the process of letting go like you start anything else in practice: by trying to see things clearly. After all, if you don't realize you're attached or experiencing dukkha, you can't do anything about it. The tools of zazen and mindfulness are useful for noticing your thoughts and feelings about the things in your life and identifying where you might be experiencing attachment. Paying attention to the precepts is also extremely helpful, because generally speaking, every time you are inclined to break a precept it's because of an attachment!

Once you've recognized an attachment, you engage it as karma work and try to unravel what amounts to a mental habit. You examine your attachment carefully, noticing anything you can about it. When and where do you feel attached to this thing? What thoughts, emotions, and fears are associated with the attachment? What do you imagine will happen if you lose the thing in question?

For example, let's say you're a woman who is very attached to her hair. You have long, beautiful hair that is a large part of your attractiveness. Everywhere you have gone, as far back as you can remember, you have brought your hair with you as part of the package you present to the world. It seems like a part of you, or at least a vital possession.

When illness or old age brings the loss of, or substantial change to, your beautiful hair, you find yourself struggling with the thought, "Who am I without my hair?" You stay with this thought, examining further, and realize the question is actually, "Who am I without my physical attractiveness?" Still further down you may notice a fear of rejection, or a sense that without your physical attractiveness you are inadequate or unlovable. At some point, you can watch the entire unfolding of this mental habit.

Loosening Your Grip

Each of the thoughts, fears, or assumptions you discover underlying an object of attachment are like threads connecting you to that object. Imagine yourself holding on to these threads in a tightly balled fist. Questioning or letting go of any one of your underlying thoughts, fears, and assumptions is like cutting or releasing one of these threads. Eventually you might release the last thread that keeps something attached to you!

Questioning your reasons for holding on to something requires humility and being honest with yourself, because you'd probably rather not know some of the things you think. However, it's good practice to test and question everything in your mind, because lots of erroneous or outdated ideas have ended up in there.

Earlier I mentioned the example of being attached to the idea, "I am lazy." With some Zen study you will probably start questioning this idea—not because you suddenly become diligent and energetic, but because you realize no adjective applies to a person's entire being. With mindfulness you notice that sometimes you are lazy and sometimes you are not. Voilà! You have just loosened your grip on an idea that you're attached to.

CONSIDER THIS

The kinds of things you can be attached to might surprise you! Think of what you might say if someone asked you to thoroughly describe yourself. You'd obviously describe your appearance, your job, and your relationships. You'd probably also mention some of the things that happened to you in the past and how they affected you, as well as your personality and worldview. Any of these things can be attachments—even narratives and character quirks—when you have a personal investment in maintaining them the way they are because they're part of your self-identity.

Letting go, in comparison, does not challenge the content of your mind so much as the *function* of your mind. For example, you come up against a thought like the one mentioned earlier, "I am inadequate," and at some point you wonder what life would be like without that thought. You've spent hours in zazen letting go of thoughts, so you've built up the ability to let go of this one (maybe not permanently, but for a moment at least).

It may take quite a while to convince yourself to try letting go, but when you do you experience the benefits of non-attachment: gratitude, greater intimacy, and relief of worry. This is rewarding, and begs the next question: why would you want to pick your attachment back up? You probably will, because you're in the habit of doing so and habits have momentum, but your relationship to the object of your attachment will be forever changed.

Favorite Attachments

It can be very tricky dealing with the small self and the way it has appropriated the things around it into your self-concept. It may be helpful to go into some more detail about typical human attachments and how to work with them. This is by no means an exhaustive list of possible attachments, but it includes things that almost every person ends up identifying as self or as a possession of self.

Your Body

Your body is probably the most obvious thing in the world to get attached to. It's been there from your beginning, and will be there until your end. You are never said to be somewhere else than where your body is. It's your vehicle in this world, allowing you to perceive, think, and act. Changes to your body affect your abilities, your thinking, and your experience of pleasure versus pain. *You-ness* and your body seem just about impossible to separate. The best you can usually do is think of your self as being carried around by your body, making your body the only absolutely essential possession of self.

Attachment to your body manifests as excessive pride, shame, or concern about your physical state. Notice I said *excessive*. It's not always obvious what is excessive and what is reasonable, which means you have to keep examining your thoughts and behavior. Also, what's excessive for one person may not be excessive for another. Generally speaking, it's reasonable to take care of your body, aim for health and fitness, enjoy physicality, and address or prevent illness. What's less useful is when concerns about your physical appearance, abilities, or health become so pervasive and strong that they start causing problems in your life, or in the lives of those around you.

For example, if you're so concerned about your weight that you spend many of your waking hours obsessing about calories and food, you're probably missing or neglecting other areas of your life. If you're thrown into a depression because an injury keeps you from your favorite athletic activity, you're probably attached to your physical abilities. If you worry about every ache and pain you feel and spend hours on the internet looking for the terrible disease you probably have, you may have incorporated self into your self-concept.

 CONSIDER THIS

This may seem a bit extreme to you, but Buddhist monks used to work on their attachment to the body by deliberately contemplating illness, old age, and death, sometimes even in graveyards. They would call to mind thoughts like this: I am of the nature to grow old, I cannot avoid it. I am of the nature to become ill, I cannot avoid it. I am of the nature to die, I cannot avoid it. The point was to get comfortable with these thoughts, so they no longer caused distress.

Appreciating the body without attachment is challenging because it's intimately tied to your literal survival (your relationship to life and death is something I'll discuss in a later chapter). However, the less attached you can be, the better. Remember that the true nature of the self is not inherent or enduring, but that doesn't mean you don't exist at all. Your emergent-phenomenon, causal-flow self manifests through your body, so it will always be central to your life.

However, if you can recognize that who you are is not limited to your body, it can help you accept your body as it is. If you can loosen your attachment to your body, when it inevitably changes you will not be quite so devastated. This is, of course, much more easily said than done.

Your Relationships

When you have a problematic attachment to a relationship or to someone in your life, things start to feel frustrating. Even more significantly, the person's actions start to trigger your sense of dukkha. "They shouldn't be doing this," you think, or, "Our relationship shouldn't be like this." It's quite natural that you would prefer the people in your life to be respectful, generous, and responsible: to express their appreciation for you occasionally, help out with household tasks, make wise choices, or refrain from abusive speech.

It's not a problem to acknowledge your desire for things to be different, or to recognize some behaviors as harmful, or at the very least unhelpful. There may be aspects of a relationship you simply cannot accept, and for good reasons. However, if you view the person or the relationship as part of your self, you have additional problems.

When you've attached someone to your self-concept, you're personally invested in them acting a certain way: the way that suits you. For example, you may *need* your children to be successful in school. Wanting them to be successful for their own sake is one thing, but needing them to be successful because *you are someone with successful children* is quite another.

If you view a relationship as a possession of self, you see and interact with the other person only as relative to *you*. Someone becomes *your* friend, *your* partner, *your* parent. The world appears to you as a system of relationships with you at the center, and it will be frustrating and bewildering when people act like they have other priorities than you.

There's a way you can actively engage with, argue with, guide, love, and depend on people without letting the small self get involved. You can look at other beings as full entities in and of themselves, each ultimately responsible for their own life. When you recognize someone is not part of the definition of who you are, you can release your desperate grasp on them and take a better look at who they really are, without the filter of your self-concern. You can give up the effort to control or hold on to the person or the relationship, and see what happens.

As the saying goes, if you love something, set it free; if it comes back to you, it is yours. If it doesn't, it never was. It is unimaginably rewarding to have a living being freely and willingly in relationship with you. Sometimes they are even kind, generous, responsible, or wonderful, all of their own accord.

ZEN WISDOM

"If you say to me, 'The law office where I work is closing. My last paycheck will be six weeks from now and then I will be on the street. Isn't that terrible?' I might be inclined to echo my teacher and answer, 'Maybe so.' Not because I am unsympathetic to your plight. It certainly sounds unfortunate. But who knows what will happen? Maybe two years from now you will look back and realize that losing your job was the best thing that ever happened to you .... What is more important and more essential: that you seem to have failed or that you are still you?"

—Zen Teacher Lewis Richmond, from *Work as a Spiritual Practice: A Practical Buddhist Approach to Inner Growth and Satisfaction on the Job*

What You Do

Many people are heavily identified with what they do—their job, or the other roles they play in the world: parent, spouse, activist, artist, spiritual practitioner, and so on. After all, the activities you undertake to fulfill your various roles and responsibilities are what consume most of your time and energy. If you have one or more roles or pastimes that deeply inspire you, you will usually use them as an outlet for your inspiration, passion, and creativity.

Thinking you *are* what you do is very tempting, but it causes great distress when you can't do what you want to. There are lots of reasons why this happens, and some of them are inevitable: you get sick and can't go to work, you get laid off, things change (say, kids grow up) and your effort isn't needed anymore, you lose your motivation or inspiration, or you get too old and frail to do what you used to do.

If you are attached to what you do and you can't do it for an extended period of time, it can be devastating. If you were raised with a strong work ethic, not being able to be productive can be humiliating and depressing. Having a role taken from you that you have identified with can feel like part of you is dying. Once again, the medicine for attachment is getting used to and embracing impermanence. You won't always be able to do what you do, but in the meantime you can do it wholeheartedly without attaching it to your self-concept.

Rather than thinking of what you do as a possession of self, you can view it as an opportunity to be generous with self. When you shift the emphasis to the giving, you will naturally be willing to change what it is you give (or do) when the situation changes and something else is needed. You will energetically give as long as you can, and when you can't give as much, or can't give what you'd like to, it's not the end of the world because it's not about *you*. Even if you can't give or do anything at all, you know your heart is in the right place and you would give if you could.

Thinking and Feeling

Particular thoughts and feelings are usually too transient for you to get overly attached to them, but it's typical to get attached to your *ability* to think and/or feel. This becomes, "I am my intelligence," or "I am my feelings." (You are usually attached more to one than the other.)

Attachment to thinking and feeling becomes obvious when you cannot loosen your grasp on the activity of thinking, or evaluation of your feelings, even when it would obviously be a very good idea to do so. You can be aware that you are overanalyzing something, running it through your mind over and over, building up anxiety and bringing on insomnia, but you just can't stop. You can realize that the way you are dwelling on a feeling like betrayal or jealousy is making you morose, unpleasant to be around even to yourself, maybe even physically sick, but you can't let go of the feelings.

In these cases you have identified so closely with your thinking mind or your emotions that letting go of your attachment to them can sound as impossible as letting go of your left arm.

CONSIDER THIS

Distraction is often an effective way to break yourself out of an unhelpful emotional or mental state. You may follow your breath, or take a walk, or read a book. These may seem like measures you take because you can't handle the emotions or thoughts that are plaguing you. However, when you're stuck in a fruitless, repetitive, troubling pattern of thinking or feeling, deliberately distracting yourself is letting go. By consciously doing something that will make you set aside your thoughts or feelings for a bit, you acknowledge they are not your entire reality.

When you are not attached to them, thoughts and emotions are just information about how your causal-flow self is reacting to its environment. You don't devalue or try to suppress thinking or feeling; you get valuable information this way, and besides, such suppression is difficult and damaging. Instead, you look at your thoughts and feelings from a larger perspective—because they are not *you*, they are just a part of your unfolding experience.

As an example, imagine waking up in the middle of the night full of anxiety about something. Let's say it's your job. Your usual way of dealing with this anxiety is either to suppress it (probably not very successfully) or analyze it. You might try to talk yourself out of the anxiety, or make a plan to fix the situation that's causing it. Chances are, these efforts just prolong the anxiety and you end up lying there, wide awake.

Stepping back from your thoughts and emotions is a different approach: you observe, "Hmmm. It's the middle of the night and I am feeling anxiety about work. Is there anything I can fix right now? No. Am I really thinking clearly enough right now to make a good plan? No. This is a self-perpetuating emotional state that isn't useful. I'll try to get myself out of it by following my breath." If you're really worried, this may not make the anxiety go away for good, but it's a whole lot less painful than identifying completely with the anxiety and being unable to see anything else.

Learning as You (Let) Go

Working with attachment presents many great opportunities for your Zen practice. You get a chance to notice and change thoughts and behaviors that cause dissatisfaction or suffering for yourself and others. You can learn to be more open-handed with the stuff of your life, so it doesn't hurt so much when it goes away or changes.

You also have the opportunity to gain insight into the truth of no-self. One moment you're holding on to something you believe is absolutely vital to your existence, and the next moment you let it go. Afterward, you still exist. Who are you now? If what you let go of wasn't self (because you're still here), what else are you holding on to that might not be self?

Letting go of attachments raises questions that are essential to Zen insight. Because of this, you can end up embracing difficulties that threaten your attachments with a certain kind of appreciation, because you know what a great learning opportunity is being presented. For a time you may not know what to do in your Zen practice, but when you experience a loud internal "Nooooo!" you think, "Oh, look—I'm attached to something. Now I've got some work to do."

The Least You Need to Know

- Good attachment is affectionate regard, and Zen does not tell you to let that go.
- Problematic attachment means you have identified something as part of your self-concept, or think of it as a possession of self.
- You can be attached to just about anything: your body, objects, people, ideas, opinions, abilities, roles, memories, personality quirks—you name it.
- Letting go involves examining your attachment until you can see the thoughts, fears, and assumptions that keep it bound to you—and then cutting or releasing those threads one by one.
- You can learn a great deal from working on your attachment to things like your body, your relationships, your job, and your thoughts and feelings.

Studying the Self

It may seem ironic that Zen involves so much contemplation of self, when the whole idea is to give up self-centeredness! Wouldn't your time be better spent doing nice things for people, or engaging in activities that make you forget about yourself? The Zen view is that these kinds of activities are great and you should continue to do them, but that they probably aren't going to give you lasting peace of mind. The best way to achieve that is to personally experience and verify the teaching of no-self that I introduced in Chapter 11.

In this chapter I walk you through how to use Zen tools to look more carefully at your fundamental misunderstanding: that you have an inherent, enduring self-nature. By paying careful attention to your thoughts, feelings, and behavior, you can notice certain signs that you're operating under the influence of the delusion of persistent self-essence. Once you notice these signs, you can challenge this delusion (incorrect belief) and prove it wrong. In zazen you can explore your pervasive sense of self. You can do this so intimately that at some point the illusion is recognized as exactly that—something that appears to be, but is not.

In This Chapter

- Why studying the self is central to Zen
- How to know when your "self delusion" is operating
- Ways to challenge your idea that you inherently exist
- Dispelling the illusion of enduring self-nature
- The joy of living with less of a sense of self

To Study Buddhism Is to Study the Self

Zen master Dogen, one of the major Soto Zen ancestors, went so far as to say that studying Buddhism *is* studying the self. Zen Master Rinzai, through whom the Rinzai school of Zen arose, also thought that seeing the true nature of the self was the essence of spiritual liberation. This is because your conviction that you have an inherent, enduring self-nature is the linchpin that holds together the mental machinery that generates your problems: stress, fear, dissatisfaction, grasping, aversion, selfishness, anger—you name it. Pull out the linchpin and the machine falls apart.

> **ZEN WISDOM**
>
> "To study the Buddha Way is to study the self. To study the self is to forget the self. To forget the self is to be verified by all things. To be verified by all things is to let the body and mind of the self and the body and mind of others drop off. There is a trace of realization that cannot be grasped. We endlessly express this ungraspable trace of realization."
>
> —Zen Master Dogen (1200-1253), from his essay "Genjokoan," as translated by Shokaku Okumura in *Realizing Genjokoan*

A personal experience of the true nature of self is considered so important in Zen, there's a word for it. *Kensho* means "seeing the true nature of self." It's often described as a dramatic event, where someone drops to their knees, weeps, or whoops for joy when they finally see the truth, and afterward they are forever changed. The idea of having this kind of sensational experience has attracted many people to Zen. This is particularly true in the West because the first Zen teachings published in Western languages focused on Rinzai Zen and the goal of kensho.

Striving for insight can be useful, but what people often misunderstand is that the important thing is seeing the truth for yourself, not having a dramatic experience. Sometimes insight comes suddenly, in a big rush, and the occasion feels remarkable. Sometimes understanding comes a little bit at a time, and there's no exciting episode to point to as your "enlightenment experience." What matters is that you correct your fundamental misunderstanding about the nature of self, because this will be transformative whether the insight comes suddenly or gradually.

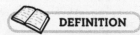

> **DEFINITION**
>
> **Kensho** means "seeing the true nature of self." The word generally refers to a dramatic awakening experience where someone suddenly realizes there is no inherent, enduring self-nature. However, the same thing can be understood more gradually, with lots of smaller insights. Another word for seeing the truth is *satori*, which means comprehension or understanding.

Signs of Belief in Self-Essence

Your belief that you have a persistent, independent self-essence has been with you since you were an infant, as discussed in Chapter 11. It's so familiar and pervasive it's hard to even realize you hold it. I call this your self delusion, because a delusion is a belief that doesn't reflect reality. Fortunately, self delusion results in telltale signs, and the Zen tools of zazen, mindfulness, and the precepts can help you notice them. This is far from an exhaustive list, but it can give you a sense of what to look for.

A Sense of Imperative

Whenever you start to feel like you *must* do something, you *must* have something, or something *must* happen, your self delusion is at work. This sense of imperative implies a big "or else," and at the bottom of all of your reasons for doing or wanting something is the idea "or else I will cease to exist." You may not believe that refraining from acting out your imperative will literally result in the end of your life, but you're worried that some vital aspect of your self will come to an end if you don't.

As discussed in Chapter 13, anything you're attached to—that is, anything you have incorporated into your self-concept, or made a possession of self—is something you need to protect from change or annihilation, because it is synonymous with your being.

It's entirely possible to respond to life and take care of yourself without the imperative to protect your inherent, enduring self-essence. For example, you may start to think that you need to find a new job. The work environment at your current job is stressful and negative, and you no longer find the work fulfilling. You can calmly start to consider whether you will be able to find another job, or whether another job will be better than the one you have. Maybe the time isn't right to make a change, but you decide that you'll do so when you can.

This coolheaded way of dealing with your problem is entirely different from the ordeal you might go through if you felt an overwhelming sense of imperative around it. If your self-concept is threatened by having to endure a job you don't like, or by not having a meaningful and rewarding occupation, your process of considering your options will be filled with stress, a refusal to consider certain possibilities, and impatience.

Anger and Resistance

Anger is a sign that you feel the need to protect something. Some anger is sincerely on behalf of others, but most of it has to do with feeling the need to protect yourself or something you're attached to. When your anger is self-centered, you don't just recognize something that needs to be dealt with, you think, "How *dare* they!" Whatever is provoking you is not just a problem, it's a personal affront.

Anger can manifest mildly or dramatically as resistance, irritability, aggravation, antagonism, outrage, and hatred. No matter what it looks like, underneath it is usually a story about how someone has done you wrong, or acted out of accord with your view of the way the world should be. Zen master Bodhidharma's commentary on the precept against anger says that in order to keep the precept, you need to give up "contriving reality for the self."

Having a basic sense of right and wrong, or being able to tell suffering from happiness, is not contriving reality for the self. Attributing inherent, enduring existence to yourself, your views, your attachments, other people, and other people's motivations *is* making up a story to fuel your sense of righteousness. You may need to take drastic action in the world to alleviate suffering, but you can do so without anger. You don't need to conceive of you versus them, right versus wrong, or good versus evil. These concepts are just part of the story your self cooks up to make sure your self-essence is safe, justified, and on the right side of the struggle.

 CONSIDER THIS

In one of the most ancient Buddhist texts, Shakyamuni Buddha gives this teaching on anger and hatred:

"'He abused me, attacked me, defeated me, robbed me!' For those carrying on like this, hatred does not end. 'She abused me, attacked me, defeated me, robbed me!' For those not carrying on like this, hatred ends. Hatred never ends through hatred. By non-hate alone does it end. This is an ancient truth."

From *The Dhammapada*, translated by Gil Fronsdal

Greed and Stinginess

When you are acting selfishly, with greed or stinginess, your self delusion is operating. In Chapter 10 I talked about how it's not a problem to have desires and preferences, but when you view them as imperatives that must be acted on with grasping or aversion, you create problems. The sense that your desire *must* be filled, or that you absolutely *have to* hold on to something, arises from your self delusion. The part of you concerned with your inherent, enduring existence is filled with anxiety because things are constantly changing, and it can't find anything to rely on. Therefore it tries to grab and hold on to things in order to feel substantial and real.

Again, you can be responsible and reasonable about the stuff in your life without indulging greed or stinginess. For example, you may get a new car and enjoy it very much. This may not cause suffering, but let's say you can't get a new car. Are you deeply disappointed or distressed? Do you need a new car to feel good about yourself? If so, the new car has become an object of greed.

An example of being responsible versus stingy is deciding not to give money to a relative who has repeatedly been careless with their finances (assuming you have the money to give). This decision involves stinginess if you find yourself needing to justify it, and thinking at length about how you don't have enough money. A sense of scarcity when things really aren't that bad is a sure sign of preoccupation with self.

Physical Tension

Finally, all of the signs of self delusion listed above generally occur along with physical tension. People describe this as tightness in places like the gut, jaws, chest, forehead, or hands. This is your body manifesting your self-concern, getting ready to fight, flee, grasp, or push away, as necessary to further your self's agenda. The involvement of your body is evidence of how deep your self delusion goes; it's not just an idea you ponder, it's a conviction you'd be willing to bet your life on! Depending on your personality, your physical sensations might be the first sign you notice that you're worried about your unchanging self-essence.

Challenging Delusion

The belief that you have a persistent self-essence is a delusion, or a belief that isn't true. The pervasive *sense* that you exist in such a way is an *illusion*, or an erroneous perception. The illusion is much more subtle, and will be discussed in the next section. Your false belief about the nature of self is based on your misperception of self, and this belief is slightly easier to deal with.

Your main self delusion gives rise to other erroneous beliefs that can be examined and challenged. These beliefs have to do with identifying something as part of your essential nature. Because of this identification, the thing must have the same qualities you believe your self-nature has: it must be enduring, and independent of not-self things. When you see that something doesn't fit these criteria, you can no longer identify it as self-essence.

In Zen practice you continue this process, examining all of your attachments, one after another. After years of concluding, "Oops, not self-essence," and "Oh, not that either," your mind opens to the possibility that there isn't anything that can be pointed to and called self-nature.

It Doesn't Go Away

If you can watch something arise and pass away, it isn't part of your inherent, enduring self-nature. You still might consider it part of your self in a larger sense, or a possession of self, but it can't be part of your essence. Your essence (you think) is always present and doesn't fundamentally change. (This belief is not a point of view you have arrived at through careful reasoning, remember. It is based on a misperception, so this doesn't have to make sense.)

If you had to put words to it, you would probably describe your unchanging, ever-present self-nature as awareness, consciousness, or the ability to perceive. Whatever it is, it can't *not* be present for even a moment, or it isn't the inherent, enduring self-nature you count on.

Maybe you think that it's okay with you if your self-essence goes away and comes back, but that's not really true as long as you hold on to self delusion. After all, you wouldn't agree if someone revived you from an unconscious state and then said, "You didn't exist a few minutes ago." You would just figure your self-essence had receded to the innermost sanctum of your being and then emerged again.

POTENTIAL PITFALL

If you are the least bit intellectual or philosophical, contemplating self-nature can really get you thinking. Unfortunately, thinking about it is a big obstacle to personally understanding and experiencing it. Any thinking you do will inevitably assume the point of view of an inherent, enduring self, even if you try to avoid it. Even the thought, "I do not exist," assumes an "I." No-self describes a human experience, not a philosophical statement about reality.

Thinking about this too much can tie your brain in knots, because there's no real self to grasp. You will most likely think, "Well, if that's not my self-essence, then how about ...." You keep on looking for something that isn't there. Still, when you watch things go away—physical attributes, health, opinions, awareness, consciousness, hope, will—you start to recognize them as not-self. Even if they come back, you know they aren't part of the essence of who you are. This leads to less attachment, but also brings you closer to understanding the true nature of self.

Independent of Not-Self Things

You also believe this enduring essence you count on is inherent, meaning that it exists within you because of your very nature. It is not something bestowed by someone else, and it can't be taken away. It does not arise because of surrounding conditions, and therefore won't disappear due to conditions. Everywhere you go, your entire life, you are inherently *you*.

For example, imagine that last Wednesday you had a terrible encounter with a co-worker. It really upset and confused you, and for the span of at least an hour you felt very out of sorts, like you weren't "yourself." By this, you mean that you weren't feeling, thinking, and acting in ways you are used to or in ways that you want to. You don't look back on last Wednesday and think, "Hmmm. There was an hour there that I wasn't me." You don't go that far; your inherent, enduring self-nature was still there last Wednesday, existing as a little speck-sized bit of essence marking the hour as part of your life. No matter what happens, it's there, and it's identifiable as you. You think.

After becoming very mindful of your mental and emotional states over time, however, you begin to realize how every part of you is affected by conditions, sooner or later. You recognize that nothing in you stays the same in all conditions. Caffeine makes you alert, and humidity makes you dull. Being surrounded by positive people makes you feel positive, and being surrounded by misery depresses you. At certain times in your life you have felt a great clarity of purpose, but at other times you have felt listless. The positive attitude you cultivated when you were healthy falls apart when you become ill. None of these states were inherent to you, so clearly none of them are your self-essence.

Dispelling Illusion

No matter how many things you recognize are *not* part of your self-essence, you can still persist in believing you have one. After all, it just *feels* like you do. Even if you manage to let the mind settle in zazen, and refrain from identifying any of your thoughts and feelings as self, there's *you* sitting zazen!

Many Zen teachings and methods are aimed at getting you to drop this self illusion. One of my favorites is to imagine that you are long dead, but somehow, strangely, still aware. If you like, you can imagine your bleached-out skull sitting in a deserted, sunny meadow (go ahead and make it sunny, this isn't supposed to be depressing).

You have been dead for 100 years, so all the people who would personally remember you are also gone. Anything you worked for or possessed in life has disappeared or belongs to someone else. Many of the things you cared deeply about look very different, because things have changed so much. Your inventions or passions or causes may be obsolete. Given all of this, who are you? You can still imagine inherently existing, but in what way? Then you think of being dead 300 years, or 500. This is a good exercise for focusing in on your belief in self-essence.

If you keep studying your self illusion, in the course of meditation you can notice something radical: when you are thinking, you have a conviction of self-essence. When you aren't thinking, or at least not doing so consciously, the sense of self isn't there. Of course, it's extremely difficult to make this observation, because the second you make it you are thinking. After a while, however, you are able to notice the moment of self-concept arising. Noticing it arise, you know there was a period of time when it wasn't there.

This absolutely convincing sense of inherent, enduring existence—on which you have based everything—comes and goes! You've already stripped away all the things the self identifies with, and now you've called into question the only piece of evidence you have left: you *feel* like you inherently exist. If you don't have that feeling for a period of time, either your feeling-sense is fallible, or ... maybe ... you don't exist the way you think you do.

ZEN WISDOM

"If you realize that your activities are not based on thought alone, you let go of thought. Strangely enough, whether you think about it or not, the heavy meal in your stomach gets digested completely. When sleeping, we continue breathing the necessary number of breaths per minute and the 'I' continues to live. What on earth is this 'I'? I can't help but feel that this 'I' is the self that is connected with the universe."

—Kosho Uchiyama Roshi (1912–1998), from *The Zen Teaching of Homeless Kodo*

Dispelling the illusion of having unchanging self-essence is a subtle and involved practice that I can't cover here in a way that even begins to be comprehensive. The process has been described by Zen masters throughout the ages in countless different ways, as they tried to find the words that would get through to their students. Hopefully this will have at least piqued your interest and given you a sense of what Zen practitioners are doing as they sit so intently for hours, weeks, and years.

The Experience of Less-Self

As I mentioned earlier, you can't recognize when you are living without the filter of your self-concept. The moment you think, "Ah, here I am, experiencing no-self," the self-concept is obviously back. Still, you can learn to live with less-self, and this is definitely something you can appreciate and work on.

Ironically, Zen practice can make experiencing less-self more difficult, at first. All of the Zen tools, including zazen, mindfulness, and the precepts, involve you looking more carefully at your life and sense of self. Rather than feeling like you have less-self, you end up feeling like self is front and center all the time!

I remember taking walks as I was learning how to be mindful. I paid attention to my physical movements and sensations, and tried to let go of extra thinking. Naturally, I evaluated the success of my effort, and I noticed how unruly my mind was and how rarely I was fully mindful. Instead of walking with less-self, it seemed like I was walking with a big extra dose of self-consciousness. Unfortunately, there's no way around this phase of the practice. As the Dogen quote at the beginning of this chapter suggests, you have to study the self *in order to* forget the self.

Once you can manage to go about your life with less-self, this annoying self-consciousness is replaced by a more direct awareness of life. Your self-concept is entirely unnecessary to your full and effective functioning at this moment, so you learn to do without it. You are just washing the dishes, just eating, just walking. It's a little like the way you used to do things, except for the *absence* of something. That something is your self-concern, which used to manifest in the background of your experience as low-level anxiety, vague dissatisfaction, anticipation, or regret, or as more intense things like anguish or a sense of meaninglessness.

The signs of self delusion—a sense of imperative, anger, resistance, greed, stinginess, physical tension—decrease as you live with less and less of a sense of self-essence. They still arise, but you can let go of them much more easily. You know all of these phenomena depend on your self-concept, which is a creation of your mind. You know how to return to life as it is, just breathing into the next moment, and things like anger or greed start to dissipate. Even if they don't disappear completely, as their form begins to shift and break up like a cloud in the sky, you can't regard them as entirely real.

Encountering people and things with less-self is especially rewarding, because you can appreciate and see them for what they are. You don't assess how they fit into your agenda, and subsequently either manipulate them to serve your interests or dismiss them as irrelevant. In fact, you stop dismissing anything. There still may be many things you end up not noticing, because less-self doesn't necessarily give you unusual powers of attention, but you don't look elsewhere out of boredom because the thing in front of you is *just another* grocery line, *just another* customer, or *just another* evening at home with your partner. Dismissing something as being unworthy of your care, attention, and appreciation involves looking at it in terms of your small self's agenda.

Living without an agenda means everything is fascinating. Even the annoying and painful stuff. It's all part of the unfolding drama of your particular human life, which is, as far as you can know, your one and only human life. Awareness of this results in a curiosity that sustains you throughout all of the work you have to do to live.

The Least You Need to Know

- Personally understanding the true nature of self is considered the most liberating aspect of Zen.

- You know you're clinging to the idea that you have an inherent, enduring self-nature when you experience things like a sense of imperative, anger, resistance, greed, stinginess, or physical tension.

- You can challenge your belief that something is self by examining it carefully, and disproving your assumptions that it doesn't go away and that it's independent of not-self things. You won't find anything that fits these criteria.

- It's possible to see through the illusion that you inherently exist, by diligently observing your mind in meditation. However, this is the ultimate Zen goal, so don't expect it to happen overnight.

- Living with less-self is a wonderful thing.

Taking It Deeper

There's a danger that you will misinterpret certain Zen teachings and practices to mean, "This is it, just go about your everyday life, and do your best to be aware and appreciate it." In a certain sense this is exactly what Zen is recommending, and it's great if you've moved from suffering to a sense of relative ease that makes you think, "Good enough!" However, to rest there results in complacency and imposes a limit on the depth of your transformative understanding.

Life is infinite, so if you want to master the art of living it, there's always more to learn and do. While it's true that it's impossible to keep the precepts perfectly, you need to keep examining your life so you are aware of all of your harmful habits. Continuing to work diligently on those habits throughout your life maintains your humility, and who knows, maybe you'll even manage to change them!

While it's true that an experience of no-self is elusive, the key to lasting liberation is a direct, personal verification of emptiness. Many people have achieved it in the past, so why not you? While it's true that Nirvana is not elsewhere, simply accepting that does not mean you've mastered the art of living. This chapter covers some important ways to deepen and challenge your Zen.

In This Chapter

- Preparing to turn up the heat on your practice
- The importance of facing your fears
- Five characteristic human fears and their resolutions
- Building up comfort with not having the answers
- Challenging yourself with koans

A Strong Foundation

When you turn up the heat on your Zen practice, stuff can happen. You can gain insights that, while ultimately liberating, can be temporarily disorienting. You may change in ways that mean your current network of relationships, work, or lifestyle no longer suit you. You can become discouraged and frustrated because you want some particular outcome (such as insight) but it isn't happening. You may end up experiencing deep self-doubt and wonder whether you are really capable of deep wisdom or compassion.

POTENTIAL PITFALL

If you think too much or too often about whether Zen is giving you the results you want, or whether you are enjoying it, you are likely to stop practicing before you have built up a strong habit of practice you can rely on. Sooner or later, Zen will seem boring, or frustrating, or pointless. If you keep practicing through those experiences, at some point Zen will seem fascinating, effective, and transformative again. *And* you will have built up a strong habit of practice in the meantime, which can sustain you through difficult times.

In order to sustain yourself through these kinds of upsets and challenges, it's good to have built a strong foundation for your life. This amounts to healthy routines and habits, and contact with positive, supportive people. Habits are important because they can carry you through a confusing time. As discussed in Chapter 7, they have an energy and momentum all their own. This fact is annoying when you're dealing with a harmful habit you would like to change, but it works to your advantage when you go through rough periods in your life.

If you've built up the habits, you will continue to sit zazen, get enough sleep, eat well, and keep the precepts, even when all hell is breaking loose. Such habits keep you functioning fairly well despite conditions, and give you a sense of grounding when nothing else makes sense. Positive people are those who will encourage your good habits. When you're going through some difficult changes, such people respond to you with patience and have faith that you'll find your way. Zen teachers and other Zen practitioners try to provide this kind of positive support for one another.

A strong foundation also means faith in Zen practice itself—faith that it gives good results. This is not a faith you can will yourself to have; it has to be built up slowly, step by step. Each time you see an improvement in your life, or attain a better understanding of something, and can attribute it to Zen, your trust in the practice will grow. The next step in your practice is, by definition, something you have not done before, and you can't be sure it will take you where you want to go. Knowing that all of your previous steps have been fruitful, or at least not dangerous, gives you the faith to take the next one.

Part of this faith in Zen is trusting that it will bring good results … eventually. Over time, especially if you're able to get to know some people who have been practicing Zen longer than you have, you start to see Zen as a path from suffering to mastery of the art of living. As long as you're certain you're on the path, you don't have to worry so much about *whether* you will arrive at your destination. You just keep going. This allows you to be patient and gentle with yourself. Balance this curiosity and determination, and you have a great combination for deepening your Zen.

Generating Determination

Some of the more challenging aspects of Zen practice require hard work and great determination. You may need to sit meditation for many hours, months, or years before you have a sense that you're making any "progress." You may need to face things about yourself that you'd rather weren't true. You may need to keep yourself going through periods when practice seems pointless or frustrating.

Although Zen teachers will generally discourage you from trying to attain something special, or from collecting insights like badges, there is a time and place for the "positive" use of greed. If your desire gets you on the meditation cushion, it has had at least one good effect. The great thing about Zen-related desires is that they lead you toward practices that undermine your delusions and grasping, so eventually your un-Zenlike greed defeats itself.

If you aren't longing for spiritual attainments, how do you generate the energy and determination you need for intensive practice? It's best to be creative with yourself. Basically, take advantage of whatever motivates you.

One Zen practice is to call to mind your own inevitable mortality as vividly as you can. You might contemplate how you would feel if you died suddenly in an hour or two. If you had a few moments before death to take stock of your life, how would you feel? Would you have any regrets? Would you be afraid? Would there be things you felt were left undone? Any sticking points that would prevent you from leaving this world with a sense of peace and gratitude are things that still need resolution, and you only have a limited time to do it.

 CONSIDER THIS

There is a verse recited in Zen monasteries at the end of the day, which is meant to inspire the students to be diligent in their practice:

"Let me respectfully remind you, life and death are of supreme importance. Time swiftly passes by and opportunity is lost. Each of us should strive to awaken. Awaken. Take heed. Do not squander your life."

—From the *Zen Mountain Monastery Liturgy Manual*, edited by John Daido Loori

Some people find metta practice very motivating. This involves the recitation of a verse that sends "metta," or loving kindness, to other people or to yourself. Silently or out loud, you say, "May [you, or I, or a specific person or group of people] be free from fear and anxiety. May you be at ease. May you be happy." As you recite, you seek to awaken sincere feelings behind the words.

It's best to start this with someone it is easy to feel kindness toward, but then it can be extended to others. This practice can generate determination because it encourages a motive based on a desire to relieve whatever suffering you can, rather than on a desire for something the self is going to attain. It can also call your attention to how much suffering there is in the world, and therefore how important spiritual practice is.

One of my favorite sources of motivation is the thought of how liberating the truth is, and how much I still don't see or understand. Wanting to know the truth can be compelling even if it is tough to face.

In some ways, the story told in the movie *The Matrix* is analogous to waking up to reality through Zen. In it, the main character chooses to take a pill that will wake him up from the dream he has been experiencing up until then. When he wakes up he realizes he has been held in a comatose state all of his life, and fed a false image of the world. The reality he wakes up to is very grim, while the false image being fed to all the comatose people is relatively pleasant. Still, as you watch the movie, can you imagine yourself choosing to stay asleep, locked comatose in a cocoon and believing in a fantasy?

No matter how painful the truth is, it's *the truth*. The difference between reality and delusion in the movie *The Matrix* is very dramatic, but actually it's not all that far from the difference between being completely caught in the delusion of self and the clarity of liberation.

Facing Fears

You know the saying, "Ignorance is bliss"? Hopefully, the reading you've done in this book so far has convinced you that this is not the case, but the saying does point toward a certain truth. Sometimes ignoring a truth about your life feels preferable to facing it. In such a situation, at least temporarily, acknowledging reality is going to be more painful and troublesome than continuing to avoid it. However, the pain and trouble can only be avoided temporarily. Eventually the truth will come out, and the longer you have suppressed or avoided it, the more traumatic and difficult the coming out will be.

It's comparable to having a medical problem that requires surgery. The surgery is daunting and will probably be painful, but chances are the problem will only get worse the longer you put it off.

The good thing is, you don't have to look at facing your fears and problems in an entirely negative way (that is, you'd better face them or they'll come back to bite you). Fear and the urge to look away are signs that there is something very valuable to be learned. In fact, the bigger the fear, the bigger the lesson. Understanding and resolving fears and problems liberates you and lets you further your mastery of the art of living. Once you have done so, you are a valuable resource for other people with problems and fears similar to yours.

Skeletons in Your Closet

It's not unusual to start having some insights about yourself once you start meditating and doing Zen practice. It's like you're able to get some perspective and can observe your thoughts and actions from the outside. For example, you might suddenly recognize how you repeat a certain behavior that's not only useless, it's also counterproductive or harmful. Let's say that when you start to worry about the state of your intimate partnership, you tend to corner your partner, make them sit down and hear you out as you shed tears over your anguish and anxiety, and then ask them to comfort you.

As you observe this scenario with some Zen perspective, you realize that in essence you're confronting your partner with a complaint about them, and then you're asking them to set aside their own feelings of hurt and defensiveness to make *you* feel better. It becomes clear to you why this approach has not brought you the results you want, but instead has caused more conflict and hard feelings. Now that you've seen what's going on, you do some karma work on this habit and explore some other options.

Once you've experienced a few insights about yourself like this, it's natural to begin to wonder what other skeletons might be in your closet. What else are you going to find out about yourself? How deluded, selfish, and annoying might you really be? What changes might you feel compelled to make in your life, based on what you find out? It takes a great deal of courage to not only face the truth when you're confronted by it, but to actually go rummaging around your mental and emotional closet, looking for delusions! Especially when you realize your closet is full of them (as all of our closets are).

You can find the courage and motivation to face truths about yourself by working on the aspects of practice described earlier: building trust in Zen practice, and generating determination. After you've undergone the mental and emotional surgery required to identify and resolve a problem, you will always think of the surgery as having been worthwhile, however uncomfortable it was at the time of the operation. This builds your faith in the process and in your own ability to survive it, so it becomes easier to face the next challenge.

Add to that the reward of embracing the truth and being able to act in ways that are wiser and more compassionate, and there's part of you that's going to be ready to roll up its sleeves and dive right in when you discover another of your fears, problems, or delusions. Finding and dealing with the skeletons in your closet can save your relationships, your health, and your life.

ZEN WISDOM

"A Zen student should not fear delusions. He should gaze at them squarely and determine their true nature. A Japanese poem says, 'The real form of the ghost was nothing but a group of withered reeds in the late autumn field.'"

—Zen Teacher Nyogen Senzaki (1876-1958), in *Buddhism and Zen*

Fear of Emptiness

One Zen way of looking at reality is that underneath all human problems—self-centeredness, grasping, aversion, greed, anger, and delusion—is fear. And at the base of all fears is the *fear of not existing.* This fundamental fear manifests most obviously as a fear of death, but actually the fear of not existing is more subtle and pervasive than that. Because of impermanence and your inability to find something unchanging and inherent that you can grasp and point to as *you,* you have an intuition about emptiness. Even if you aren't consciously exploring emptiness, you have a nagging sense that you might not really exist the way you think you do.

Actually, what you fear is not emptiness, but what you *think* emptiness is. Until you experience emptiness for yourself, you're bound to think it's synonymous with meaninglessness or annihilation. When you hear the Zen teaching that you (and all things) are empty of inherent, enduring self-nature, it can sound like the teaching is that you don't exist. Naturally, you get very concerned about the reality and continuation of your existence.

There are five characteristic fears about emptiness, and typical reactions to each. The fears are about insubstantiality, annihilation, isolation, vulnerability, and oblivion. You can primarily be afraid of being insubstantial—of being liable to disappear in a puff of smoke, with nothing to hold on to. A typical reaction to this is to try to acquire as many things as possible to make yourself feel less vulnerable to disappearance, including material possessions, relationships, power, and status.

You can be afraid of annihilation, or being brought to a precipitous end by some agent or event, perhaps unidentified. To prevent this you strive to protect yourself by any means necessary, particularly by aggression and by carefully honing your intellect and skills so you can perceive and fend off threats. Your central fear may be of isolation, or the inability to make real, intimate contact with anything or anyone. Consequently you may seek compulsively for the experience of being connected and not alone by trying to consume all the intimacy you can get out of your relationships and experiences—often chasing away intimacy in your efforts.

Alternatively you may fear vulnerability, the inability to protect your territory in this world of impermanence. The reaction to this fear can be pervasive anxiety and paranoia. Finally, your primary fear might be of oblivion, of being nothing and experiencing nothing in a big universe of nothingness. If this is your fear, you tend to sink into depression and torpor.

Everyone has a little bit of all of these emptiness-related fears, although there will usually be one or two that are the strongest for any individual. The wonderful thing is that a true understanding of emptiness (see Chapter 12) cures these fears. However, in order to gain that understanding of emptiness, you are first going to have to face your fears about what it might be or mean. The closer you get to letting go and experiencing no-self, the more inflamed your fears are likely to get. Just knowing this is the case can help you find the courage to go on.

And when you face your fears of emptiness in order to see what emptiness really is, your fears are transformed. You realize that while there is nothing substantial that can be called *you*, you're also not separate from anything, so in a way the whole universe is you, and yours. You recognize that there is no inherent, enduring self-nature to protect, but instead there is a buddha-nature that is unbounded in space and time—so there is no need to fear annihilation.

Experiencing no-self gives you all the intimacy you could want, because there is no *you* separate from that with which you want to connect. You can only isolate yourself within your own mind. Your existence is just flow, a dance with the universe, so you don't need to worry about protecting your territory. This frees up boundless energy. When you see that emptiness is not *nothingness*, but the vast, luminous potential within which everything is able to arise, you can live wholeheartedly in the spaciousness.

> **CONSIDER THIS**
>
> The five characteristic fears about emptiness—fear of insubstantiality, annihilation, isolation, vulnerability, and oblivion—are part of a Vajrayana Buddhist teaching called the five wisdom energies, or the five buddha families. It's a useful teaching for exploring personality and karma. You can read more about the wisdom energies in *Spectrum of Ecstasy* by Ngakpa Chögyam and Khandro Déchen, or in *The Five Wisdom Energies* by Irini Rockwell.

Willingness to Not Know

Another way to deepen your Zen practice is to work on your willingness to be patient and non-reactive when you don't know the answer, the solution, the next step, or how to make sense of things. Facing your fears and deepening your understanding are not activities that are going to give you instant results. That means that a lot of the time you're going to be in an in-between state of not-knowing. As a matter of fact, much of the suffering you encounter, especially in others or out "in the world," requires you to take a don't-know attitude *permanently*.

If you're anything like most people, you're uncomfortable with not knowing. Anything but that! You feel on edge, fearful of what might be coming, full of anxious anticipation, or desperate to do something to fix the situation right now. Not knowing can make you feel inadequate and defensive. It can challenge your sense of self. To end the discomfort, you may exhaust yourself with a frantic search for answers. You may also seize on any answer you can find, although that answer is often wrong or overly simplistic.

As long as you avoid the place of not-knowing, you will never obtain the answers that require time and effort to find. The information you need may not yet be available, or perhaps your ability to see clearly needs more development. Some insights seem to just take time to ripen, so that one day you know something that you've been seeking to understand for ages.

In addition, sometimes there is no one answer or solution to a complex problem, such as world hunger. Your inability to tolerate not-knowing may compel you to latch on to an explanation for why things are the way they are (and therefore, an explanation of how things need to change). Unfortunately, this answer may not be as much about hunger as it is about your need to avoid not-knowing. Because you are attached to your particular answer, it may blind you to other answers or to the complexity of the situation. It can also make you defensive (again, on your own behalf).

Fortunately, not-knowing isn't so bad once you get used to it. If you explore it, you realize that it's not necessarily about some fault of yours preventing you from giving the correct response. Instead, it can be a generous act to rest in the place where you don't have the answers, whether they have to do with your karma, spiritual teachings, or the state of the world. This allows wise responses to arise in time, and avoids oversimplifying your view of the world in order to avoid discomfort.

Challenging Yourself

When you're suffering, you have natural motivation and don't have to think about what to concentrate on in your practice. You just turn your attention toward the source of your suffering and learn a great deal in the process of trying to relieve it.

When you feel more or less okay, it's easy to get complacent. You may acknowledge, intellectually, that you aren't a buddha yet, and you still go about most of your day unaware, and most of your thinking is still self-centered. But what can you do about it? Where do you begin your work when you're not sure what you should even work on? How do you seek out remaining delusions when you're still deluded by them? How can you deepen your understanding when you don't know what deeper would look like?

Working with Koans

This is where koans can help. Koans are questions or problems that bring you up against the edge of your understanding, or your ability to respond with skillfulness. Formal koans are teaching stories that have been collected by some lineages of Zen and offered to students over the generations to challenge their understanding.

A classic example is the story of an exchange between Zen master Joshu and a questioning monk. The monk asks Joshu whether a dog has buddha-nature. The Zen teaching is that all things have, or partake of, or even *are* buddha-nature, so the technically correct answer to this question would be yes. However, Joshu says, "Mu." This means "no," "not," "nothing," or "non-being." The koan is the question why did Joshu say "Mu"?

You may think of all kinds of possible reasons (he wanted the monk to stop being so intellectual, or he wanted the monk to show his understanding by arguing the point), but none of these are the "answer" to this koan. In fact, the koan often gets boiled down to just one word, "Mu." You are just supposed to sit with "Mu." What on *earth* does that mean?

CONSIDER THIS

Formal Zen koans are notorious for not making sense. For example, in one story a monk asks Zen master Joshu why the ancestral Zen master Bodhidharma went all the way from India to China. Joshu's answer is, "The oak tree in the garden." This may seem nonsensical, but many koan exchanges are aimed at pulling the student out of intellectual contemplation and pointing them to the reality around them. In a way, you can think of this as saying, "Hey you! What does your question address, right here, right now?"

A koan like "Mu" brings you up against the edge of your understanding and ability to respond. You may think it's the dumbest activity in the world, or you may long from the depths of your being to unlock its mystical truth. In either case, if you're engaging a formal koan, it's because you want to deepen your understanding and some Zen teacher you respect told you to work on it. So you keep trying. You don't even know what you're trying to do.

All of your longing, pride, effort, anger, desire to please, determination to succeed, and conviction that you are separate from enlightenment get involved in this crazy process. What from the outside looks like an intellectual puzzle ends up being a real, personal struggle. Then, at some point, usually after years, you "break through" and "Mu" isn't a problem for you anymore. This breaking through can't be explained, it can only be experienced.

Engaging with koans keeps you actively working on mastering the art of living. One way or another, they bring you up against your remaining delusions and limitations: your conviction that you have an inherent, enduring self-nature, your attachments, or your fundamental fear of emptiness.

If you've gotten pretty comfortable with emptiness, a koan can challenge you to demonstrate how you can enact your understanding in the world. If you've been happily dancing with everyday life for a while, a koan can point out where you still think it's *you* that's dancing, in some subtle way. If you feel a deep sense of peace and joy about life, a koan can show you the limits of what you currently see and know. There's no limit to mastery of something, and koans help you make Zen a lifelong study.

Everyday Life Koans

Koans arise in your everyday life and provide the same opportunity as formal koans to find the edge of your understanding and apply pressure on yourself. In fact, some schools of Zen do not employ formal koans at all, but there is still an expectation that you will keep up diligent practice your whole life.

How do you identify a koan in your life? A koan is where you come up against an obstacle and cannot get past it. It may be a real-life problem, like a difficult relationship, a tendency to depression or anxiety, or a particularly harmful, entrenched habit. It may be something you cannot accept or understand. What differentiates a koan from your garden-variety problem, or a question you are merely curious about, is how much the koan matters to you. The more you care about resolving it, the more potent and important the koan. The best koans of all feel like a matter of life and death.

Sooner or later you *will* be faced with a matter of life and death that will present you with an obstacle you can engage as a koan. You may face the loss of someone who should not have died so young, or a crippling illness, or a situation full of injustice. As you encounter this koan, you feel the tension that results from not being able to resolve it, understand it, accept it, or work with it.

This is when you use the tool of insight described in Chapter 8, and invite the koan into your zazen. You don't analyze it, you explore it. You examine it in detail as a scientist or artist would study their subject. You ask questions, waiting for the answers to arise of themselves, "What is it I can't accept? What do I think acceptance would mean? Is it true that acceptance would look like that? What am I afraid of?"

If you follow the process of insight through to the end, eventually the koan is not a problem anymore. This isn't to say that a challenge you're facing in life—such as illness or loss—disappears, just that it is no longer a problem in the same way it used to be. Despite the challenge, you know you are fundamentally okay, and you feel a measure of spiritual peace despite the pain.

ZEN WISDOM

"Situations that come up in our daily life can be koans. In fact, that's precisely how many koans in the classic koan collections came into being. But often, when something comes up in daily life, we tend to take it only at face value, not investigating further. Koan study is essentially a skillful means to really make us question what this life is, until we fully resolve the question."

—Zen Teacher Bernie Glassman in *On Zen Practice: Body, Breath, and Mind*

Fortunately, you don't have to wait until life presents you with great difficulty to find a koan. Zen seeks to be proactive, so you can resolve some of your problems and deepen your understanding *before* you're faced with a traumatic situation. After all, your attachments, delusions, and fears are already there, just waiting to be triggered by the events of life. You can seek them out by engaging some of the apparently lighter koans of life, and then tracing the cause of your obstacle deeper and deeper, until you find the life-and-death concerns that underlie attachments, delusions, and fears.

For an example of this process of looking beneath a shallower koan for a deeper one, imagine you have a difficulty in your intimate partnership. Let's say you've been with your partner for many years, and you find yourself getting bored and thinking about being with other people. If you examine this koan very diligently and carefully, trying to be very honest with yourself, you may notice that you long for the intensity of a new relationship, where intimacy and connection are front and center. So you are actually longing for more intimacy and feel you can't get it in your current relationship. And yet, a new relationship would eventually lose its intensity, so would you have to keep going from relationship to relationship to get your needs met?

Now you can start to question your assumptions about intimacy, and how you get it. Following this line of inquiry may eventually lead you down to your fundamental fear of emptiness—your fear that it means isolation. Facing this fear and working on a personal understanding of what emptiness really is may end up *improving your relationship with your partner.* This may seem like taking the long way around, but doing it this way results in transformative, lasting change because it's about changing the entire way you relate to the world.

Avoiding Complacency

Complacency is just another koan, but it's one that can put you to sleep instead of waking you up. There's always more to see, understand, and master, so there's no excuse for slacking off. Still, it's easy to do. You can keep yourself from getting complacent by engaging koans, working with a Zen teacher, and asking yourself questions like, "What do I still not see?" (There's always something you don't see.)

You can also challenge your own understanding to make sure it's experiential, not just intellectual. (It's always a little intellectual.) You can keep your eye out for any view you hold and try to drop it in favor of meeting each moment on its own terms. (There's always another view to drop.) Perhaps most importantly, you can try to keep the fire of your curiosity burning, because letting it go out means you think you've seen this all before. And you haven't.

The Least You Need to Know

- If you want to deepen your Zen practice, it's very useful to be able to rely on a strong foundation of healthy habits and faith, built up over time, that practice works.

- You may need to get creative when generating the determination you need to intensify your practice, but typical methods include contemplating mortality, reminding yourself of how the truth can set you free, and cultivating goodwill toward others.

- To understand more, and become more skillful in your life, you need to have the courage to face fears both personal and profound. Liberation from these fears is very rewarding.

- Koans are obstacles that show you the limits of your understanding and your ability to respond skillfully. They are opportunities to use insight to see the truth and relieve suffering.

- Once things feel okay, it's easy to get complacent. Part of Zen practice is to try to keep your curiosity alive.

Enlightened About Delusion

Enlightenment has many names, even just within Zen. The word is often used interchangeably with the terms awakening and liberation. The English word enlightenment also means to have received greater understanding or knowledge about a situation; when it's used in a Zen context it refers specifically to attaining greater understanding about the nature of reality. Awakening means to have woken up to this reality from the stupor of delusion. Liberation means gaining freedom from the painful and restrictive delusion of inherent, enduring self-nature (discussed in Chapter 11).

If you don't care about enlightenment, you can feel free to skip this chapter. However, if you find the idea intriguing, confusing, troubling, tempting, inspirational, or off-putting, what's presented here might help you understand better what Zen means by enlightenment, and how to relate to the concept.

In This Chapter

- How the concept of enlightenment is used in Zen
- Relating to ideals
- The way in which you are already awakened
- Enlightenment experiences
- Life after enlightenment

The Concept of Enlightenment

Whatever the language used to describe it, enlightenment is a tricky subject. It points toward what Zen teachers say is possible, but also limits your relationship to what is possible by attaching it to a concept. Many Zen teachers throughout history have refused to talk about enlightenment at all. Others stress the importance of awakening above all else. The differences in approach have less to do with disagreement about the value of spiritual insight, and more to do with the best way to motivate, and get through to, a particular audience.

In a time and culture in which everyone was desperately striving for spiritual liberation, a teacher may have decided that the best way for people to attain that liberation would be for them to give up the striving. In another time and place, faced with complacent students, a Zen teacher may find it most useful to encourage them to push for enlightenment. The only thing that matters is the effect on the practice of living people, not whether enlightenment really exists or should be sought after.

CONSIDER THIS

The *Heart of Great Perfect Wisdom Sutra* is chanted daily in Zen monasteries and temples. It reminds practitioners that *everything* is empty of inherent, enduring self-nature, including the teachings considered fundamental to Buddhism: ignorance, the end of ignorance, suffering, the cause of suffering, the cessation of suffering, the Eightfold Noble Path, knowledge, and attainment. As long as these teachings are helpful, they are used, but they do not refer to some enduring, self-existent truth that exists "out there," separate from your experience.

The concept of enlightenment is simply a tool. Like all things, it is empty of inherent, enduring self-nature. Is there really such a thing as enlightenment? Yes and no. There are very clearly differences in levels of understanding, but there is no fixed *thing* you can point to and call enlightenment. Just as it's useful to speak in everyday conversation as if you have an unchanging self-essence (as if there is a fixed thing called *you* that will be here tomorrow to receive a phone call), it's useful to talk about enlightenment. In the end it cannot be grasped, but that doesn't mean it isn't real.

The Human Ideal

The concept of attaining profound spiritual insight and freedom, usually through strenuous effort, is one that has captivated human beings since long before Buddhism. Human history, literature, and religious traditions are full of stories of people who experienced something that was spiritually transformative, and who subsequently related to the world in a radically wiser, more selfless, and more compassionate way than your average person. They rose above the rest of humanity simply by virtue of their wisdom, personal conduct, and interaction with others, not because of political power, wealth, productivity, or any of the other ways people usually gain fame.

Together, remarkable individuals throughout history have contributed to the ideal of the enlightened sage, who seems to dwell in a different world than most people. While going about his daily life, the sage exhibits almost no self-concern. This lack of self-centeredness is not due to recklessness, self-loathing, or general ambivalence. It is utterly sincere: a simple absence of the delusion of self most people are carrying, as covered in Chapter 14.

The sage may live a quiet, unassuming life completely devoid of ambition, serving as a teacher for those who seek her out. Alternatively, the sage may work actively for the welfare of others, giving more generously and tirelessly than most people would be capable of doing—and all without requiring the slightest thanks, and without burning out.

Direction, Not Goal

As long as you think of enlightenment as something to be attained and held on to—such that there are enlightened people and unenlightened people—it will probably be a problematic concept in your practice. The ideal of the enlightened sage sets a pretty high bar. For a few ambitious people it might serve as great motivation, but for most people it sets up a standard you strive for but never reach, resulting in frustration or a sense of inadequacy. Alternatively, the ideal can seem so high that little-old-you could never reach it, so you figure you might as well not even try.

It's better to think of enlightenment as a direction, rather than a goal. No one can argue that it's always possible to understand more, to be aware of more, to become less self-centered, and to live with more generosity, kindness, patience, and gratitude. The people in the world who demonstrate this fact in a remarkable way just serve to remind you how much more is possible. While it's true that certain realizations result in more dramatic transformations than others (particularly seeing the true nature of self), no single transformation turns an ordinary, suffering, self-centered being into a sage. Behind every unusually enlightened person is a long story about the circumstances, support, and personal work that resulted in who they are.

POTENTIAL PITFALL

When talking about Zen concepts like enlightenment, there's always an "on the other hand." If you think about awakening as a direction rather than a goal because you figure you can never attain it, you run the risk of buji Zen. Zen teacher Bodhin Kjolhede, in the afterword to *Three Pillars of Zen* added in 2000, describes buji zen as "the stance that to speak of becoming enlightened is a contradiction in terms since we are all innately enlightened." Kjolhede suggests that this stance "should be exposed for what it is: a loss of faith in one's potential for realization."

You Already Have It

The most important reason of all to avoid getting stuck on the idea of enlightenment as a dramatic, one-time event that leads to sainthood is the fact that *you are already enlightened*. As long as you think of it as something outside of yourself, you will keep yourself separate from it. Time and time again Zen masters and teachers have emphasized this point. The paradox is that you have to work on becoming conscious of and actualizing (manifesting) this awakened nature, but enlightenment does *not* involve an understanding of something that is outside of your current experience of reality. Instead, it's being able to see what is already here.

Clarity About Delusion

Attaining spiritual liberation is completely unlike attaining knowledge in an area like physics. For example, there's a great difference between a PhD in physics who is at the top of her field, and you (assuming you're not a physicist). The physicist is familiar with, and understands, a huge amount of information you don't even know. No technique in the world is going to give you instant access to that information; you have to acquire it gradually over time. In addition, it may be that the PhD is constitutionally different from you, and she is capable of comprehending the implications of this information in a way that escapes you, no matter how much you study.

In contrast, what is realized in enlightenment has nothing to do with information. It involves insight into being truly alive, so it's accessible to anyone living. Perhaps there are people with more spiritual aptitude than others, but this is usually due to curiosity and willingness to let go of self-centeredness, so it's definitely not a matter of intelligence, ambition, or any of the other things that usually lead someone to mastery of a particular field.

According to Zen, what stands between you and a wise, compassionate, selfless life is delusion. Your true nature is buddha-nature, but what gets in the way is the self-centeredness based on your fundamental misunderstanding about the nature of self. This is why Zen master Dogen wrote that buddhas are those who greatly understand delusion, while ordinary beings are those who are greatly deluded about realization. Awakened beings know that enlightenment is not somewhere else; it has been here all along. Because of your misunderstanding and selfish habits, you can't see it, and you imagine that buddhas awaken to something beyond your current knowledge and experience.

You think that enlightened sages have access to special information, or have had a special experience, that relieves their suffering, gives them peace of mind, and allows them to operate without so much self-centeredness. When you experience some enlightenment for yourself, it's a little like suddenly catching on to a great joke: "Oh! *That's* what they meant! Recognize the perfection of *this* moment, *this* life!" You realize that all along you knew everything you needed to know, and had all the tools required for awakening.

If you're like most people, it doesn't help much to simply be told—or even to believe—that you are already enlightened. Maybe it's a little encouraging to know that, theoretically, you could awaken completely this moment, in this very life, body, and mind. But knowing this potential is latent in you, and becoming conscious of it, understanding it, and appreciating it is another thing entirely.

Perhaps everyone has buddha-nature and the potential to liberate themselves from suffering, but there are many people who lead sad, desperate lives in spite of this. Conscious realization is an extremely important piece of the puzzle. In fact, the teaching that you are already enlightened is not meant to be a consolation—it's meant to keep you from fruitlessly searching for enlightenment somewhere else.

To illustrate how enlightenment can be part of your nature but still require some effort on your part, I'll use an analogy I learned from one of my Zen teachers, Kyogen Carlson. The pervasiveness and accessibility of enlightenment is like the pervasiveness and accessibility of gravity. Gravity is so ubiquitous, so much a part of you, that it took a remarkably creative thinker (Newton) to conceive of its existence. All along, before and after Newton, before and after you learned about the concept of gravity, it was present and operating. When you fall down on your face, that's gravity operating. When you walk, gravity's at work. When you dance, that's gravity operating, too. It's all a perfect relationship to gravity. You can't *not* have a perfect relationship to it.

Still, in your human experience there's an awfully big difference between falling on your face and dancing. In Zen you try to harmonize your life with the truth, with enlightenment, to result in the least amount of suffering possible and to maximize the wisdom, compassion, joy, and beauty you can manifest in your life. Part of this harmonization requires a conscious appreciation of the truth.

No Longer Looking Elsewhere

Just as it was difficult for people to conceive of gravity even though it has always been operating, it's difficult for people to recognize enlightenment in their lives. As discussed in earlier chapters of this book, because of impermanence and no-self, you usually experience dukkha, or the sense that this is not quite the way things should be. Because of your belief that you have an inherent, enduring self-nature, you grasp after things, push other things away, and worry constantly about your well-being.

Because of your attachment and habits, you often act in ways that cause suffering for yourself and others. *How can this be enlightenment?* How can it be that you have buddha-nature, or that your life, just as it is, is precious and complete? Enlightenment is about luminous, transcendent visions, not being 20 pounds overweight, unemployed, or irritable! Right?

> **CONSIDER THIS**
>
> Being honest and realistic about yourself is essential, so you can maintain humility, keep working on your unhealthy habits, and continue to erode your selfishness. At the same time, you have to work on acceptance and seeing your life, just as it is, as precious and complete. It can be tough to find the right balance between these two sides of practice. It helps to remember that the most important thing is seeing clearly. You don't have to reconcile these two aspects of life, just keep your awareness open to both of them.

This is precisely why awakening, realization, or liberation is so difficult. You can't imagine it's really about you. You'd actually prefer it to not be about you the way you are; you'd rather it be about you transformed into the person you want to be. You hope enlightenment will give you access into a different world than this one, because even when this world is okay, it seems far from precious and complete!

Ironically, the awakening that liberates requires you to drop every last bit of resistance to your life as it is, and to the world as it is. Buddhahood shines through your child, your paperwork, and your daily commute. Enlightenment doesn't transform your life into something else, it reveals what is already there—it's just so close, so obvious, so intimate that you usually can't see or accept it.

Enlightenment Experiences

After all this talk about waking up to your life just as it is, and not conceiving of enlightenment as a dramatic experience that will fundamentally change you, you may be wondering about how enlightenment experiences fit into the picture. This was discussed to some extent in Chapter 14, where I emphasized that the important thing is seeing the true nature of the self, not how exciting, sudden, or dramatic the experience of insight is.

Still, one of the first Zen books available to Westerners was Roshi Philip Kapleau's *Three Pillars of Zen*, published in 1980, and this book includes over 100 pages of descriptions of enlightenment experiences, or kensho. Some people are drawn to Zen primarily because they hope to have one of these experiences.

There is no denying that kensho happens. I personally know, trust, and respect at least ten Zen practitioners who experienced a shift in perspective and understanding that was so sudden and substantial that it shook them to the core of their being. For each person the experience was different, but generally speaking it was disorienting, emotional, blissful, and more or less traumatic. The traumatic aspect came not from the kensho being negative or frightening (although it can occasionally have these qualities as well), but more from it being such a sudden and large change in mental perspective, self-conception, and perception.

The more dramatic the awakening experience, the more difficult it can be to integrate what is learned into your daily life. It can also be very tough to get past the event, to forget about it and move on. It can be made a possession of self, just like anything else, and become a problem. In fact, there are probably just as many Zen stories about getting people to let go of their awakening experiences as there are stories about encouraging people to have them. This is not a reason to try to avoid having a kensho, because no one who has had one regrets it, no matter how long they had to work at integrating it into their practice. The kensho was about seeing the truth, so why would you want to step back from that?

Here's the thing: many people arrive at a personal understanding of the true nature of reality without having a kensho experience. Instead, they have a whole bunch of smaller awakenings, less dramatic but also less traumatic. In this slow path of realization, you awaken to a truth, integrate it, and then awaken to another truth. It's like the petals of a flower opening one at a time, almost imperceptibly. One day you look and there's a fully blossomed flower. It's less exciting, but just as effective.

Whichever way you might prefer your awakening to happen, sudden or gradual, it's probably not up to you. Sudden awakening sometimes happens to people who never thought they would experience it, while other people strive tirelessly to achieve sudden awakening for many years, only to discover the flower of their enlightenment has bloomed in the meantime. It probably has to do with your karma—all the causes and effects that led up to you being who you are. Your constitution, experiences, personality, brain chemistry, and who-knows-what-else affect your tendency to wake up suddenly or gradually.

The important thing is to keep up your energetic search for the truth. Someone once asked Shunryu Suzuki Roshi why *satori*, another word for the experience of enlightenment, didn't appear in his book *Zen Mind, Beginner's Mind*. He replied, "It's not that *satori* is unimportant, but it's not the part of Zen that needs to be stressed."

After Enlightenment

This brings us to a discussion of what happens *after* you gain a conscious, personal experience of the true nature of self and reality. Whether your enlightenment flower opened suddenly or gradually, once it's opened, are you home free? Does everything suddenly make sense? Are you instantly freed from selfishness? Do you respond to everything with patience, generosity, and compassion? Unfortunately not. The process of harmonizing your life with the truth is endless, and the moment you think you've got it, you've lost it.

No Enlightened People

Beware of people who would have you believe *they* are completely, or even mostly, enlightened. They don't have an inherent, enduring self-nature, right? What is it that qualifies in a permanent way as enlightened? The particularly dangerous thing about the claim of enlightenment is that it suggests that everything the awakened person does is a manifestation of their wisdom and compassion—even when it involves actions like stealing, lying, or misusing sexual energy.

If people act like this, especially if they do so repeatedly, or over a long period of time, and expect to suffer no consequences for their behavior, it's evidence of their lack of actualization. They're still caught in self-centeredness, despite whatever they've realized or done in the past. On rare occasions you might be justified in breaking a moral precept for compassionate reasons, but you still don't escape the consequences, and you have to be extremely careful not to just end up trying to rationalize your own selfishness.

You have to put into practice whatever you've learned through insight. As discussed in Chapter 7, habits have energy of their own, and require you to put energy into changing them. It takes work to actualize your deepest understanding. If you've spent your whole life doing things a particular way, it may be hard to change even when you see very clearly how your behavior is causing harm or is based on a delusion. Over time, your insight can help a great deal with changing your behavior, but I don't think anyone on this planet thinks and acts in a perfectly enlightened way all the time. There's always more to work on—or, at the very least, to recognize as imperfection.

Meeting Each Moment

For another thing, enlightenment is not a state or a point of view; it is a way of being in the world that has to be lived, moment by moment. It is fresh, undefended engagement with reality, which is only right now. Some insight you experienced in the past is only relevant in how it has shaped your causal flow, and thereby contributes to your wholehearted response to life in the present.

Enlightenment doesn't give you a philosophical framework in which you evaluate what you encounter and come up with an "enlightened response." You don't base your actions on some idea of yourself as a wise or compassionate person, an idea developed over years of spiritual practice. Any of these things involve the activation of your belief in inherent, enduring self-nature: there's *you* responding in an enlightened way to *that*.

ZEN WISDOM

"A foolish passing thought makes one an ordinary man, while an enlightened second thought makes one a buddha."

—Zen Master Hui Neng (638-713), from *The Sutra of Hui Neng*, translated by A.F. Price and Wong Mou-Lam

Meeting a moment in a completely enlightened way means no self-concern is there at all, including any concern about being enlightened. This is why Zen master Dogen says that buddhas don't need to realize they are buddhas. Is there any person whose every moment is perfectly enlightened, utterly free of any self-centeredness? Has there ever been such a person?

Some people may disagree, thinking of certain remarkable individuals like the Buddha, or Christ, or the Dalai Lama, but I think probably not. Whether anyone has ever achieved complete and permanent perfection is not really that important. What matters is how *you* meet the next moment. There is a self-centered way to do it, and an enlightened way to do it. What do you choose?

The Least You Need to Know

- The concept of enlightenment is simply a tool to get people to wake up to reality, so sometimes it's talked about and sometimes it's not.
- Awakening is an endless process—always more to see, always better ways to harmonize your life with the truth.
- Waking up to reality means seeing through delusions—so all that buddhas, or awakened beings, have attained is deep insight into delusion.
- Enlightenment experiences happen, but they are not the end of Zen training and not all people have them, no matter how hard they work. The important thing is what you come to personally understand, not how dramatically you come to understand it.
- A liberated person meets each moment in an open, undefended, unscripted way. Enlightenment is not a state or an attainment; it must be embodied and enacted.

Living Zen

Zen is all about living. The whole point of Zen practice is to live with more awareness, appreciation, wisdom, and compassion. Not only is it important to bring Zen into your everyday life (otherwise, what's the point?), your everyday life is a great place to strengthen and test your Zen. It's also where you learn the most, about profound or personal matters.

On a daily basis you encounter opportunities to cultivate awareness and transcend self-centeredness. In your relationships you can work on patience and non-attachment; at work you can learn about the spirit of generosity; while using technology you can learn to pay attention to your state of mind and notice how certain activities affect you. Facing mental health issues is a strong challenge to your sense of self, which also makes it a great opportunity for self-study. Challenges like stress and difficult emotions are your chance to employ and test your Zen spirit, as are the ultimate challenges like injustice, illness, and loss. Every day of your life offers chances to practice Zen and deepen your understanding of life.

Zen in Relationships

Nothing challenges your self-centeredness like other people do. From a Zen perspective, this is great. Your relationships provide you with ongoing opportunities to see where you're still attached to things, or selfish, defensive, stingy—you name it! Sometimes other people have perspective on your life and behavior that you do not, so they can give you some useful feedback. At other times people are just acting out of their own self-centeredness, and you end up conflicting with them. Either way, you can learn something valuable about yourself.

Relationships also give you the opportunity to test and manifest your deepest understanding in a very concrete way. Generosity in theory gets tested when you think about whether to lend something of value to a friend. You learn more about patience when sitting down to help your child with her homework. No-self becomes more real to you when you notice how you feel a little bit like you're still a child when you visit your family of origin. You're always in relationship with other people in some way, so relationship is naturally a huge part of your life and, consequently, your Zen practice.

In This Chapter

- Why relationships are so great for Zen practice
- How to engage a relationship as a koan
- Four Zen approaches to relating with others
- Zen practice with family, partners, and friends
- Working Zen on your archenemy

Relationships as Koans

All of your relationships are koans, whether or not you recognize them as such. In Chapter 15 I explained how to engage koans to deepen your Zen, and how koans are questions or problems that bring you up against the limit of your understanding, or against your ability to respond in a way that demonstrates your aspirations or insight. Few things in your life provide this kind of challenge as predictably and clearly as other people.

Once I was considering whether to get involved in a new intimate relationship, and a Zen teacher told me, "Relationships bring out the worst in you." She wasn't saying this to discourage me, she was just being realistic. From a Zen point of view, it's not necessarily bad that something would bring out the worst in you. In fact, depending on the situation, you might even look at it as a good thing.

Throughout this book I've talked about how troublesome delusion can be, and how critical it is to be able to see things clearly. The tricky thing about delusion is that it means you believe something that isn't actually true—and how do you see through your own thinking? Other people can help, because they aren't motivated to maintain your delusions the way you are. They have their own delusions to maintain, and you're especially going to find out about your delusions if they work at cross-purposes to someone else's!

You will have developed a predictable dance of interaction with any person you encounter regularly over time. The longer you've known them, and the more involved they are with your daily life, the more this dance is going to be tied up with your sense of self. Because it seems like so much a part of who you are, you're going to be extremely invested in how this typical pattern of interaction goes. One way or another, this kind of attachment to a relationship causes suffering.

If you like your dance with someone—you enjoy it, it makes you feel safe, it supports other ideas you have about who you are—you will want that dance to stay the same. Unfortunately, it's a rule of the universe that everything changes, so inevitably your favorite relationship dance will shift, and then what? If the dance is part of who you think you are, this will be very uncomfortable. If you *don't* like the dance in a relationship, you will feel an imperative to change it—and that usually involves expecting the other person to do things differently. They rarely oblige.

How do you engage a relationship, along with its dance, as a koan? You use Zen tools to carefully examine your relationship, and try to work with it so it causes less suffering and brings more happiness to all involved. You take a step back from it, because if you're too wrapped up in it you will only see your own agenda. You cultivate determination to face the truth about the relationship and see things as clearly as possible.

With Zen practice you develop more ability to return to the present moment and let go of commentary and reaction, so instead of always being triggered by someone you can keep your eyes and ears open to what is actually going on. You decide that you will do your best to give up your selfishness if you find any (and you will), and to challenge your delusions if you encounter them (they'll be there). You summon as much humility as you can, acknowledging that it takes two to manifest the relationship dance you are working on.

Like working with other kinds of koans, a relationship koan requires patience and determination. It doesn't help to give up because you can't understand or improve a relationship right away. Sometimes it takes many, many years to resolve a koan. It also doesn't help to latch on to overly simplistic answers in an effort to fix things ASAP; such answers won't bring about substantial, lasting change, and they will only distract you from the longer-term process of searching and learning. It helps, as discussed in Chapter 15, to have built up faith in Zen practice so you have some confidence that all this work will pay off—eventually.

It's also essential that you *stay in the relationship* if you are going to engage it as a koan. This may or may not mean that you continue living with someone or interacting with them in a way that is bringing problems. It's still important to set appropriate boundaries and take care of your responsibilities, although it's not always easy to see where those boundaries should be.

Consider, however, that even if you set boundaries with someone, you can still be in relationship with them. You may not even see them very often, or perhaps at all, but you don't cut them entirely out of your view of your life or write them off as not worth your effort. You let the person and your relationship with them continue to be alive and present for you—something that brings you up against the limit of your understanding, or against your ability to respond skillfully and compassionately. You don't blame anyone for the fact that this is so; you just turn toward the relationship as something that can teach you something.

 CONSIDER THIS

> The more difficult the relationship, the more you can learn from it. This does not mean that the other person is right, or justified, and you should just accept their behavior. The rightness or wrongness of their actions has nothing to do with your process of learning from the relationship. In a troubling relationship, someone is triggering your doubts and fears. This gives you the chance to investigate and resolve them within yourself. In a way, it has nothing to do with the other person.

Finally, it's essential that the questions you bring to a relationship koan, and the answers you come to, have to do with *you*. The other person in the relationship *may* cooperate and work on it with you, but your koan work does not, and cannot, depend on this. You take responsibility for the only part of the dance you actually have any control over: your part. In fact, to see the relationship dance clearly, you're going to need to get very still inside. This requires that you spend some time just watching and listening, without trying to actively change things or shift the blame.

Once you start to see things clearly, you may indeed need to make a change that affects the other person, such as making a request, or refusing to continue doing something the other person expects you to do. However, these actions will not be about the other person; they will be about you being honest and setting boundaries as you need to. You change *your* part of the dance. How the other person responds is up to them. You can certainly hope they respond in a way you like, and that supports the health of the relationship, but you can't demand or expect this. That's the definition of a relationship dance! There are two of you: two independent individuals, interacting. When the other person freely responds with wisdom, kindness, or generosity—what a lovely outcome!

A Zen View of Relationships

Looking at relationships from a Zen perspective is probably very different from how you learned to look at them over the course of your life. Your family of origin, friends, significant others, and culture have encouraged you to view relationships as a means to gain what you need and want. Whether you want companionship, intimacy, material support, encouragement, respect, excitement, security, validation, gratitude, or something else, you look around for people who can provide it with a minimum of fuss. The people you're stuck in relationships with—relatives, partners, children, co-workers—often fail to provide what you need or want, so then you have to struggle with them until they do.

From the Zen point of view, the self-centeredness behind such an approach to relationships leads to dukkha, or stress and dissatisfaction, as discussed in Chapter 10. As long as you're searching outside yourself for ultimate happiness, you will never find it. As long as you blame (or credit) other people for your inner experience, you will see them primarily in terms of how they serve your self-interest, and true and lasting intimacy will be impossible. Here I highlight four Zen approaches to relationships that tend to run counter to what people often do.

No One Makes You Angry

No one else can *make* you feel anger, or any of the related negative, self-centered emotions like frustration, disgust, impatience, jealousy, or resentment. Someone does something, and you experience an emotional response. Your response, by the standards of your friends, culture, or moral views, may be perfectly reasonable, or even justified. However, from the Zen point of view, the other person is not responsible for your reaction—you are.

It's entirely possible to alter the way you engage with life so much that an event that once upon a time would have made you furious no longer bothers you. Much of the time you may not be able to do anything to prevent the initial emotions from arising, but you can recognize that they have to do with self-concern and then decide what to do about them, if anything. Once you develop a conviction, through practice, that acting out of self-concern leads to misery, you're much more likely to let negative emotional reactions fade away *before* you decide on the best course of action.

There are so many ways to possibly misunderstand this Zen teaching, I'll start with a paragraph devoted just to what it *doesn't* mean. It's *not* that you are to blame for your emotional reactions, as if you *should* be able to control your emotional responses and not let people bother you. Your emotional reactions arose because of many reasons, and there is no inherently existing, unchanging *you* to be blamed for them.

This teaching is *not* saying that other people should be relieved of responsibility for their actions. If you need someone to stop doing something, go ahead and try to get them to stop—but it isn't necessary for you to be angry when you do it (actually, it's better if you aren't). This is *not* about maintaining absolute internal control so you never lose your dignity or make yourself emotionally vulnerable. After all, that's all about self-centeredness.

 ZEN WISDOM

"Not long ago, despite many years of practice, I unexpectedly became embroiled in a wave of hatred and anger .... I folded my blankets and sat before my altar focusing on my breathing. The act of doing this, of moving away from the angry stories we tell ourselves in our mind, and just returning over and over to the practice of breathing, can be called letting go. It is an extraordinarily powerful practice .... Letting go is sort of like cleaning out the garage. There is stuff there that you think you want to keep, but once you get rid of it you forget you ever had it in the first place."

—Calvin Malone, Zen practitioner and prison inmate, from *Razor-Wire Dharma: A Buddhist Life in Prison*

The idea that "no one makes you angry" *is* pointing to the fact that you have influence over every part of your internal experience. You have the ability to work on yourself to change your habits and your understanding of the world, and therefore how you react to things. This doesn't make change easy or quick, but it does mean that nothing in your emotional experience is completely out of your sphere of influence.

Ultimately, the best thing you can do is work on your fundamental misunderstanding about the nature of self, as discussed in Chapter 14, because that lets you function with much less self-concern. However, even before you manage to radically shift your worldview, you can at least stop blaming others when you continue to hold on to negative, self-centered feelings. Maybe someone else triggered your initial emotional response, but only you are responsible for the long-term health of your internal environment.

No One Makes You Happy

Just as you can take responsibility for your internal environment so you aren't doomed to be angry because of someone else's actions, you can work on yourself so that no one else is responsible for your happiness. If you do so, it will be of great benefit to your life. If you're only happy when people are near and acting in ways that suit you, you will have to continuously chase after the experience because inevitably people go away or disappoint.

In addition, your happiness will not be complete, because you will always be aware that it's soon going to pass, or that you have to keep the right people around to maintain it. If you can only be happy when you're in the *right* relationship with the *right* intimate partner, you're probably going to find yourself disappointed when even that relationship can't remain perfect, or it doesn't take care of all of your problems.

It's not that Zen suggests you try to get to a place where you don't need anything or anyone (as if that were even possible); it's just that true, lasting happiness is possible, but no one can give it to you. Nice and compatible people certainly are one of life's greatest joys, but even if you're surrounded by loving, generous, wonderful people, you can still be miserable. And chances are, if you are miserable, you don't notice how loving, generous, and wonderful the people in your life are.

If you *are* happy in a lasting, peaceful kind of way, it's not because of the great people in your life. They may indeed bring you lots of enjoyment, but your happiness comes from a sense of satisfaction with life that is your responsibility, not theirs.

From the Zen point of view, happiness—or at least a profound satisfaction—arises whenever you transcend your self-concern. When this is the case, there is no thought about *you* and *your happiness*. There is no *other* who is delivering *you* an experience that results in happiness. Sometimes there are delightful interactions with people and there is gratitude and joy. Sometimes there are periods of solitude, but you are still okay, because life as it is seems luminous and precious. You don't find your happiness apart from other people, and you don't find it through other people. You experience it as you engage with life in an open, undefended way.

No One Owes You Anything

It can be tough to get your mind around the idea that no one owes you anything. You probably believe your parents owe you love and support, your partner owes you attention and affection, your children owe you gratitude and respect, your boss owes you fairness and clear communication, and your government owes you justice. To give up such ideas seems like it would mean the end of the civilized world. If obligations aren't made clear and collection on them enforced, people will be selfish and cruel, right? If you don't make it clear to your partner that he'd better do such-and-such or he will be betraying his commitment to you, who knows how callously he may behave?

POTENTIAL PITFALL

If you try to work with the idea that no one owes you anything, be careful you don't let bitterness creep in. When you practice with this concept in a fruitful way, your attitude is one of curiosity—and gratitude when someone does something positive or nice. If you feel like no one owes you anything because you're tired of how stingy and selfish people are and you don't want to depend on them anymore, this is actually believing that they *do* owe you, but they haven't met their obligation so they aren't worth caring about.

When you believe someone owes you something, it's because you have incorporated them, or their relationship to you, into your self-concept, or made them a possession of self. As discussed in Chapter 13, this attachment means you see the other person primarily in terms of your own agenda.

For example, your life is intimately and profoundly affected by what your child does, so it's easy to incorporate your child's behavior into your self-concept. If you have done so and she acts out in defiance of your request, this threatens your sense of self. "She *should not* act this way," you probably think, or, "How can she act this way?" You have a sense that because of your relationship with your child, she owes it to you to keep her behavior within certain parameters.

It's much more effective, and less painful, to be up-front and honest with your requests of other people, but let go of any sense that they owe you a particular response. Carrying the idea that people are obligated to you is actually unnecessary to fruitful and harmonious interactions. In fact, the sense of being owed usually just makes people feel defensive, resistant, or begrudging— even if they do what you want! Instead, your request can be like asking them for a favor or a gift. If they fulfill your request, it will be a free act of generosity, kindness, or respect, or a demonstration of eagerness to stay engaged with you.

Everyone Is Like You

Finally, in relationships it is essential to cultivate the appreciation that everyone is fundamentally just like you. From a Zen perspective, this means that they are doing their best to avoid suffering and seek happiness. You may not, for the life of you, be able to understand why someone acts the way they do, but you can be confident that from their point of view it makes some kind of convoluted sense. They may be completely deluded!

For example, they may think that intimidating people in conversation makes them seem smart and will therefore make them more popular. When you encounter this behavior and see the person as just like you, you can feel some patience and sympathy for the poor deluded person, rather than seeing them as a threatening force out to ruin the conversation for others.

Other people being fundamentally like you in terms of core motivation doesn't mean they are like you in other ways, of course. But it turns out that the many ways in which people differ are not all that important when it comes to manifesting compassion, generosity, and patience in human interactions. You may choose your partners and friends based on relatively superficial similarities, but time and time again events in the world have proven that people will recognize the core motivation and experience they have in common with strangers, and will reach out to help them. They don't always do it, but when they do, it's out of this sense of not being fundamentally different from others.

There is one glaring exception to this rule, which Zen teacher Geri Larkin discusses in her book *Tap Dancing in Zen.* The rare person seems to lack certain critical tools that come in most people's standard human toolkit, and in some circles such people may be referred to as a psychopathic personality. I am no psychologist and do not recommend you casually diagnose or categorize anyone, but you also don't want to be blinded to reality because you're holding on to an ideal that everyone is ultimately good and kind.

Larkin's list of qualities of a psychopathic personality suggests the characteristics of some of the people who have caused great, senseless harm in the world. Apparently the psychopath does not feel the sense that others are fundamentally like them (trying to avoid suffering and be happy), and feels no concern at all about causing pain and discomfort to others.

As sinister as a psychopath sounds, their existence in the world is not an excuse for shutting down. Larkin's own father was psychopathic and she advises you to put as much time and distance between you and a psychopath as you can, as soon as you realize what's going on. Nevertheless, she still writes, "If you can only give one gift to the world, let it be this: to live more from your heart and less from your mind. Let mystery in. Along with not-knowing. Let other people have an opportunity to be kind, and be on the alert for your own opportunities."

The psychopath should not be allowed to wreak havoc on others, but he should receive our sympathy (from afar) because he is deprived of the connection and openness available to most people.

 CONSIDER THIS

> There is a Zen ceremony that enacts how all people can be on a path toward greater wisdom and compassion, but it may not necessarily seem like it. The ceremony involves a long procession that everyone joins, single file. The leader of the line makes his path curve around the room and cross back over itself multiple times, so the long line of people end up walking every which way. Two people in the same line end up passing each other while walking in opposite directions, but both end up in the same place eventually.

Zen Practice with ...

Sometimes it helps to have examples, so this next section will offer some ideas for how to apply Zen practice to the significant relationships in your life. What's discussed under each heading is far from an exhaustive treatment of practice within a particular kind of relationship; it's just a snapshot of what it can look like. Most of the things mentioned also apply to more than one kind of relationship, so read about all of them if you're interested in working with relationships as koans.

Family

Strangers can challenge your ability to keep the precepts and give up self-centeredness, but no one can do this better than your family of origin. There's a saying that goes, "Of course your parents know how to push your buttons. They're the ones who installed them." The predictable relationship dance with your parents, siblings, and other close relatives has been developing for many, many years, and may have started up long before you had the ability to observe it or make any conscious choices about your part of the dance. The habit energy of such interactions is very strong. This is why, when you find yourself in your childhood home, or around your family of origin, you can often watch yourself regress to old patterns of behavior you thought you had left behind.

It's natural to make up narratives to explain your past and how you relate (or don't) to each family member. These stories become part of your self-identity, and there's at least part of you invested in maintaining them no matter what. Your family members have narratives about you, too, and they are similarly attached to them. In a family, often no one wants to change their stories about the others or about the family as a whole. This is part of the nature of attachment, as discussed in Chapter 13.

As a result of this, people can—usually inadvertently—prevent one another from changing. If you manage to act a little differently within your family, chances are good no one will notice, or they may even resist or ridicule the change. This is because of their investment in things staying the same, even if the way things are is frustrating, painful, or unhealthy. Things-the-way-they-are has become part of each family member's self-concept, and too much change to your self-concept feels threatening to your very existence.

You can bring Zen practice to your familial relationships by seeing more clearly and objectively the predictable dances you are all doing. Then you can employ karma work (Chapter 7) to create space around your habits so you can try something new. First you use meditation and mindfulness to settle your mind and notice what is happening. In order to change habit patterns, especially when they involve someone else, the first thing you may need to do is simply *stop* the pattern. You may not know what else to do, yet, but at least you aren't being triggered into a reactive dance.

For example, perhaps your mother tends to bait you with criticism and then points to your anger as proof that she's right. If you can just manage to hold your tongue and not react, that's a huge change already. The pattern doesn't keep perpetuating itself, digging the groove of the habit deeper and deeper.

It may take a long time of doing this before you can actively respond in a new way, like calmly telling your mother that you care about what she thinks, and her criticism hurts. If you try something new too soon, it's probably only going to be the same dance step after all: telling your mother that her criticism hurts will just be a different way of expressing your anger, rather than a sincere communication of your internal experience. She'll know.

CONSIDER THIS

> It can be extremely difficult to accept the behavior of others, especially when they're close to you. You may hear the refrain in your mind, "He *shouldn't* ..." or "She's *got* to stop ...." You probably have some insight into the situation and why it would be good for it to change, but change is very unlikely until you fully acknowledge and accept the way things are. Internal resistance to other people's behavior only hurts you, and gets in the way of your being able to address the situation. Your brother regularly insults you, and your sister lies to your parents. It's just the way it is, and the *shoulds* are extra and unnecessary.

Sometimes it doesn't take much for family relationships to shift. As long as you keep your attention on your *own* part of the dance, and give other people the freedom to respond to your new dance steps however they choose, you will often find people moving along with you in harmony. Just a change in the way you look at things can subtly affect others. As relationships shift and old narratives no longer quite fit, you get to practice letting go of attachments. You also get to learn a great lesson in how self constantly changes, and how it arises in mutual dependence with everything around it.

Intimate Partners

Like most people, you may expect your romantic partner to meet many of your needs, particularly those for intimacy, emotional support, encouragement, companionship, and validation. You may not know where to meet these needs except within an intimate partnership, so if you don't have one it can be very distressing and lonely. Alternatively, you may have a partner but feel like they fall far short of meeting your needs.

If you don't have a partner and long for one, you don't have to stop looking, but you can engage your situation as a koan. It brings up all kinds of important spiritual questions: What is intimacy? Can you get your need for it met in other ways? Do you feel a sense of lack or inadequacy being alone? What is beneath your longing for partnership? If you can trace your concerns down to your very basic assumptions and fears about life, and then challenge and face them, you may be able to discover a self-sufficiency that will ease your pain.

The intimacy with life that is possible when you gain a personal understanding of emptiness is described in Chapter 12. With an ability to touch the ground of your true nature, your sense of inadequacy and separateness can dissolve. Then, when you engage with people, you don't have to use them to satisfy your deepest spiritual longing. It becomes okay if you never get an intimate partner, even if you'd still like one. If you do enter into a romantic partnership, you can do so with more respect and freedom, because you don't need the person to satisfy your fundamental needs.

If you have an intimate partnership that's dissatisfying, you might consider how your partner doesn't owe you anything, as discussed earlier. For example, your partner doesn't owe it to you to sit down right now and discuss your relationship problems at length, no matter what you might think. Even if you try to politely request that certain issues be dealt with but don't insist on the time and place, your partner doesn't owe it to you to meet your need. However, if you simply express that you feel worried and concerned, the ball is in your partner's court. If she doesn't respond at all, maybe she's defensive, or doesn't know what to say.

The important thing is that you try to pay as much attention to what's going on as possible, and avoid leaping to conclusions. The ability you have cultivated in zazen to allow things to arise and pass away without having to comment on them serves you well here. Give your partner as much space as you can to respond, and keep your eye out for a response that may be different than what you're hoping for.

In the example where you want to address relationship issues, your partner may give you a pat on the shoulder later and say she's sorry you are worried. Your habitual response will probably be to say, "That's not good enough!" If you refrain, however, you might notice how this is your partner doing the best she can to reach out at the moment. If you keep in mind that she doesn't owe you anything, you'll be able to appreciate the gesture. Maybe the two of you eventually will find that discussing "relationship issues" for a few minutes at a time while on a walk is the most effective way to deal with them. Sometimes very small shifts in your approach can result in significant changes in your relationship.

If you're too attached to your ideas about what a good intimate relationship looks like, you may fail to see in what way your current partnership is supportive, companionable, intimate, and healthy. Sometimes cultural messages suggest that if you've got the right partner, you will always have passionate sex, share exciting activities, and have long, intimate conversations. The rewards of a long-term relationship are usually more subtle than this, such as a patient willingness to put up with your partner's eccentricities, or a tender kiss whenever your partner gets home. If you can drop your views and look with an open mind, you may find that your partner has been attentive, kind, and loving all along.

Friends

One of the best practice opportunities provided by friendships is the chance to work on suspending judgment. It's easy to get frustrated or judgmental of a friend when you see them making poor choices, or when you notice the way that they are stuck in unhealthy or harmful patterns of behavior. The closer you are to the person, the more likely you are going to be able to recognize these kinds of things.

It can be difficult in such situations to keep the precepts about not dwelling on past mistakes, or not praising self or blaming others, particularly when you talk about your friend. Chances are you'll feel bad about criticizing your friend behind their back, or feel frustrated that they won't take your advice. You care about them, but you find yourself at odds with them because of the mistakes you can see them making.

It's possible to see everyone as being on their own path to greater wisdom and compassion, while recognizing that such paths can be rather convoluted. You can do this by working to realize your own buddha-nature, which is everyone's buddha-nature, because this allows you to see how beings are precious no matter what they're doing. You can also use the powers of patient observation you've cultivated in zazen and mindfulness to watch your friend's life carefully, over time. You will be able to see better how they might struggle for a while, but then learn from their struggle and emerge stronger in the end. You might see how they continue to indulge unhealthy habits but also demonstrate great generosity at times.

In order to be able to see the truth of your friend's life, you will need to give up your personal attachment to the narrative you've created about them. As you manage to make the friendship less about *you*, you can access more patience. You recall that you hope for this person's happiness, no matter how long it takes them to find it.

Co-workers, Customers, and Strangers

You have all kinds of relationships in your life with people you don't choose to be involved with. Some of them you end up liking, some you feel neutral about, and others are incredibly annoying to you. The worst are the people who, for some mysterious reason, push all of your buttons. Their physical posture, communication style, assertiveness (or lack thereof), and personality all combine to make you react to them strongly and negatively. When you encounter them, it's like all of your maturity, wisdom, and spiritual practice fly out the window. You may feel repulsed, judgmental, threatened, humiliated, oppressed, angry, or some combination of these and other powerful reactions.

Applying Zen practice to relationships like these requires patience and humility. It can take a while to make your interactions with a troubling person less stressful and traumatic, and it's possible you will never feel perfectly comfortable around them. Such people are great for reminding you of your limitations and keeping you humble. To work on the relationship, it can be very helpful to avoid blaming the other person or yourself for your reaction. You can consider the true nature of the self: how it's a continually changing flow of causes and conditions, influenced by everything around it. For some reason your karma doesn't mix so well with this person's karma. It's probably distressing for both of you.

 ZEN WISDOM

"Thank Buddha for difficult people, for they can bring us to our emotional knees. They are the bodhisattvas you and I need to see how strong our spiritual practice really is. As long as we are surrounded by Buddhas who insist on being peaceful and calm and wise and skillful all the time, we'll never know what work is left to be done. Give me someone cutting me off on a highway any day."

—Zen Teacher Geri Larkin, from *Tap Dancing in Zen*

After you've given up blame, you can get in the habit of watching your interactions with this troubling person unfold, and ask yourself what you can do to make things less stressful. It usually doesn't help to ask the other person to change, so this will have to involve things you can do. It may be that you need to set a boundary for yourself.

Before interaction with this person triggers you so much that you become enraged, or paralyzed, or whatever it is that happens, you say, "Okay, that's enough." You get away, or end the conversation, or, if you can't get away, you just shut up and try to stop reacting. Perhaps you follow your breath. The important thing is that you are doing this out of compassion for yourself and for the other person, because letting them upset you to the point where you can't function well is not doing them a favor.

When you no longer feel quite so trapped or threatened by this person who you might consider your archenemy, a little space can open up in your relationship. You can experiment with a little act of camaraderie, or generosity, or sympathy. If you do this without an agenda, you won't be disappointed if they don't respond well.

However, if you make it a genuine offering, chances are good the other person will recognize it as free of judgment or manipulation, and they will soften up a little bit. You still may not become best pals, but sometimes relationships can shift radically over time. When you are still strongly triggered by someone, this may not even seem like something you want to happen, but at the very least it's beneficial to shift your relationship enough that you no longer find it difficult to breathe when you see your archenemy walking toward you!

The Least You Need to Know

- All relationships are koans, in that they bring you up against the limit of your understanding and your ability to respond with wisdom and compassion.
- No one can ultimately make you either angry or happy. Lasting internal peace and happiness is an outcome of your spiritual practice and is not the responsibility of others.
- If you can live like no one owes you anything, you will be able to appreciate every gesture of generosity or kindness someone shows you.
- Deep down, everyone is just like you: trying to seek happiness and avoid suffering. Sometimes people do that in crazy ways, but it's still true.
- Relationships give you a chance to let go of attachments, practice mindfulness, and work on changing problematic habits. They're also great for keeping you humble.

Dealing with Challenges Zen-Style

Having developed a Zen practice is especially helpful when you are faced with challenges like busyness, worry, betrayal, criticism, and powerful negative emotions like anger. When things are going well, you may not feel so motivated to meditate, practice mindfulness, and study. However, when you are able to bring your Zen practice to bear a few times in these kinds of difficult situations, your motivation to maintain your practice will probably increase.

Having Zen tools at your disposal can radically alter the way you respond to challenges, letting you maintain some centeredness and grace while you decide on the best course of action. Zen could mean the difference between suffering stress-related health issues and learning to dance with the demands of your life. It could mean the difference between being unable to trust because of a past betrayal, and the ability to open up to intimacy again.

In This Chapter

- Creating space in all the busyness
- Learning to let go of worry
- Working with anger, hatred, fear, and jealousy
- Healing after betrayal
- Strength in the face of criticism

Busyness

You are probably busy, at least at certain times in your life. Chances are, you occasionally manage to be busy and still feel like you maintain your sense of equilibrium and efficiency. When things are like this, you feel capable and even energized by all of your activities. At other times, however, it's like you lose your stride. Stuff starts falling through the cracks; you start forgetting things, getting irritable, feeling overwhelmed, and longing for things to slow down. It can seem nearly impossible to practice Zen when you feel extremely busy. When are you going to find time to meditate? How can you maintain any kind of mindfulness when you're trying to juggle a dozen different responsibilities at once, and face constant interruptions?

The Effects of Busyness

To practice Zen while you're busy, you start where Zen practice always starts: noticing and acknowledging reality. Part of the reality is that Zen is no magical remedy for being overcommitted. The more work you have to do, and the greater the number of responsibilities you have, the more difficult it can be to maintain perspective and inner stillness.

This doesn't mean you *shouldn't* be busy, it just means you need to realize that when you choose to commit to lots of activity in your life, you're taking on a significant challenge from a Zen perspective. Generally speaking, the more still you are (think hours and hours of zazen in a retreat), the easier it is to let the mind settle, see clearly, and transcend self-concern. The more you have going on, the greater the chances that you will get pulled into habits of body, speech, and mind before you can notice what's going on.

> **POTENTIAL PITFALL**
>
> Unless you stop and sit zazen, you may not even realize how busy you are, or how much you feel trapped in a sense of imperative. As you go about your many daily activities, you are probably wrapped up in them, thinking constantly about how exciting, important, or necessary they are. In a certain sense you are right, but sometimes when you put everything down and sit still you can feel a little like a hamster that has just gotten off an exercise wheel. You realize you have been convinced that all the activity was getting you somewhere, but ultimately there is nowhere else to go besides right here and now.

Part of what you're trying to do in zazen, mindfulness, and karma work is to notice space—the space between your thoughts, between stimulus and response, and between impulse and action. (See Chapter 7 on karma work.) In a sense, this *space* is actually *time*, so it follows that the faster the pace of your life, the more difficult it will be to perceive the space, and therefore the more challenging it will be to take advantage of it. You take advantage of space by pausing before you're caught by habit energy and then choosing to make a healthier, non-habitual choice, like taking a few breaths and letting go of anger before responding. When it seems like all the space has disappeared from your life—pretty much the definition of busyness—your options will be limited.

Creating More Space

So how can you create more space in your life when you're really busy? The most obvious thing is to let go of some of your activities. Sometimes your schedule may be full from dawn to dusk with work you're deeply committed to, such as dedication to a career you love, taking care of your family, or contributing to a worthy cause. You may be unwilling to give up any of these activities, and that's okay. You can recognize that you're sacrificing some of your equanimity in the interest of serving others (although if you sacrifice too much you won't be of much help to them).

Alternatively, you may take stock of the things you're committed to and realize something has to go. What should it be? Look at those things you feel less than inspired about, but that you think you *have* to do. Question whether you actually have to do them, or whether there is actually some attachment at work. It may be that you've formed the idea, "I am someone who ..." and the contribution the activity makes to your self-concept has become more important than the activity itself. The extra hours at the gym, the noble service to the neighborhood association, or the preparations for the elaborate dinner party may be things you can let go of, and the resulting space in your life may more than make up for the loss of whatever these endeavors added to your life.

Assuming you do *not* want to give up any of your activities, how can Zen practice help with your busyness? There are several Zen tools you can use to incorporate more awareness—and therefore more awareness of space—into your day. First, try to sit zazen as often and as much as you can. Sit five minutes a day at least (you rarely have a good excuse for not doing at least five minutes). Just putting everything down for a short time can affect your mind-state for the rest of the day. As described in Chapter 3, there are various things you can do to support making zazen a regular habit.

Second, keep working on bringing more mindfulness into your everyday life, even if it's hard. Return to the sensations of your hands, or your breath. There are all kinds of clever mindfulness tools you can incorporate into your busy day (see Jan Chozen Bay's *How to Train a Wild Elephant: And Other Adventures in Mindfulness* for some great suggestions).

Third, work on the precepts. The precepts are all about interactions with people and situations, so challenges to keeping the precepts arise constantly in the midst of your activity. Keeping them in mind helps you notice when you're starting to lose your equilibrium and may need to slow down, take a few breaths, or remind yourself of your deeper aspirations.

Giving Up Attachments

In addition to these three practices, you can work on giving up the attachments that busyness tends to make you aware of: your attachment to calmness, to control, and to being capable, reliable, responsible, and infallible. Chances are you're also attached to things like being a good housekeeper, a good parent, a good employee, or a good citizen.

As discussed in Chapter 13, you have become attached to something when you have incorporated it into your self-concept, or made it a possession of self. This means that when your attachment is threatened (for example, your house gets dirty), you feel like *you* are threatened at a very fundamental level. This is why busyness can feel so overwhelming; it's not just about potentially losing some control or doing a poor job at some of your activities, it's about *who you are*.

 ZEN WISDOM

"We describe our activity as either 'busy' or 'not busy,' either productively working or taking a blissful break from working. But actually it is possible to experience both 'busy' and 'not busy' simultaneously, to reach beyond the labels and connect with our work in a way that is deeply satisfying."

–Zen Teacher Darlene Cohen (1942-2011), in *The One Who Is Not Busy: Connecting with Work in a Deeply Satisfying Way*

It can be difficult, but if you can detach yourself from your responsibilities just a little bit (see Chapter 13), you can gain some of that space you're looking for in your life. Letting go of attachment doesn't mean you don't care about taking care of your responsibilities, it just takes *you* out of the equation. You can still do your very best to complete your projects, take care of your family, and keep your life in order, but you engage these activities with the *hope* that you will do a good job, not out of a sense of imperative: "I *must* do this, or else …."

The "or else" that you tend to carry around with you is not something you often examine, but ultimately it's, "Or else I, as I conceive of myself, will cease to exist." This may sound dramatic, but that's really what you're thinking when busyness threatens to paralyze you. The good thing is, even if you fail at your goals, who you really are won't cease to exist. If you can bring this fact to mind when you're faced with lots of activity, it can help a great deal.

Worry

Worry can be one of the most challenging things to deal with in Zen practice because you think you *have* to worry. When circumstances are difficult—let's say you're short of money, or unemployed, or facing relationship problems, or experiencing health issues—you have to *do* something. You have choices to make. Life demands a response, and no response is going to be easy, simple, or guaranteed to give positive results.

Maybe you can't even think of a good response (you seem to have no viable options), or the situation is not one you are even invited to respond to (it involves other people, or it's entirely outside of your control). This leaves you in a stressful, in-between place of anticipating what terrible things might happen in the future and not knowing how to live your life right now.

Zen practice is not going to give you miraculous solutions to your practical problems, and it's not going to make it you don't care about what happens. After all, you *should* care about your life. What Zen practice *can* help you with is using your mind in a more effective way. You will probably admit that worrying doesn't help. Carefully considering your problem and options helps, but worrying is a stressful, generally fruitless process. You think about the same things over and over. The possibilities for action all seem equally difficult, risky, or distressing, so it seems impossible to make a decision about anything.

It isn't surprising that the origin of the word "worry" is an old German word meaning "to strangle," because when you're worried it does indeed feel like your life is being constricted and you can't breathe easily. This sense of constriction impedes your ability to think clearly, so your worrying usually doesn't do much good. You probably recognize this, which is why you're likely to say, "I wish I could stop worrying." Before Zen practice such a wish may seem impossible to fulfill, but with some time and effort in practice you can actually make the choice to set aside your worry—or, at least, observe it in a way that lets you feel some distance from it.

 ZEN WISDOM

"When we sit, we do not try to become calm or peaceful or to quiet the mind, but rather, we practice staying with and amid whatever feelings arise .... Following the breath and labeling thoughts builds a stable internal 'observer' who is not buffeted by conflicting emotions or swept away by the flow of association or rumination. A meditator becomes increasingly able to interrupt repetitive or obsessive trains of thought and sit with the anxiety or bodily tension that ordinarily accompanies such thinking in an inner, wordless silence .... Zen practice is a *structured, relational context for eliciting, tolerating, and working through one's patterns of affective experience,* including affects that have been previously repressed or dissociated."

—Zen Teacher Barry Magid, from *Ordinary Mind: Exploring the Common Ground of Zen and Psychoanalysis*

To work with worry and anxiety Zen-style, you first need to be willing to be present with what you're feeling. This is done with meditation and mindfulness. However, it's important to remember that you aren't turning the power of your attention to the *content* of your worries (the problems, possibilities, pros and cons), because that's just more worrying.

Instead, you turn your attention to the experience of worrying itself. You notice the sense of constriction, tension, or fear. You notice the train of thought your mind is on. You notice how you return over and over to the same concerns. You observe, "I am feeling very anxious about _____. I am afraid I'll never find a solution, or I'm afraid of what might happen." At the same time, you notice your breath, and the sounds you're hearing, and the rumble in your stomach because you're hungry. You might even notice some of the pleasant and supportive parts of your life, which were probably invisible to you when you were enveloped in worry.

By turning your attention to your direct experience, you are bringing your mind back to the present, which is actually reality. You're much better equipped to deal with reality than you are with theoretical possibilities: what *might* happen, what *could* happen, or which of your many options might lead to the best outcome. Even if your problems are very serious and complex, you can only deal with them one moment at a time. What are you going to do right now?

Presumably, knowing that worrying doesn't help, you're going to do something to break yourself out of the worry. This will leave you in a better place to make decisions, and also give you some relief from a stressful, unpleasant state. This relief may take some time, and when things get difficult you may need to practice returning to the present over and over in order to break the cycle of worry.

 CONSIDER THIS

Zen practice creates a positive feedback loop that encourages more Zen practice. In the case of worry, it may be difficult to set it aside even though you *know* it isn't helping, but if you can manage to do it even for a moment, you will receive just a little bit of positive feedback. With repeated efforts, eventually you will become more willing and able to set aside your worry for a time. This is because you get familiar with how doing so actually allows you to settle down and deal with things more wisely and efficiently.

One other thing that can be useful when you're worried is to reconcile yourself to the possibility of the worst outcome you can imagine. This doesn't mean you stop taking care of your life and just allow this worst possible outcome to happen! This is simply a mind game you can play with yourself to examine what is at the base of your fears. Sometimes you realize the worst possible outcome would not be nearly as bad you might have thought, or that some of your fears are actually relatively easy to let go of.

For example, sometimes what you fear most is what people would think of you if such-and-such happened. If you hold a fear like that up next to a more legitimate fear—like fear of illness, loss, death—it can seem pretty insignificant. You may also recognize that if the worst happened, people would come to your aid.

Sometimes the most difficult place to be is where the worst hasn't happened, but it might. You can't yet avail yourself of the support that often comes from friends, family, and social services when you hit rock bottom, but you can spend your time worrying that such support won't be there when you need it. Sometimes exploring your fears can help you set a few of them aside, to make your burden lighter.

Afflictive Emotions

The classic afflictive emotions are anger, hatred, fear, jealousy, and paranoia, and they're marked by being self-perpetuating. They're generally very strong and painful to experience, but at the same time they're intoxicating and lead you to believe they're entirely justified and require even more energy and attention than you are already giving them. They're all triggered by a sense that you—or your attachments—are under some kind of threat. You end up taking the emotions and their associated thoughts as *proof* that you are, indeed, in some kind of danger. When you're caught up in them, it seems impossible that they could be arising based on a misperception or a misunderstanding.

In contrast, nonafflictive emotions are not considered a problem in Zen, unless you become attached to them (see Chapter 13). Painful emotions like grief, sadness, and disappointment can be powerful but are generally not intoxicating, self-perpetuating, and destructive the way afflictive emotions are. They tend to have a more wholesome, purifying feel to them—like they're a natural process, and you're learning something from them. Such emotions generally have a period when they're strong, and then they change or fade. They do not demand that you justify or feed them. Afflictive emotions, on the other hand, feel like they have a life of their own, and pursue a strong agenda to keep on living.

Powerful and Compelling

I once had an experience with fear that illustrates the power of afflictive emotions. I was camping in the wilderness all by myself, and in the middle of the night, I heard a rustling in the bushes. Fear immediately coursed through my entire body like a chemical (which it probably was). I was instantly on complete alert, tense and ready. What was in the bushes? If it was just a mouse (they can be quite loud in the woods), why was I so scared?

Surely this kind of response meant there was really something threatening there. To just shrug, close my eyes, and go back to sleep seemed ridiculous, because then I would be deliberately ignoring the man in the bushes who was waiting to attack me. This went on and on, to the point that I wasn't even sure if I was hearing any more noises or not. Eventually I was able to settle down and sleep, but because I was familiar with Zen practice I watched the whole process with a sense of curiosity. It had clearly just been a mouse or a falling branch in the bushes, but my mind had managed to create an elaborate, intense, scary scenario that seemed quite real to me.

Afflictive emotions feel terrible, but they're very hard to let go. When you feel threatened, to let go of these powerful reactions can seem like dismantling your natural defense system. Surely, if you let go of your anger, hatred, fear, jealousy, or paranoia, you'll make yourself vulnerable to being attacked or taken advantage of!

While the afflictive emotions are in control, you can't see beyond them. You can't see how they're negatively affecting your health and your ability to see clearly. You can't see how they're giving you tunnel vision, making you obsessed with self-concern, and causing you to alienate yourself from others. Instead, you feed the afflictive emotion with your energy and attention, and get pulled further and further into what seems like a threatening reality but is in fact only a very skewed view of your situation.

POTENTIAL PITFALL

You may have seen the bumper sticker, "Don't believe everything you think." That pretty much sums it up, especially when afflictive emotions are involved. You may be used to deciding whether something is true based on a sense of deep emotional conviction that it is true. This is an unwise method of discerning truth when you're under the influence of an afflictive emotion, because this emotional conviction can sometimes be completely and utterly baseless.

Not Helpful

At some time in your life, you, or something you are attached to, may indeed be threatened, but your afflictive emotional response to such threats is not helpful. To put it bluntly, afflictive emotions make you a little crazy. For example, someone at work may be conspiring to get you fired. What you need is to be able to respond as skillfully as you can—perhaps by having a calm, professional talk with your boss.

The last thing that will help is falling into a paranoid rage and creating a story about your opponent being evil incarnate. Besides, there's a possibility you're misunderstanding the situation, or perhaps your opponent is a complex person who has also shown generosity to others and has made lots of friends. Indulging your anger may end up getting you fired after all.

In another example, suppose you suspect your partner may be cheating on you. Jealousy in particular is an afflictive emotion that can lead you to create a mountain out of a molehill, or even make you believe there is a mountain where there's nothing at all. When you speak and act out of jealousy, you're suspicious, self-centered, irrational, and liable to destroy the very relationship you're concerned about. Even if you're right and there is a problem, your jealousy is probably going to cause you to make much more of a mess of the situation than necessary.

Getting Free of Affliction

So if you admit afflictive emotions aren't helpful and you want to let them go, how can you do it? It's not going to be very effective to just tell yourself you shouldn't be angry, or scared, or jealous. Afflictive emotions aren't rational, and they will make very good arguments for themselves!

The good thing is, the moment you conceive of the idea that you would like to let an afflictive emotion go, you have already started to free yourself from its grasp. Just the intention to let go recognizes that your current view of reality may not be entirely accurate or complete. The simple desire to be more clearheaded acknowledges that you are experiencing a particular emotional and mental state that does not reflect the truth of reality in some absolute sense. At this point, describing to yourself what is going on can be helpful, such as saying, "I am feeling very fearful and paranoid right now."

As mentioned earlier, afflictive emotions can seem like they have a life of their own, and it can be useful to imagine that they do—that they are a force from the outside that has come to afflict you, and that the sooner they leave, the better off you will be. Of course, you can't get rid of them by denying or suppressing them, and the process may take a while. Even when you've recognized how much harm afflictive emotions cause, it's not good to just try to kill them. Any kind of violence—including inner violence—just causes more problems.

You want to approach the emotion with patience and compassion, but you can still identify the afflictive emotion as being like a physical sickness that you want to overcome for the sake of your own well-being. This way you don't reject or deny reality, but you can still make a wise choice about what will be the most beneficial thing to do, for everyone concerned. You can say, "Oh, there you are again, anger. I know you want me to believe everything you say and take your side, but last time I did that things didn't work out so well. I hope you move along."

Once you've fully acknowledged the afflictive emotion, you can do something that you know will defuse it, or at least distract you from it. For example, through practice you can notice that certain activities such as taking a walk, concentrating on your breath, sitting zazen, or even reading a mystery novel will decrease the intensity of your anger.

CONSIDER THIS

There is an ancient Buddhist image that can be useful when dealing with difficult thoughts and emotions. According to Buddhist mythology, a demon named Mara came and tried to disturb Siddhartha Gautama as he sat on his meditation seat, just about to achieve enlightenment. Mara wanted the future Buddha to give up, so Mara sent all kinds of challenges to the meditating Siddhartha, including the appearance of weapons flying at him, temptations of power and sensuality, and encouragement to self-doubt. Siddhartha was able to sit still through all of these challenges by recognizing them as simply the work of Mara, as opposed to believing any of them were inherently real.

The critical thing is this: *if you don't feed them with your attention, afflictive emotions will go away.* As they go, they may yell a threat over their metaphorical shoulder as they leave, "You'll be sorry you didn't listen to me!" But you won't be sorry. Even if there was a kernel of truth under the story constructed by your anger, hatred, fear, jealousy, or paranoia, you will be able to address any problems much more skillfully after the afflictive emotions have hit the road.

Betrayal

One of the biggest challenges in life can be the experience of betrayal: you trusted someone, and then they hurt you. Betrayal not only triggers the afflictive emotions discussed in the previous section, it messes with your sense of self and your ability to trust. You can be betrayed by anyone you have trusted, including your parents, siblings, friends, lovers, co-workers, or neighbors. Generally, the more intimate you were with the person who hurt you—the more you loved and trusted them, or the more involved they were (or are) with your life—the worse the betrayal is going to feel. The other person may not even see their actions as having been a betrayal, but that doesn't much affect how deeply hurt you are.

Impatience to Get Over It

Sometimes when you're trying to be mature, well-adjusted, self-sufficient, or a good spiritual practitioner, you will try to get over your sense of betrayal in ways that are not effective or helpful. You try to "just let it go," or to "forgive and forget." Naturally, you'd like the hurt to be over. You'd like to get on with your life, and to take back the piece of yourself that you entrusted to someone, only to have it treated with disrespect, callousness, or even violence.

You try to rally your determination and self-esteem, and you deny that this person really managed to hurt you. But despite all your efforts, there remains an injury that feels sore and tender (or worse). There is still a part of you that tenses up in fear or anger when you recall how you were taken advantage of. And completely relaxing—trusting that your current choices and relationships are good ones, and you don't have to worry constantly about being betrayed again—can be very difficult.

> **POTENTIAL PITFALL**
>
> People quite often neglect the emotional work they need to do on themselves because they want to be able to answer the question, "How are you?" with, "I'm great!" Being happy and well-adjusted can become a matter of pride, while feeling like an emotional wreck can seem like a sign of weakness or failure. Because of this, you may refuse to admit to yourself that you have an emotional wound that needs attention, and the wound may fester. When this is the case, try to let go of ideas of success and failure, and just do what needs to be done. Doing *that* is a reason for pride.

You can't be too impatient to be "over it." While it's natural to want to feel better, some of your desire to get over a betrayal arises from your attachments, such as the need to be someone who is strong and self-reliant, the idea that you're too smart to be taken advantage of, or having others see you as a cheerful, capable person (or whatever your particular attachment is).

As discussed in Chapter 13, when you attach to something you make it into an aspect of self. So when your attachments are threatened, it can seem like your very existence is threatened, too. It's not that you shouldn't want to be strong, self-reliant, or cheerful, but when you *have to be* these things or else your whole sense of self feels like it's coming apart, you are attached.

Letting go of attachments can be tough, but doing so can be a great relief. Especially if you are trying to recover from a betrayal, you might as well let go of the idea that you should have been impervious to injury. Holding on to that idea will just get in the way.

Opening Your Heart Again

There's no way to truly get past your sense of betrayal without fully acknowledging the injury you experienced and giving that injury some care and time to heal. Delving into your emotions and memories may seem like a daunting task that will end up being painful, endless, and possibly fruitless, but the Zen view is that the truth is always liberating.

Depending on who you are, Zen tools may or may not be the best ones for exploring and processing emotions (see Chapter 20 on mental health care; you may want to avail yourself of some professional counseling). However, your Zen practice can help you face discomfort and build your faith that working on yourself will eventually result in greater understanding and healing. This part of the process may take a while, and to some extent you may never "get over it" to the point that you can forget about your experience of betrayal, or feel complete equanimity about the fact that it occurred.

As you continue to live your life, it may help to reframe the story of betrayal you are carrying, and Zen practice can give you the flexibility of mind to be able to do it. The classic story may go something like this: "I was foolish or weak, and ended up trusting or depending on someone who took advantage of that trust and hurt me. I should have recognized the person as untrustworthy to begin with, or I should have seen the betrayal coming, or I shouldn't have depended on someone the way I did."

If this is the story you are telling yourself, you may find yourself unwilling to trust or depend on anyone. You may feel lots of jealousy and suspicion when you do dare to trust, or you may put people through a rigorous vetting process to determine whether they should be trusted. This approach will probably compromise the intimacy of your relationships and be unsatisfying.

Instead, you might rewrite the story of betrayal like this: "I had the courage, generosity, and humility to trust or depend on someone. Because of their own suffering and limitations, they took advantage of my openheartedness and hurt me. I have suffered an injury that makes me want to protect myself, but I aspire to open my heart again, even if there's a possibility I will be betrayed again. I want my relationships to be based on openness, not on defensiveness and suspicion."

 ZEN WISDOM

"This moment is alive and whole. The moment I begin to defend and protect my-self and withdraw, what becomes of trust? Can one see? 'Trusting' is slipping again into imagination and hope for security, away from the aliveness of simply being there with what is, without any sense of separateness .... As long as the sense of self dominates and distorts perception and reaction it precludes direct awareness. There is the demand for trust, but at the same time, the utter inability to trust. The need for and the inability to trust both spring out of the isolation of self."

—Zen Teacher Toni Packer, from *The Work of This Moment*

When you get to know your own mind, body, and heart really well through Zen practice, it becomes possible to change your thinking in the way described above. The change isn't instantaneous, but you become able to "try on" different ways of thinking and see how they feel, even if it's just for a moment, because you know how to loosen your attachment to a certain version of events.

When you try thinking of your betrayal as evidence of someone else's suffering and limitations, rather than as a result of you letting your guard down, you'll probably feel some relief. This relief occurs because this version of the story is in accord with the deeper truths of human experience. Inherent in trust is the possibility that it can be betrayed; if it couldn't be, there would be no value in trust.

The truth is you *have* to trust in order to live your life fully, and as long as you are alive you will be at risk of being hurt. Better that it should be because you opened your heart than because you closed it down. No amount of caution, defensiveness, or suspicion can completely protect you, but you can summon the courage to move on because you want to experience intimacy and love. Most people will eventually disappoint you in some way, but they won't betray you.

Being Misunderstood or Criticized

If you are sensitive to criticism, people and events can easily distress and derail you. People's negative feedback or lack of support can make your confidence flag, or even deflate it like a popped balloon. You may find it difficult to maintain your enthusiasm for ideas, choices, or projects if there are others who do not feel the same enthusiasm. Critical comments—whether deliberate and harsh, or offhand and subtle—can leave you wallowing in self-doubt for days or weeks. It can feel as if your sense of self is in the hands of other people, leaving you subject to their whims.

With Zen's emphasis on letting go of self-concern, it may not be obvious how Zen practice can help with sensitivity to the opinions of others. In fact, applied incorrectly, Zen can even worsen your problem by suggesting that there's no real *you* to get in touch with when you're trying to summon confidence. When you hear that the way you really exist is as a causal flow, mutually dependent with everything around you, how can you get your bearings and find out what is true for you?

People who do not suffer from self-doubt generally have a very strong sense of who they are, what they are good at, what they believe, and what their limitations are. Isn't all of this just self-attachment, or stories they are making up about themselves that have no inherent, enduring reality? When there's really only this moment, how do you make decisions?

Ironically, if you are overly sensitive to criticism, you have an advantage in Zen because you already have some insight into no-self. You are very familiar with how quickly your sense of self can change, and how it's affected by things around you. You are right: any story you tell yourself about what you are good at, or about how your idea is brilliant, or about how you expressed yourself clearly at a meeting is just a story with no inherent reality to it. It's all dependent on your point of view, in a shifting landscape of constant change. There is actually no absolute right or wrong, good or bad. No matter whose approval you obtain, there will always be an arbitrary aspect to your choices and what you believe.

The challenge for you is to let go of the attachment to *being right* and the attachment to *being seen as being right*. Alternatively, it may make more sense to you to think of giving up your fear of being wrong (and seen as wrong, or bad, or weak, or stupid, or …). Those confident people aren't confident because, unlike you, they have managed to find the right way to be; they're confident because they have decided to be. They have stepped up to offer what they can, and they are determined to be their own advocates.

This option is also open to you. You have as much right as anyone to step up and say your piece, offer your ideas, and make your choices. Inevitably some of what you offer is not going to be well received. You may even look back on your actions and realize you made a mistake, or made a fool of yourself, or revealed your limitations. But who cares? You learn from it and move on.

Offering yourself in a confident way is an act of courage, and a way of embracing emptiness. Remember, it's not that Zen says the world is empty and therefore it's meaningless. Zen says everything is empty of inherent, enduring self-nature, and therefore everything is full of potential.

It may help to think of life less as being a test that you can pass or fail, and more as being a dance. When you dance, you are going to have a particular style. You may not present the most beautiful, most graceful, or most athletic dance, but that's not the point. If you don't dance, you've missed out. You haven't played your part and offered what you have to offer. Amazingly, everyone has something to offer. Despite your imperfections, someone is going to be grateful for your gifts.

Holding yourself back, or beating yourself up when someone criticizes or misunderstands you, is just as much about self-concern as asserting yourself with arrogance. When you are able to transcend self-concern (the goal of Zen), you try to do your very best and then let go. You can't control the reactions of others, or all of the results of your actions. When you realize your efforts have fallen short or been misinterpreted, you can apologize or try to change the way you go about things without it having anything to do with who you really are.

The Least You Need to Know

- Zazen and mindfulness take time, but adding them to your busy schedule makes more space around everything. The space can help you feel less stressed and more efficient, so the time spent is worth it.

- Worry doesn't help, no matter how serious your situation. You can gain some freedom from its grasp by fully acknowledging it, and then turning your attention from the future back to the present moment.

- Afflictive emotions like anger, fear, and jealousy are painful, destructive, intoxicating, and self-perpetuating. There are two keys to maintaining some clarity despite feeling afflictive emotions: recognizing their nature, and questioning what they tell you to believe.

- It's natural to feel hurt after betrayal, and you may need to do some healing work. Eventually, you can trust again if you can make trust an offering that doesn't demand guarantees (which are impossible to make, in any case).

- Criticism and being misunderstood become easier to bear when you learn to offer what you have to give without attaching what you offer to your sense of self.

Daily Opportunities for Zen Practice

It's important to test and manifest your Zen practice and understanding in your life. Otherwise, what's the point? However, that's not the only reason to pay attention to your daily activities and relationships. They are actually wonderful opportunities for practice in and of themselves.

There are a number of examples in this chapter of how to make your daily life into Zen practice. Work and dealing with money give you the chance to notice your self-centeredness and attachments, practice mindfulness, and work on habits. Trying to live authentically and peacefully in a culture that encourages materialism, intoxication, and distraction presents you with important spiritual questions.

Practicing Zen in a culture where most people do not gives you the chance to closely examine your own motivations for practice and learn how to be authentic without being defensive. Finding a way to be mindful while surrounded by modern technology can stretch your definitions of awareness. Finally, it's an art to learn how to deeply accept and appreciate your life just as it is, and yet work to fulfill your dreams.

In This Chapter

- Making your work into generosity practice
- Fighting the temptation of materialism
- Choosing stillness over distraction (sometimes)
- Dealing with reactions to your Zen practice
- Ways to let go of judging the behavior of others

Your Work as Your Gift to the World

It may be difficult to see your work as your gift to the world. Generally speaking, work is what you *have* to do, or what you get paid to do. It often doesn't feel much like a gift, or something you are cheerfully and willingly offering. Your work may or may not seem to you like something that's worth being called a "gift." Perhaps you work as a clerk, a bureaucrat, or at manual labor, or just do your job to pay the bills. Isn't work that qualifies as a gift something like researching a cure for cancer, or creating beautiful things as a successful artist? If you find any joy in your work at all, though, it's probably because you are able to do it with a sense of generosity.

A Story of Two Waitresses

I had an experience that forever afterward defined, for me, the way any kind of work can either be a wonderful gift or a source of misery. I was staying at a motel with a restaurant attached, and the first morning I was there, I went to the restaurant for breakfast. The waitress serving that day may have been the owner, because she seemed to take extra special care of the customers. She cheerfully greeted them as they came in, as if she was very happy they were there. She was attentive to their needs, but also seemed comfortable and competent in her work, so she didn't need to hover or ask too many questions.

She offered just enough personable warmth to make you feel like you had made a personal connection with her, but didn't cling or talk too long in a way that made you feel like you were serving her social needs. The clear delight she was taking in her work filled the whole restaurant with a positive energy, and I was clearly not the only person affected. I left the restaurant with a cheerfulness that lasted for hours, and I looked forward to my return for breakfast the next day.

On the second day I went to the restaurant, there was a different waitress serving. I probably would not have remembered the first waitress so long if this one hadn't been her polar opposite in terms of how she dealt with her work. I don't mean to be critical—it might have been a very difficult day for this second waitress. Still, there was a dramatic difference in the way she went about *exactly the same work* the woman had been doing the previous day.

This second waitress was clearly unhappy in her job. Her movements suggested the work was beneath her, an annoying necessity that she would rather get through as quickly as possible. She sighed and reacted with exasperation and irritation to the challenges and setbacks of the restaurant, such as a customer who wanted some cream, or a new customer arriving while she was busy with something else. You got the idea that she was doing you a favor even dealing with you. Then, largely because of her carelessness and lack of mindfulness, some things started happening that really *were* challenging—like dropped trays and forgotten orders. The whole atmosphere in the restaurant was one of stress and negativity.

As far as I could see, the *only* difference between the first and second waitresses was their attitude. The first waitress saw her job as an opportunity to offer gifts to people—a warm smile, a good meal, consideration, respect, and appreciation. The second waitress did not see her work that way, and therefore it just seemed like an annoyance and a burden.

Shifting Your Attitude

When you're working with bitterness, boredom, or carelessness, chances are you are not enjoying your work or you think it's unimportant. There is something you'd rather be doing. Even if you're lucky enough to have a job you love, there are going to be parts of it that are a drag, or other tasks in your life that you'd rather not have to do.

When you're doing something you think is worthwhile, you have that happy spirit of generosity. When you're doing something you don't feel that way about, you probably act like the second waitress. You probably get annoyed easily and find it difficult to be mindful. You probably try to hurry through the task and end up making mistakes. The people around you most likely taste your stress rather than your generosity.

When you're feeling like the second waitress, it's not easy to instantly shift your attitude. Like everything else in practice, it takes time and energy to work on your mind and habits. However, it's helpful to realize that cultivating a spirit of generosity in your work is not about talking yourself into how your job makes an important contribution to the world. Maybe it does, but that's not the point. The point is not *what* you do, it's *how* you do it. Whether you're filing papers, providing childcare, or driving a bus, it's possible to do your work with wholehearted joy, and it's possible to do it with bitterness and carelessness.

What if, as suggested in Chapter 5 on mindfulness, you didn't regard anything as beneath your attention? What if your conscious evaluation of the worthiness or pleasantness of your work was irrelevant to whether you did it with care and mindfulness? What if your own opinions didn't matter much to you, much less the opinions of others? If these conditions were true, you would do each task in front of you in a wholehearted way that would naturally transform it into an act of generosity. After all, work, by definition, is activity that brings about some kind of desirable product or effect. So no matter what you're doing, no matter how small or mundane, it can be offered as a gift to the world.

To gradually change the way you approach work, it helps to practice mindfulness while doing simple tasks like washing the dishes, cleaning the house, or gardening. As you try to keep your attention on the task and on your physical experience of doing it, you start to taste the rewards of just being present with your life, no matter what is going on. Then you start to notice the beauty in simple things, and the positive effects of your small or large gifts to the world. You get in the habit of paying attention to your work—even when it isn't work you like, or isn't work that seems important.

Just as you do in any other Zen practice, you repeatedly turn your mind back to the present. In doing so, you have to let go of anticipating the future (when the task will be over and you can get back to what you like doing) and let go of ideas (comparisons, judgments, attachments). Wholeheartedness in your work is about simplicity of spirit rather than maintaining some kind of idea about the value of your effort.

 ZEN WISDOM

"By throwing our life force into our work, every situation literally comes to life and that in turn generates clarity and vividness. When the situation is full of life, we become more alive as a result. This means, then, that our life force has breathed a vividness into the situation. I feel very deeply that each of us must look clearly at this point for ourselves and then practice diligently with both our bodies and minds."

—Kosho Uchiyama Roshi (1912-1998), in *From the Zen Kitchen to Enlightenment: Refining Your Life*

The Zen Approach to Work

There is a strong tradition of honoring work in Zen. The twelfth-century Zen master Dogen wrote all kinds of profound spiritual treatises, but one of his most famous essays describes the daily work of the monastery cook. In the *Tenzokyokun*, Dogen lists all of the mundane tasks the cook needs to take care of each day, including washing the rice, storing the pots and pans, and planning how much food to make by recalling how many monks are currently practicing at the monastery.

Then Dogen talks about the spirit in which all of these tasks need to be done. The cook must plan and prepare the food with a spirit of joy and magnanimity, and with the mind of a parent. According to the translation of the *Tenzokyokun* by Thomas Wright (in Uchiyama Roshi's *From the Zen Kitchen to Enlightenment*), a joyful spirit is "one of gratefulness and buoyancy"; a magnanimous spirit means being "stable and impartial" and "without prejudice"; a parental attitude means handling everything—"water, rice, or anything else"—with "the affectionate and caring concern of a parent" raising their only child.

These three Zen approaches to work are to be maintained at all times. Dogen advises, "When you prepare the food, never view the ingredients from some commonly held perspective, nor think about them only with your emotions. Maintain an attitude that tries to build great temples from ordinary greens, that expounds the [Buddhist teachings] through the most trivial activity."

So the next time you engage in a task you are inclined to resent having to do, or to dismiss as unimportant, try to let go of the self-centered discrimination. After all, deciding what work you like and what work you don't, or deciding what work is worth your energy and what is not, is all about *you*. For practical, everyday decision making this kind of discrimination may make sense, but as discussed in Chapter 11, it is self-concern that causes most human misery.

Adjusting your attitude toward work is an opportunity to improve your life. Turn your attention to your task—whatever it is—with mindfulness, and reclaim that part of your life from the oblivion of inattention and disinterest. At the same time, your engagement with your task will take on a positive wholeheartedness that will help you enjoy it, do a better job, and make it an act of generosity.

Contentment Instead of Materialism

Zen practice is pretty much the polar opposite of materialism. Materialism is seeking something tangible and outside yourself to decrease your suffering or make you happy. It's not just about acquiring physical possessions. Materialism is the drive to acquire, and by definition, anything you can acquire (that is, anything you are able to obtain and keep) has to be material, or tangible, in some sense. Or, if what is acquired is not directly tangible, such as status or power, there are tangible signs of what has been acquired. Given this definition, it's even possible to be materialistic about spiritual achievements! Zen practice challenges you to cultivate a contentment that runs counter to all the cultural messages that suggest your happiness is dependent on things outside of yourself.

 POTENTIAL PITFALL

> In case you are someone who has been attracted to Zen in part *because* it is anti-materialistic, you may need to be careful not to fall into the trap of judging others. Once you have a sense that there is a deeper source of satisfaction than tangible or external things, it may be frustrating for you to watch people get so attached to their stuff, or so caught up in acquiring things. This is an opportunity for you to practice what Buddhists call *sympathetic joy*. If you sincerely desire other people to be happy, you will feel some satisfaction when they are—regardless of what made them happy.

Happiness Dependent on Conditions

Materialism comes in many forms. You may seek money in order to be able to feel more comfortable and safe. You may seek a romantic partner, a house, a car, a job, status, power, or fame. You may seek more rewarding interpersonal relationships, greater health, a more attractive body, or skills. You may seek particular experiences, such as parties, exciting vacations, or the thrill of a new sound system.

It's entirely possible to acquire and enjoy such things without your efforts being materialistic, but you can identify when materialism is at work in your life when the things you want are attached to "if onlys." For example, if only you were able to move to the country, you would be happy. If only you had a more exciting romantic partner, you would be happy. If only you lost weight, had a job you liked, or were able to travel, you would be happy.

In most industrialized societies, materialism is highly encouraged. The prevailing idea is that your happiness is pretty much entirely dependent on your conditions. Of course, it *is* more challenging to be happy when you don't have safe, clean housing, or don't have enough to eat, or are living in dangerous or unjust circumstances.

Or is it? Most people who have experienced life in wealthy, industrialized countries and then spent time in poorer, developing nations are surprised how much they learn about real happiness in the culture with less material wealth. With more stuff also comes more isolation from other people, and more need to worry about and acquire stuff. (See the section in Chapter 11 on the misery of "I, me, and mine.") This observation is not in any way meant to justify the greed of some people that results in the impoverishment of others, but it is in part why Mother Teresa said "in the West is a different kind of poverty—it is not only a poverty of loneliness but also of spirituality."

Materialism and Zen

It's not that Zen practitioners don't own, enjoy, or seek to acquire anything, it's just that they do their best not to make their happiness contingent on their conditions, or on the acquisition of anything tangible or outside of themselves. It's a tall order, but that's the goal.

As discussed in Chapter 10, according to the Zen view the worst of your suffering (or the main reason for your lack of satisfaction) is your sense of dukkha, or that *things are not as they should be.* True happiness is reached through a cultivation of, acceptance of, and appreciation for your life just as it is. True happiness and peace can never be found in tangible or external objects or experiences, because these things are always subject to change. Even when you acquire exactly what you want, you will feel some anxiety that you will lose it, and eventually you will—and then you will lose your happiness, too. And if you can't obtain what you want, happiness eludes you.

I've explained at length in other places in this book ways to seek happiness through spiritual practice instead of looking for it from outside sources. These include examining the nature of suffering or dissatisfaction (Chapter 10), letting go of self-attachments (Chapter 13), and experiencing the freedom and joy that come from transcending self-concern (Chapter 14). What I want to discuss here is specifically how to cultivate contentment when you are surrounded by lots of temptations to seek happiness outside yourself.

You're constantly being bombarded with messages encouraging materialism. Advertisements try to convince you that the object or experience they're selling will bring an end to your troubles and provide you with great pleasure and satisfaction. There is very little cultural emphasis on seeking happiness within instead of without: people understand that money, a good job, and a harmonious family make you happy, but not many of them are going to understand how your insight into the emptiness of self has made you happy. Perhaps most importantly, the simple availability of so many opportunities and objects invites you to get caught up in them, and begin to rely on them for your happiness.

CONSIDER THIS

Buddhist monks have traditionally divested themselves of all of their money, personal belongings, relationships, and status in order to concentrate on spiritual practice. However, there is also a great tradition of wealthy lay Buddhists enacting their enlightenment by benefitting the people around them with great generosity—generosity that was only possible because they had stuff. From the beginning of Buddhism, lay people donated land, food, clothing, and medicine to support the practice of monks. A number of the bodhisattvas in the Avatamsaka sutra practice by giving people whatever they need, or whatever will make them happy—food, drink, garlands, jewels, chairs, or medicine. So there's more than one way to practice with regard to materialism!

To cultivate a lasting spiritual contentment in the midst of all this stuff, it helps to think of all the stuff flowing freely in and out of your life. You aren't trying to reject the stuff, you are just trying not to rely on it for your true happiness. To wish you didn't live in a materialistic culture is just another way of causing yourself dukkha. Instead, you can try to let all the stuff come and go. When it's here, you enjoy it. When it goes, you're fundamentally okay.

Being able to hold things lightly is the test of whether you are being materialistic or not. If you're dependent on something for your happiness, you will not want to let it go. If you've touched a deeper source of satisfaction, you may be sad to see something go, but its disappearance won't be so devastating to you. (Or your inability to obtain what you want won't be so discouraging.) You can feel deep gratitude and appreciation for the things you have, which also decreases materialism. You can practice generosity, actively testing your materialism by challenging yourself to let go.

Going on a Distraction Diet

Modern life is full of interruptions and distractions. You get used to almost constant stimulation of some kind—conversation, music, television, radio, the internet, smart phones, texts, reading—and days, weeks, months, or even years may go by without a break from them, except while you are sleeping.

Even when you're on a relaxing vacation, chances are there are very few times when you just sit there doing absolutely nothing. You probably engage in enjoyable activities like swimming, eating, or reading, and spend just a few moments between each of these activities gazing with appreciation at a sunset, or closing your eyes in contentment. You may even feel the need to wear earbuds so you can listen to music while doing any activity that isn't stimulating enough by itself, such as driving, walking, working out, waiting in line, or riding the bus.

Not Enough Stillness

There's nothing inherently wrong with doing things you enjoy when you have the chance, but the problem is that for many people, stimulation is not balanced with enough stillness or silence. In fact, stillness and silence may be neglected altogether. I know many people who would be horrified at the thought of sitting silently in meditation for 10 minutes, let alone for hours. It's as if people have become uncomfortable with stillness. They don't know what to do with it, or perhaps they are afraid of what might come up in their minds if they sit still too long.

The prospect of boredom may seem intolerable, but boredom is just a term for a vague sense of dukkha, or dissatisfaction. When you're bored, you have a sense that the good stuff is happening somewhere else. It's the opposite of the simple contentment you are trying to cultivate in Zen.

In some ways, people are right to be apprehensive about having to experience too much silence or stillness. The longer a moment of silence goes on, the more likely you are to wake up to reality, which is just this present moment. Part of that reality may be thoughts and feelings you've been suppressing or avoiding. Part of that reality may be realizing that you're stressed, or lonely, or depressed. Part of that reality may be recognizing how impatient or dissatisfied you are, or realizing how much has been going on in your environment that you've been missing.

Of course, what you wake up to isn't necessarily going to be negative! You may also suddenly notice the flowers blooming on the trees, or that someone nearby needs help opening a door because their arms are full of groceries. However, until you settle into reality, you can't be sure of what you're going to find, so just the possibility that you might find something difficult or painful may be enough to keep you going from distraction to distraction.

Setting Aside Stimulation

The stillness you cultivate in zazen can help increase the silence-to-stimulation ratio in your life, and it certainly helps you realize how distracted you've been, but sitting zazen isn't enough. To create more space in your life—and become more comfortable with stillness and silence—you may also need to go on a distraction diet, setting aside your various sources of stimulation from time to time.

There are many simple ways to do this, without completely renouncing life's little pleasures. You can opt to just eat your breakfast without reading at the same time (and then go ahead and read at other meals). You can drive home from work in silence, instead of turning on the radio. When you take a hike, you can pause for a little longer than you ordinarily would as you take in a beautiful vista. When you wait for the bus, you can try to simply be aware of what's going on around you, and put aside listening to music or looking at your smart phone. When you're on an airline flight, you can wait an additional 10 minutes before opening your book or falling asleep, and just sit there.

CONSIDER THIS

Most of the time during my Zen training as a junior monk, unless I was sitting zazen, I was very busy. The temple schedule runs from dawn until dusk, with very few breaks for you to do your own thing. Despite this, my teachers always emphasized the importance of "fallow time"—time spent doing absolutely nothing useful at all. When they would hear that someone had spent part of their day off sitting on the grass in the sunshine, staring at the clouds, they would say, "Great!" Sometimes even your zazen is not truly still, because you have some kind of agenda. Perhaps only during truly fallow moments will you taste the kind of silence that lets you see reality directly.

It may feel strange at first, to just be sitting or standing there, paying attention to an experience that you might ordinarily think of as being too boring to tolerate all by itself, or as merely being an opportunity to pay attention to something else. You'll probably be surprised as you look around you, to see how few people are consciously present in their bodies. Even if they're engaging some obvious form of distraction, they're caught up in thoughts that are serving the same purpose—to avoid the boredom of the present.

If you can get yourself to face that boredom, you have a great opportunity to work on mindfulness (Chapter 5) and letting go of dukkha (Chapter 10). The reality of your life is always right in front of you, in the silence; if you are avoiding silence, you are avoiding your life. Fortunately, Zen practice can help you cultivate the tools and courage to face the silence and learn not only to be comfortable with it, but to love it and find refuge in it.

Zen in a Non-Zen World

More and more people in the West are identifying themselves as Buddhist, or as Zen practitioners. Still, if you think of yourself as either of these, you will generally find yourself in a tiny minority. On the one hand, it can be challenging to present yourself authentically in the world, not hiding your Zen practice or feeling defensive about it. On the other hand, it can also be challenging to present yourself as a Zen practitioner without compromising your connection with people.

This compromise can be due to people's lack of understanding about what Zen practice is, to your eagerness to share the brilliance of Zen with people who aren't really interested, or to a sense of superiority you may develop because you see Zen as being better than other spiritual paths (or the lack of a spiritual path).

Negative Personal Reactions

If you feel inclined to hide your Zen practice, some of your reasons for keeping practice private may be fears about what the people close to you will think of you, or how they will react. It can be very scary and painful to face the judgments of others, and the closer they are to you, the more this is true.

I had one friend who broke off her relationship with me because I got so involved in Zen. To this day I don't understand why she did so, but sometimes people are attached to an idea of you that doesn't include something like Zen practice. It's hard for them to see you change. It makes things even more complicated if people close to you look down on active religious or spiritual practice, or if they belong to a different religion. Then your Zen practice can seem like a betrayal to them.

If people in your life are inclined to react negatively to your Zen practice, it can take lots of patience and courage to be authentic and not hide it. It may help to keep in mind that this process can take years, and people can get used to just about anything. When others see that you are calmly going about your Zen practice over the course of years, and not cutting off your relationships, or acting crazy, or proselytizing, they will gradually get more comfortable with your unusual choice of spiritual path.

It helps if you refrain from speaking about Zen too much with people who are resistant to your practice, even if you are excited about it or it's becoming a very important part of your life. It helps if you don't get too strict or overzealous about your practice, and go ahead and have a beer with friends even though you've been trying to cut down on intoxicants, or skip meditation practice in order to go on a hike with your partner.

It also helps if you cultivate compassion and patience for people, and recognize that they're acting out their own fears or are just concerned about the relationship they have with you. A teacher of mine once told me to remember that when people ask you about your Zen practice, they rarely actually want to know about Zen. What they are really asking is, "What does your Zen practice mean to our relationship?"

You may feel frustrated or hurt because people close to you are resistant to, judgmental about, or just disinterested in your Zen practice. However, if you can *include* your relationships in your practice, they provide many opportunities (see Chapter 17). As mentioned above, you can work on compassion, patience, and sensitivity to others. You can work on becoming more independent of what other people think of you. You get to examine some of the karma in your relationships that gets triggered by the issue of your Zen practice.

ZEN WISDOM

"If you want to be a Buddhist, when you visit your parents, don't argue with them. If they are Christian and you put down Christianity while talking about how great Buddhism is, you don't understand Buddhism. Instead, keep your mouth shut. Why don't you just be present with your parents in peace and harmony?"

—Dainin Katagiri Roshi (1928–1990), from *You Have to Say Something: Manifesting Zen Insight*

The most important thing is to let go of any ideas about how the people around you *should be reacting*. In essence, holding on to such ideas is saying, "I'm not being supported in my Zen effort to accept my life just as it is, because these people won't act the way I want them to." You can see the contradiction here! It's perfectly natural to *want* the people in your life to be understanding and supportive, but they are the way they are. The rewards of patience can be profound; when a loved one who has long resisted your Zen finally asks about how your meditation retreat went, out of simple, genuine interest, you will probably be filled with gratitude and joy at their gesture.

Cultural Tension

The tension with other people around your Zen practice may be of a more cultural nature, rather than personal. This may be a work culture, a local culture, culture you share in your social group, or the culture of your country. You may be surrounded by people of a different religion who pressure you to share their faith. Your friends may be radical atheists who believe religion is the opiate of the masses, and disparage it or make fun of you for your spiritual practice. In other settings, any kind of spiritual or religious endeavor just seems strange and out of place—especially if you engage in it more than once a week for a couple of hours.

It's important to realize how little most people know about Zen, and the assumptions they generally make. Most of the time it's not helpful to try to correct their misunderstandings, because most of the time they're not actually interested in learning more about Zen, and few people enjoy being told they're wrong about something. Still, there are two major assumptions that people often make, and just keeping them in mind can help you choose ways to act and present your practice that won't further compound misunderstanding.

First, most people cannot conceive of a religion without a deity. Religion is often considered synonymous with belief in a God (or more than one), so people of other religions are generally going to assume you have forsaken their God in favor of a different one. It can help to mention (when the time is right) that Zen does not require any beliefs, and that it does not deal with whether there is a God or not.

It's perfectly fine to believe in God, or even to be actively involved in a theistic religion, and also practice Zen. In fact, many people do just this. If you don't believe in God, the nice thing about

Zen practice is that you can start to understand what people mean by "God." You could say that in Zen, God is the Dharma, or ultimate truth, but it simply isn't personified. In the great tradition of mystics throughout the ages, you can start to see how all spiritual traditions ultimately point toward the same thing: there is more to this world than first meets the eye, or the mind. Zen can actually help you understand and appreciate other religions.

Second, if people understand that there is no God in Zen, they often assume that means you have no motivation to behave morally. Basically, if there are no divinely inspired instructions about what is right and what is wrong, if you're just using your own personal sense of morality, where can you draw any clear boundaries between what people should and shouldn't do? It can give people great relief to know that Zen includes a set of moral precepts (see Chapter 6), and that compassion and generosity are considered essential values in practice.

I have successfully explained the Zen view to Christians before by saying that, through careful observation of the world, it becomes obvious that compassion and interdependence are part of the structure of the universe. That is, in reality we are all connected and interdependent, so we cannot act selfishly without hurting one another, and we cannot hurt someone else without hurting ourselves.

Finally, people who know just a little bit about Buddhism and Zen (say, from television shows), often end up with a stereotype that Zen practice involves a rejection of life. By "life," they mean all the lively parts of your experience, including pleasure, sensuality, emotions, fun, creativity, passion, excitement, humor, opinions, love, and taking risks. Because of this stereotype, people sometimes worry about one or both of two things: one, that you will withdraw from actively enjoying life with them, and two, that you will judge them for continuing to enjoy life.

Now, this stereotype arises from the fact that Zen does indeed ask you to set aside many of your activities and pleasures *for a time* (even if only for a meditation period), in order to examine your relationship to them. The goal is, indeed, to give up your attachment to things (see Chapter 13), so you no longer depend on them for your happiness or peace of mind. But the point of Zen is *not* to reject life, because doing that would only be attachment to your own equanimity, and therefore not enlightenment. Letting people know this is the case can put them more at ease.

You can also look for things you can share with people that will reassure them you are still actively engaged in, and enjoying, your life. Even if your main interest is in understanding emptiness, you can chat with your neighbor about your garden or your dog, in order to let her know that you still live on the same planet.

The Behavior of Others

Another great opportunity for Zen practice is learning to witness the behavior of others without judgment. While you are trying to make changes in your life, the people around you may act in ways that tempt you to give up your aspirations, or make you question the value of what you're trying to do. You may be trying to keep Zen precepts while everyone around you seems to be abusing intoxicants, righteously indulging anger, cheating on their taxes, lying whenever it suits them, or eagerly engaging in gossip—and they have no interest whatsoever in hearing about an alternative approach to life. Or, even as you make a concerted effort to meditate and be more mindful, the people around you may seem perfectly happy to zone out, constantly distract themselves, or dwell in self-centeredness.

From the beginning of Buddhism, practitioners have been encouraged to surround themselves with good spiritual friends, or sangha (Chapter 9). This is so you will have positive social support for your aspirations. Good spiritual friends are people who are working on themselves, taking responsibility for their actions and experience, and supporting you in your efforts to do the same. Even if these friends aren't perfect (and they aren't), their efforts challenge you and show you what is possible.

On the other hand, being around people who don't share your aspirations can be discouraging, or can pull you back into bad habits. You will need to decide for yourself whether a particular relationship is one that you want to maintain, or whether it has outlived its usefulness and it would be better for you to seek out other company.

 POTENTIAL PITFALL

Be very careful about ending any relationships in order to practice Zen; I suggest waiting until you have attained some clarity about your own mind and motivations. Ending relationships so your practice is easier for you can end up being a largely self-centered action that you will later regret. Still, sometimes it may be necessary.

Doing Your Own Practice

Once you have a sufficient social support for your practice, it's time to let go of watching and evaluating the behavior of others. Doing so will only fill you with judgment, a sense of superiority or inferiority, or doubt. For example, perhaps you've heard the Zen teaching that you can't harm others without harming yourself. Instead of exploring how this teaching is true within your own life and experience, you may look around you and wonder why it is that so many people act selfishly and seem to be perfectly happy doing it. Does this disprove the Zen teaching? Does this mean you should give up working so hard to keep the precepts, or seeing the true nature of self so you can transcend self-concern?

If such doubts arise in your mind because of the behavior of others, you need to energetically follow another Zen teaching: *do your own practice*. Basically, you can't know what is going on in other people's minds, experience, or life. You don't know what their motivation is, or what their circumstance might be. The negative consequences of their selfish actions may be something they're unaware of, or hiding from other people. Alternatively, the consequences may happen only after a long period of time, or where you can't observe them.

Trying to understand the workings of karma in your own life is tough enough; trying to figure out how it works in the lives of others will keep your mind going around and around in circles, and will distract you from your practice. The good thing is you don't have to worry about whether Zen teachings apply in the lives of others, or whether Zen practices would be good for them. Once you verify things for yourself, it doesn't matter at all what other people do.

Respecting People's Paths

You may also have experienced significant relief from your suffering through Zen practice, and it pains you to watch people go about making the same mistakes you used to make, ignorant of the ways they're contributing to their own lack of happiness or satisfaction. It can be very difficult to see people you care about suffering, stuck in unhealthy habits of body and mind, unable to let go of anxiety or afflictive emotions, or numbed out to their lives. If you gained insight into how to work with your mind and change your behaviors, you may be very tempted to share your understanding with others. If you've given in to that temptation, you've probably discovered that people generally dismiss what you say, get defensive, or nod and smile but don't actually take your advice.

The readiness and willingness to consider the possibility that you need to make a change in your life is called "the way-seeking mind" in Zen. This mind doesn't arise in people very often, and it usually does so in response to suffering—a trauma, a loss, or when things in your life have gotten unbearable. You finally conclude that continuing the way things are is unacceptable to you, and you feel the determination to find a better way.

It's impossible to predict when and where your way-seeking mind is going to arise, and until it does, you probably aren't going to be very receptive to spiritual teachings and practice of any kind. (Why bother? Things are fine.) In Zen, the way-seeking mind is considered very precious, because it opens the door to practice. Later you may not be suffering so much, but your practice will already have been established.

 CONSIDER THIS

When you develop some ability to settle your mind and see clearly, you will probably gain some insight into what behaviors of body, speech, and mind cause suffering. The thing is, you may gain insight into the behavior of others *before* you gain insight into your own behavior. It's often much harder to see and admit your own attachments, mistakes, and shortcomings. Keep this in mind if you start to feel frustration when observing the behavior of others. Just because you think you see the truth of their situation, it doesn't mean you see the truth of your own.

Recognizing that the way-seeking mind has not arisen in some of the people in your life can help you feel more patient with them, as well as more hopeful. There is an assumption in Zen that everyone is on their own spiritual path, and their way-seeking mind will eventually arise. Whether or not this is literally true, thinking of it this way reminds you that you are not in control of the process, and you can't predict when and where the desire to change will manifest.

When you deal with someone who does not yet want to change, you don't pity them because they haven't woken up yet, you feel gratitude and humility because of what you've managed to realize in your own life. After all, what caused *your* way-seeking mind to arise? There is no inherent, enduring *you* that can take responsibility for it; you are a causal flow affected by everything around you. At some point, things came together in such a way that you wanted to change, and then you were lucky enough to find a way that worked for you. This isn't evidence of superiority, it's just good fortune.

The Least You Need to Know

- If you can manage to approach all of your work the same way you approach a task you consider enjoyable and worthwhile, the work will all become an act of generosity.
- Materialism is seeking happiness from things outside you—things you can obtain and keep. Zen encourages you to let stuff flow freely into your life and back out again, without depending on any of it for your ultimate happiness.
- You can benefit greatly from making sure there's a balance of activity and stillness in your life by setting aside your distractions periodically throughout your day and allowing there to be some silence.
- Sometimes you may meet with resistance or misunderstanding from other people regarding your Zen practice. If you do, you have another great opportunity for practice in trying to be authentic but sensitive to what's going on for others.
- It can be frustrating or even painful to watch others behave in ways you have come to recognize are harmful or unhealthy. For the most part, you benefit others the most by doing your own practice and trying to be as patient and compassionate as you can be.

Zen and Mental Health

The relationship between Zen practice and mental health presents some very interesting questions. In a way, isn't Zen aimed at mental health? Especially with all the meditation and mindfulness being used in the mental health care field these days, what is the difference between those tools and Zen? What's the difference between working with a therapist and working with a Zen teacher? Is there a time when you should get mental health care instead of practicing Zen?

I am not a mental health care professional, so what I offer here is from the point of view of a Zen teacher and practitioner. Quite a number of Zen or Buddhist teachers *are* also psychotherapists, psychologists, or psychiatrists, however, and they've written some good books about the intriguing relationship between Western Zen practice (which has been influenced by psychology) and mental health issues and treatment. These include Barry Magid's *Ordinary Mind: Exploring the Common Ground of Zen and Psychotherapy* and Philip Martin's *The Zen Path Through Depression*.

In This Chapter

- How Zen relates to mental health care

- Making psychological issues into Zen practice

- When to seek professional help

- How psychological treatment can help your practice

- When Zen tools might hurt rather than help

Zen Versus Mental Health Care

It may or may not have occurred to you that there is sometimes a tension between Zen and professional mental health care. By mental health care, I am referring to the treatment of psychological problems through therapy, medication, behavioral modification programs, and sometimes the formal diagnosis of mental illness. There are lots of people faced with issues like anxiety or depression who wonder whether they should opt for Zen or therapy. Others get involved in Zen and then wonder whether it can really address their mental health issues properly. From the point of view of a Zen teacher, it can also be tricky to decide when to refer someone to a mental health care professional.

> **POTENTIAL PITFALL**
>
> Beware of thinking you can find one solution that will fit all of your problems. It's tempting, if you discover something that works well for you, to assume you can rely on it for support, answers, and resolution no matter what you're faced with. Maybe you can rely on it almost all the time … but if you limit the resources you're willing to use because you want to stick to one solution only, you may shortchange yourself.

Here I will illustrate some of the *differences* between formal Zen practice and mental health care, but also challenge the idea that using whatever tools you can find to relieve your suffering *isn't* Zen. In a way, Zen and psychotherapy present a prime example of a Buddhist paradox: they aren't the same, and they aren't different. In this wonderful, complex world of ours, both of these statements can be true at the same time.

The Useful Dichotomy

It's definitely useful to make a distinction between formal Zen practice—using the tools described in Part 2 of this book—and availing yourself of the resources available in the field of Western psychology. Generally speaking, both options involve some study of yourself and aim at reducing your suffering and increasing your happiness. Despite some apparent similarities, there are three main differences between Zen and mental health care.

First, there may be overlap in some of the methods used, but there are many tools used in psychology that are not used in Zen, and vice versa. The number of different types of therapies, medications, treatments, and approaches in modern psychology is so great and variable it's difficult to summarize what is offered there that *isn't* offered in Zen. Suffice it to say that Zen does not deal with medications, diagnoses, or triage for severe mental health crises. For the most part, Zen is going to assume you're feeling well enough to cope in your daily life, and if you aren't, it can't offer you the tools that are regularly employed in the mental health field for helping you get your life back on track.

Second, and closely related, a Zen teacher receives vastly different training than a mental health professional. Someone who becomes licensed to practice psychotherapy or psychiatry has had a rigorous education in modern psychological methods. A Zen teacher, unless they are also trained in psychology, will be more or less clueless about those techniques and approaches. What they *will* know intimately is the Zen method, and their goal will be for you to learn that method and apply it yourself.

A Zen teacher, ideally, will also have significant insight into Zen teachings and into their own karma. They will have started out like you, applied Zen tools to their life, and obtained some measure of satisfaction. So when they guide you in Zen, they're guiding you through a process they themselves have experienced. Still, their knowledge is specialized and doesn't necessarily cover all the problems you might have (although the same could be said about a mental health professional).

Third, while both formal Zen practice and psychological treatment can help you become healthier and happier, which one you need the most can change at different times in your life, depending on your mind-state and conditions. It may seem ironic, with all the Zen emphasis on giving up attachments and seeing the emptiness of self, but it's actually beneficial to have a *strong* sense of self when you engage Zen practice. It's also good to have some healthy confidence in yourself and in life before you start challenging your delusions and narratives.

The introspective Zen practices, particularly zazen, karma work, and cultivating insight, can be difficult or even harmful if your natural sense of self is incompletely formed, or has suffered a trauma. This can also be the case if you're finding it difficult to engage with daily life because of anxiety, depression, or other psychological issues. In these cases, it's not that Zen introspection doesn't work, it's that it isn't what is most needed.

 CONSIDER THIS

> Nothing in this chapter is meant to discourage you from practicing Zen if you have mental health issues. Many Zen practitioners credit their Zen practice for their lasting freedom from despair, depression, anxiety, and other psychological problems. However, most of these people also made use of Western psychological techniques and treatments in order to support their life and practice through difficult times.

What *is* needed when you're in a mentally or emotionally fragile or volatile state is healing, support, and stability. There are many ways to meet these needs, and it may well be that therapy or medication will be very beneficial for you. Healing wounds, encouraging self-esteem, putting boundaries around unhealthy behaviors, boosting confidence, and soothing anxiety are not really Zen's areas of expertise. However, I should state very clearly that such things *can* happen in a Zen context.

Mindfulness can ease anxiety, precepts can stabilize your daily behavior, and various other Zen practices can be a source of strength and solace, such as chanting, walking meditation, scripture copying, working with a teacher, and participating in a sangha. It's just that it will probably be up to you to monitor whether a practice is helping, and whether you're getting *enough* help.

The False Dichotomy

The dichotomy between Zen and mental health care becomes false when you think of Zen in a larger sense than its set of formal practices. As described in Chapter 3, you can think of Zen practice at different levels, and at the most subtle and profound level it's approaching each moment of your life with awareness and the intention to decrease suffering for yourself or others. How could taking care of your mental health *not* be part of your practice in this sense?

The sad thing is, people who face mental (or physical!) health challenges sometimes conclude that they can't practice Zen after all. Sometimes there's the perception that Zen is only for people with perfect mental health—people with robust egos and a sense of fearlessness when it comes to facing their delusions and embracing emptiness. This is not true at all. Zen is about being completely present and aware with your life *just as it is*.

It may be that your psychological condition means it's not helpful for you to sit zazen. It may be that past emotional trauma causes you to dissociate when you are trying to let go of attachments, so you need to spend some time encouraging your emotions and celebrating your attachments. Because of your limitations you may feel disappointed or inadequate, as if the deep liberation and joy Zen offers will be forever beyond you. Amazingly, this does not have to be the case. All you have to do is make your mental health issues *into* practice. Facing, accepting, and working with mental health challenges requires an enormous amount of letting go, and it can result in profound insights into no-self.

 ZEN WISDOM

"I had always depended on my practice of Buddhism to help me in difficult situations. But [when I found myself in a severe depression] it didn't seem enough, or relevant to what I was going through …. But I had always believed in a spiritual practice that was about settling deeply into life, going into the depths if necessary. So I persisted, trying to find a way to connect this practice to what was happening with me …. My practice and path are Zen Buddhism. I found I was finally able to bring my depression into the vastness of my practice, and I learned that others can, too—whatever their own spiritual leanings."

—Philip Martin, from *The Zen Path Through Depression*

Mental Health as Zen Practice

If you are facing mental health problems, you have some perfect opportunities for Zen practice. These may not be the opportunities you'd like, but engaging them wholeheartedly can result in deep transformation and liberation from suffering. Chances are, you'd rather sit peacefully in meditation until you experience transcendent insights about the nature of the universe (who wouldn't?), but generally speaking it's the difficult stuff that ends up challenging your sense of self and the way you cling to attachments.

Who Cares What People Think?

One way you can practice with mental illness, mild or severe, is to give up concern about what other people think. There are few things in this world that can make you feel as much shame as mental illness. When you are beset by anxiety attacks, paranoid delusions, paralyzing depression, a nervous breakdown, or something less dramatic, you may end up feeling like you have lost control and are weak, flawed, unreliable, unlikely to receive respect ... the list goes on. It's bad enough if you think these things yourself, but when you contemplate what people would think if they found out, it can be devastating. If they already know, you may feel the label of mental illness weighing heavily on you.

Letting go of caring about the opinions of others isn't about rejecting your need for human warmth and support, it's about refocusing your attention on your reality, without reference to others. This is essentially mindfulness practice. When you mindfully wash the dishes, you pay attention to your experience of the activity in and if itself, without thinking about what you are going to do next or whether this activity is worthy of your attention.

You can do the same thing with the activities that involve taking care of your mental health, such as attending therapy, trying to sit still through a wave of anxiety, or getting enough exercise to fight off depression. All of these things are part of your life as it is, and being completely present in them lets you appreciate them. Who cares what other people are doing? Who cares how their life compares to yours? Dwelling on comparisons and the opinions of others is the small self trying to build itself up into significance in the relative world. If you can see how opinions and standards have no inherent, enduring reality, this is an important spiritual insight.

Letting Go of Ideas

Another way to make mental health work part of your Zen practice is to let go of your ideas about who you are and who you would like to be. This is tough! Still, from the Zen point of view, all of those ideas are just creations of your mind that you have attached to your self-concept.

In Chapter 13 I explained how we all attach certain things to our self-concept in order to feel more substantial and real. Some of your favorite attachments are naturally going to be ideas about who you are and what you want to do in your life. These attachments simply cause dukkha, or the sense that *things should not be like this*. When you realize that the attachments are not necessary to your life, you can engage each moment without reference to them. You are free, appreciative, and attentive, even if you are facing situations that run counter to your stories about yourself.

 POTENTIAL PITFALL

> It's also possible to incorporate mental illness into your self-concept, which means in some subtle way you will be invested in keeping that label. Assuming you would prefer mental health, it's good to remember that the label "mental illness," or the label of any particular diagnosis, is ultimately just a concept. It may be useful at times, but it has no inherent existence. You can let go of your attachment to it just as you can let go of anything else. This lets you embrace change if it comes, and reminds you that you are not defined by a label.

You probably don't like the idea of having mental health issues, which can be very daunting and scary, so they are unlikely to be part of your self-concept. Therefore, if you are having psychological problems, you're receiving a strong challenge to your sense of self. While this can be confusing and painful, it's also a great opportunity. Life has deprived you of being able to say things like, "I am always clearheaded about things and can trust my perceptions." You may no longer be able to say, "I can predict how I am going to react to things," or "I have a stable, positive outlook on life."

Can you let go of having a story to tell about yourself? Can you encounter each situation in a fresh, open way; do your best, and just see what happens? If you can, you've made significant headway in letting go of attachments.

Appreciating No-Self

If you can't control your own mind, or can't always trust your perceptions and thoughts to be true, where is your self-essence? Not in your mind, apparently. If you need to avail yourself of medication, treatment, or therapy that alters the way you think or behave, who are you? Are you really *you* only when you are without treatment?

Mental health issues can be a profound lesson in how the self is empty of any unchanging, independent essence, as discussed in Chapter 11. As you find yourself dependent on support or interventions from the "outside," your sense of a separate, autonomous self can get whittled away. When you watch large swings in mood or outlook, your sense of a continuous, unchanging self that moves through time can be severely challenged. This is part of why mental illness can be so traumatic.

Zen practice can help just by putting all of this in context. *Of course* it hurts. *Of course* it's disorienting. But it's also okay. Mental health problems are irrelevant to your buddha-nature. When you are emotionally or mentally volatile or fragile, it isn't the time to push yourself into a fuller experience of emptiness. You don't need to; you are experiencing it personally already. Just being gently present with your day-to-day life will inform you.

When to Turn to a Mental Health Professional

When is it time to avail yourself of professional mental health resources in addition to, or instead of, Zen practice? There is no hard-and-fast rule here, unfortunately. It never hurts to see whether therapy or mental health treatment might be helpful to you. It can be part of your Zen practice in the larger sense of the term.

CONSIDER THIS

There are a growing number of mental health professionals who also have experience with meditation, Buddhism, or Zen. You may want to seek one out if you have decided to seek therapy or treatment, because they will have some insight into what you are doing in your Zen practice. Some psychotherapists are long-term practitioners of Zen themselves and may be able to help you integrate your therapy with your Zen.

However, if your mental health issues are interfering with your functioning in daily life in a substantial way, you *should* seek help from a mental health professional. If your anxiety or depression is making it difficult to work, for example, or your neuroses are threatening your relationships, or you are actively contemplating suicide, it's time to look beyond the traditional Zen tools for a solution.

It's up to you to decide if and when you've reached the threshold of your psychological issues "interfering in a substantial way" with your daily life, but keep an eye out for an unwillingness to admit you have reached it. It takes humility and courage to acknowledge you're facing problems you need help with—problems that may challenge your idea of yourself or even get you labeled with a psychological diagnosis. Getting help when you need it can be another important part of your Zen practice, requiring you to face the truth and embrace humility.

How Mental Health Care Complements Zen

Zen practice and Western mental health care both have strengths and weaknesses. Neither one is perfect and complete, and they can actually be quite complementary. Many of the shortcomings of Zen have to do with misunderstandings about what the practice really entails, or what Zen teachings really mean, but anything that is easily misunderstood is therefore imperfect.

One of the primary weaknesses of Zen, from the point of view of maintaining mental health, is that it doesn't deal so well with emotions. It has the potential to do so, but because of all the emphasis on letting go, there's a danger that you will try to let something go before you have fully acknowledged, processed, and embraced it. Zen doesn't offer many explicit tools for exploring emotions, while psychology offers many of them.

You can certainly allow emotions to arise during your meditation, or attend to them with mindfulness, or explore them in karma work. Unfortunately, these methods can seem to imply that you should experience a certain dissociation from the emotions, rather than feeling them deeply and seeing how they are a part of you. While it is possible to do the latter in Zen practice, the process will probably be mostly self-guided. In contrast, some Western psychological methods are explicitly aimed at uncovering and experiencing your emotions, and the thoughts or memories underlying them, and can be very useful.

 ZEN WISDOM

"Zen does not have all the answers to all the problems of the human condition. Psychoanalysts need not simply defer to Zen's greater wisdom and longer history. Zen needs psychoanalysis as much as psychoanalysis needs Zen. In particular, Zen needs psychoanalysis to keep it emotionally honest."

—Zen teacher and psychoanalyst Barry Magid, from *Ending the Pursuit of Happiness: A Zen Guide*

Another weakness of Zen is its inability to address the importance of your conditions. It encourages you to accept your life as it is and find liberation and joy right here, without searching around elsewhere for it. Ultimately this *is* possible to do, no matter your conditions. However, your conditions may be making it extremely difficult not to succumb to depression or anxiety, which don't help you practice. Past or current trauma may have left you with significant psychological issues or barriers that upset your life and make it difficult to concentrate on acceptance or understanding. Your emotional issues may be exacerbated or triggered by current dysfunctional relationships.

Basically, sometimes it's time to *do something* about the state of your life, and Zen isn't necessarily going to encourage you into action. Western mental health care, on the other hand, is much more likely to address your conditions, particularly your psychological ones.

The kind of suffering Zen is really good at dealing with is subtle: the kind of unhappiness that people can have even when everything is going great. This is where psychological treatment tends to reach its limits. You might say that Zen takes over where Western psychology leaves off, addressing the deeper issues that some people would call spiritual. Still, the line between suffering that requires action and suffering that's "just in your mind" is often unclear.

Sometimes Zen practitioners can feel a little bit like they've failed when they turn their attention toward improving their conditions instead of just accepting them, but this is creating a false duality that isn't actually the truth of Zen. The acceptance and the doing are not opposed to each other. The most effective doing happens when you've accepted the way things are, and sometimes you aren't really accepting something unless you start doing something about it.

When to Be Careful with Zen

Again, I am not a mental health professional, and there are books available that are written by such professionals on how Zen or Buddhism relates to depression, anxiety, and other psychological issues. However, in a book like this one, which tries to be comprehensive, it's worth mentioning a few kinds of mental health issues that require you to be careful with Zen tools.

This is not an exhaustive list, but some of the issues that come up most frequently for Zen practitioners are dealing with an incompletely developed sense of self, depression, and posttraumatic stress. This is not to say you shouldn't practice Zen if you are experiencing, or have experienced, any of these things. It's just that you should be aware that not all Zen tools and teachings will be helpful to you all the time, and reaching outside traditional Zen for additional support may be very useful.

Strengthening the Self

I was once deeply touched when I heard the Dalai Lama at a public lecture, when he said that in order to practice Buddhism you need a strong sense of self. This seemed so radical to me! Weren't we trying to get rid of the self? Wouldn't a strong sense of self just be an obstacle to practice? And yet, I had an intuition that what the Dalai Lama said was true, and it gave me hope because I definitely had not gotten free of a deep conviction that I existed, concretely and very significantly.

What is a strong sense of self? It is a well-developed self-concept, complete with stable narratives about who you are, what's yours, what you like and don't like, and what you want. It is a sense of a clear boundary between yourself and the rest of the world. It is a belief that you have some measure of control over the things you identify as self, and confidence that you can move about in the world effectively and autonomously. It is a conviction that you have a self-essence that continues through time, and that you own enough territory in this world to figure in its ongoing drama.

This list could go on, but suffice it to say that a strong sense of self lets you navigate successfully in the world, protecting your self-interests and trying to gain what you desire.

It takes time and maturity for human beings to develop a strong sense of self, and there are many ways its development can be undermined. In particular, abuse, trauma, and seriously dysfunctional relationships can confuse boundaries and result in an unstable or tentative sense of self. Some mental illnesses with genetic or physical components contribute to this. The weaknesses in your sense of self can be subtle or substantial, but in either case what you need is some of the nurturing support, encouragement, and validation that children require in order to grow up confident and strong. This may mean that you need to spend some time and energy on pursuing things that make you feel good, loved, successful, and whole.

If your sense of self is underdeveloped, it may not be helpful for you to attend austere Zen meditation retreats and spend hours contemplating how you don't really exist, or how everything changes and nothing can ultimately be depended on. You're welcome to try these practices, but watch carefully what effect they have on you, and check in with a teacher if you can. It may also be wise to form a relationship with a mental health professional who can help monitor and build up your psychological strength and sense of self.

 CONSIDER THIS

When trying to judge how much intensive Zen practice to do when you're feeling fragile or volatile, think of the metaphor offered by the Buddha. He explained that in practice you want to keep yourself tuned like a lute. If a lute string is too loose, it won't make a beautiful sound. If it's too tight, it will break. What you're looking for is the "just right" place in the middle, and it takes constant adjusting to stay in tune. Too much intensive practice can be like tightening the lute string too much. You don't want to break; you want to make beautiful music with your life.

When Zen asks you to let go of searching for happiness and validation from outside things, it's assuming that you have already done plenty of this. It assumes you have a vital and energetic relationship with life, and a strong determination to take care of yourself. Zen uses that very self-interest—your desire to be happy and free from suffering—to motivate you to explore the true nature of human existence and suffering. It asks you to see how you are naturally good, worthy of being loved, successful, and whole, and to see that therefore you don't have to depend on outside things for happiness.

But this is about *seeing the true nature* of your relationship to the world, not about withdrawing from the world out of fear or despair. Zen is about *seeing the true nature* of the self, not destroying it. When your self is destroyed, you have nothing to work with. It is your vehicle for life and practice, so it needs to be taken care of with loving attention.

Fighting Depression

Another mental health challenge that requires you to be careful with Zen practice is depression. In a strange way, depression can make you feel like you are acting out Zen practices and teachings, but with a negative result. The Zen teaching on emptiness can resonate with you because everything seems pointless and hollow. Giving up self-attachments can seem like a nonissue because you can't care about anything. Sitting still and alone on a cushion meditating can seem preferable to dealing with the world. And yet, all that happens is you sink deeper and deeper into the dullness and torpor of depression. But then, who cares?

What you need when you're depressed, and what Zen is unlikely to give you, is a nudge to get you moving. You need active encouragement to engage with life, to exercise, to take care of yourself, and to do whatever you can to jolt yourself out of your depression. Depending on the seriousness of your condition, you may need medication to provide that jolt. Many successful Zen practitioners have availed themselves of this tool and found that it *allowed* them to do Zen practice. The Zen tools of introspection can just make your depression worse if all you can see when you are meditating is how bleak everything is.

Fortunately, there are Zen tools that can be helpful even when you are depressed. Mindful activity in the form of walking meditation, bowing, chanting, or simple physical work can pull your attention out of depressive loops. Practices like metta—sending wishes of loving kindness to others—can shift your attention away from the state of your mind. However, nothing beats finding something to do that you enjoy, even if your capacity to enjoy it is somewhat compromised. Try getting a massage, going on a hike, reading a mystery, or painting a picture—activities outside of traditional Zen practice, but which can help you connect with life again.

Dealing with Trauma

Living with the effects of trauma is another effort that requires taking some care with Zen. You can end up triggered into an extreme emotional, psychological, or physical reaction through Zen practice, and then find yourself in a situation where the people around you don't know how to help you. Of course, this is true wherever you go, not just in Zen practice settings; but you may assume that because Zen teachers encounter all kinds of emotions and experiences in their students, they will understand yours. However, they may not recognize your experience for what it is (a reaction due to past—or current—trauma), or may not recognize its seriousness (there's a huge difference between feeling anxious, for example, and a full-blown panic attack).

In addition, in the context of Zen practice it may be seen as positive to experience stress or negative emotions as you face and process your karma; but if you are dealing with the effects of trauma, it's easy for the stress and negative emotions to become too overpowering. It may be difficult for you to handle the feelings and still go about your daily life, let alone examine them more closely while hoping to gain some insight into them.

Introspective Zen tools can sometimes increase the chances of being triggered into an overpowering emotional response. This is especially true of long, silent meditation retreats. If you are dealing with trauma and are interested in meditation and retreats, however, you shouldn't necessarily refrain from doing them. Just do so carefully and thoughtfully, and preferably with the assistance and feedback of a mental health professional *and* a Zen teacher. Be honest with both of them about your history and symptoms. They can help you monitor what is helpful, and how much is too much.

ZEN WISDOM

"Putting words like Zen, trauma, and spiritual together ... seems at first glance to be a stretch, yet the experience of trauma survivors is often singularly spiritual. Moreover, the experience of recovery from a traumatic experience has a darkside and a lightside. Trauma recovery is cyclical, often a lifelong process, much as the yin and yang of Dao. A traumatic experience both touches and invites our essential, true nature."

—Zen Teacher Harvey Daiho Hilbert, Vietnam veteran and clinical social worker with other survivors of trauma, from *The Zen of Trauma*

In the meantime, seeking support and guidance from a professional who understands the effects of trauma can be very useful. It can be an immense relief just to know you aren't alone and that your experiences are typical reactions to trauma. There are also tools, medications, and techniques available to help you manage symptoms and reactions. As mentioned earlier, if you think of Zen practice as approaching life with awareness and an intention to relieve suffering, dealing with the effects of trauma is Zen practice, too.

The Least You Need to Know

- Both Zen and mental health care involve some study of the self, and aim to relieve suffering and increase happiness.

- Zen does not deal with medications, diagnoses, or severe mental health crises, and Zen teachers are trained completely differently than mental health professionals.

- Professional mental health care can give you the strength and resilience to engage Zen methods, and Zen can give you the spiritual context and motivation for taking care of your mental health.

- Taking care of your physical and mental health should never be considered outside of, or less than, "real" Zen practice. Real Zen practice includes your whole life.

- If you are a survivor of abuse, suffer from depression, or have experienced trauma, be gentle with yourself, and receive some guidance when employing introspective Zen tools like meditation or karma work.

Zen When Life Is Tough

Unless you are going through great difficulty, reading a chapter about dealing with it may not seem like your idea of a good time. Illness, pain, loss, death—these are things you naturally would rather not dwell on unless you have to. However, in Zen practice you are advised to explore *everything*, and are told that doing so will have a positive effect on your life. Even if things are going well for you now, you may find it helpful to know how to apply Zen practice to your life when things are very tough in a literal, tangible way.

After all, as human beings we know that adversity will come into our life at some point, so it's hard not to be at least somewhat anxious about it. If you gain some confidence in practice, it can be a great relief to know that you can rely on it even when things fall apart.

If you are facing some of the hardships described in this chapter, hopefully you will be encouraged. Zen doesn't deny that certain situations make life painful, distressing, or grueling, but there are no circumstances so difficult that Zen practice becomes irrelevant or ineffective, or loses its potential to help you find peace of mind and gratitude for your life. In fact, like all of the challenges discussed so far in this book, literal hardships are great practice opportunities—the greatest, and hardest, opportunities of them all.

In This Chapter

- Practice in challenging circumstances
- The reward of forbearance
- Dealing more effectively with injustice
- Profound peace despite illness, pain, and old age
- The lessons of loss

Difficult Circumstances

Sometimes the circumstances of your life can be overwhelmingly stressful and discouraging. Just taking care of your responsibilities can seem an impossible task. Maybe this is because you don't have enough money, or you are facing legal problems. Maybe you are stuck in a dysfunctional living situation, or have been left alone to care for your children without any help.

When the stressors build up, things tend to start falling apart: because you don't have any money, you don't have a car and can't get to job interviews to find work; in your anxiety about the future you've gotten short-tempered with your partner and your relationship is in trouble; anxiety about your relationship makes you seek solace in buying things too expensive for your budget, so you have even less money … and so around and around it goes. You can feel like you're doing everything you can to just keep your head above water.

There is nothing Zen can do to fix the practical aspects of your life for you. However, Zen practice can help keep you from the brink of despair, so you can be at your best when you're trying to improve your circumstances. It can also help you maintain some centeredness and dignity through your struggles.

POTENTIAL PITFALL

When your life becomes very difficult, you may be inclined to think you can't practice Zen. You may not be able to find the time or energy to sit zazen very often, or attend a Zen group, or do any Zen study. However, this is thinking of Zen practice in a limited sense. As discussed in Chapter 3, at the most subtle and profound level, Zen practice is approaching each moment of your life with awareness and the intention to decrease suffering for yourself or others. You can do this no matter what's going on or how busy you are—and your life will benefit if you do.

Dropping the Stories

One of the most important things you can do when the practical aspects of your life seem to be falling apart is to give up the extra stories you're telling yourself about your circumstances. It may take some mindfulness, karma work, and insight to even be able to see the stories, but if you look carefully you will find them. Chances are good that you're thinking, "Things shouldn't be like this." Of course, this is dukkha in a more obvious manifestation than the rather subtle existential dissatisfaction you might feel when things are going well.

In your current circumstances, you are clearly of the opinion that things aren't the way they should be. However, as discussed in Chapter 10, this opinion causes you stress and suffering, and it doesn't help. It's not that you should give up trying to change your situation, just that you're better off starting your efforts here and now, in your present circumstances, rather than waiting until—by some miracle—your inner resistance has forced the world to be different. Things are the way they are, and ironically you can gain a measure of composure and peace from simply accepting that. Not that this is easy to do at all, especially when things are really tough! But the fact that it's very difficult to do doesn't make it any less worthwhile.

When your circumstances are hard, you probably also think, "What did I do to deserve this?" and, "Why are other people's lives so much better than mine?" Both of these thoughts are based on stories about individual control, based on a belief that each of us has an inherent, enduring self-nature. This belief is erroneous (see Chapter 11), and leads us to further erroneous assumptions. These assumptions include the idea that there is an intrinsic, graspable *you* that misfortune is happening to, and the idea that you should be able to control the things that you have identified as being *I, me, and mine*.

When you hold on to the idea of enduring self-essence, you conceive of you versus the world; but the reality of your existence is that you are a flow of causes and conditions, deeply influenced by everything around you. There are no clear boundaries between you, "your" life, and the rest of the world.

Thinking about how you are empty of any inherent, unchanging essence may not seem comforting intellectually, but when you can directly experience how this is true, you are much less likely to fall into the trap of blame. Blame leads you to create one or more of the following stories: you are to blame for your situation; you are not to blame for your situation (and therefore others are, or "the world" is); others are responsible for their good fortune (and therefore superior to you, because you don't have the good fortune); or other people are *not* responsible for their good fortune, and therefore have been unfairly rewarded (the universe is biased, and out to shortchange you).

Telling yourself these stories can lead to feelings of pain, anger, shame, disempowerment, persecution, envy, and confusion. None of these feelings is going to help you maintain your health in body and mind—and you really need that health in order to take care of your life.

 CONSIDER THIS

Dropping your stories about your circumstances may sound a little bit like "Just get over it!" However, telling yourself (or others) to "just get over it" is unkind and unhelpful. When you work on dropping your stories, you should do so because you are ready to, and then employ patience and compassion with yourself. Dropping stories does not require you to deny the reality of your circumstances. Instead, you are voluntarily changing your mental habits in order to feel more positive and empowered—without giving up your intelligence or your determination to take care of your life.

How do you drop the stories? You apply karma work to them, because they are habits of mind (see Chapter 7), and you work on challenging the delusion of inherent, enduring self-nature

(Chapter 14). First you get to know these habits of mind through careful, patient, and honest attention. You encourage yourself through this process by trying to summon compassion for yourself—admitting things are tough, and examining how they are affecting you.

Eventually, by getting to know your mind, you can learn to set aside certain thoughts or stories at will, even if just for a moment. Then you can see how they aren't absolutely true, and how much better off you are without them. Ultimately, it helps to challenge your self-delusion and learn to live with less of a sense of self. This loosens some of the anguish around the worry about *I, me, and mine*, and lets you engage each moment without dwelling so much on the past or future.

The Perfection of Forbearance

When faced with difficult circumstances, or with any other hardship, it can be transformative to work on the Buddhist perfection of forbearance, or *kshanti*. Forbearance can help you maintain a sense of purpose and dignity, even when everything else seems to be out of your control. There are five other perfections that all help you master the art of living: generosity, morality, diligence, concentration, and wisdom. All take work to cultivate and are beneficial, but forbearance is unique among the perfections in that, when practiced, it doesn't generally get you any special admiration, respect, or spiritual kudos.

Forbearance is the least glamorous of the perfections (not that you should be practicing perfections for the sake of your reputation, but it's human to notice these things). Few people set out thinking, "I'd really like to practice kshanti." You can probably picture someone acting out any of the other perfections, and how noble they would appear. If you picture someone acting out kshanti, they will simply be in touch with their spiritual center in the midst of difficulty. Kshanti *is* worthy of deep respect, but you may not easily recognize when it is being practiced.

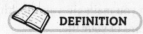 **DEFINITION**

> **Kshanti** is the perfection of forbearance, or tolerance. It can also be translated as "able to bear" or "composure." It's one of six perfections, which are to be cultivated in order to help support your spiritual practice. The other five perfections are generosity (*dana*), morality (*sila*), diligence or energy (*virya*), meditation or concentration (*dhyana*), and wisdom (*prajna*).

Forbearance is about recognizing that you have influence over how your life unfolds, but not control. At times, this influence may be extremely limited, sometimes to the point that the only thing you have any chance of changing is your own mind. Generally speaking, the more adverse your conditions, the more limited your influence.

Forbearance does not forbid acting to change whatever it is you can manage to change, but it means that you will try to have realistic expectations about your sphere of influence, and will graciously take care of whatever you can. You give up guilt, comparisons, attachments, stories, dreams, and ideals in order to be present in your life as it is. When you do this, your sense of groundedness returns. You have a stable place from which to meet your challenges.

The great thing about forbearance is that you don't have to enjoy it. The fact that it is included as a perfection is the Buddhist acknowledgment that sometimes, no matter how well you take care of your life, no matter how spiritual you are, no matter how good you have been, things are going to feel awful. No amount of letting go of attachments, resistance, delusions, or stories is going to suddenly make things feel great or easy.

The radical thing about forbearance is that it points to the possibility that nonetheless your life can be lived with wisdom, grace, gratitude, dignity, and even a little bit of joy. Life doesn't *have* to feel great in order to be worth living. Experiencing great difficulty does not obstruct your enlightenment; in fact, it gives you the supreme opportunity to let go of your self-concern. Doing so when things hurt, as opposed to when you're looking for a more sublime spiritual state, is a more direct route to liberation. Knowing this can give you a sense of purpose and dignity when you are practicing forbearance.

Injustice

Few things can be more disturbing than witnessing, experiencing, or fighting injustice. Whether you are the victim of injustice or are taking up a cause on behalf of others or of the planet, it can be incredibly hard to let go of dukkha: your sense that *things should not be like this*. Because they shouldn't! Things need to change! The injustice needs to be recognized, acknowledged, and addressed. Lives may be at stake. Existence as we know it may be threatened. To accept things as they are, or to try to see how life is complete and precious just as it is, seems to risk slipping into complacency and ignorance. As the bumper sticker says, "If you're not outraged, you're not paying attention."

And yet, persistent agitation, anger, resentment, outrage, resistance, and fighting don't seem to be the most effective way to bring about change. These negative emotions and postures tend to exhaust and embitter you. Your repeated reminders to other people about the existence of terrible injustice often seem to fall on deaf ears, as if people were just too wrapped up in themselves to care, or too unwilling to face the ugly truth.

Noticing this can further discourage you. Your efforts to change things probably meet with great resistance, whether it's simple inertia or active opposition. Change comes very slowly, not nearly fast enough to satisfy your longing to see things put right. You can envision things being taken care of, justice being restored, peace and harmony prevailing, compassion and wisdom being manifested. This vision seems so close, why doesn't it come about?

ZEN WISDOM

"There are so many problems. Sometimes I feel overwhelmed. But I try to work one day at a time. If we just worry about the big picture, we are powerless. So my secret is to start right away doing whatever little work I can do. I try to give joy to one person in the morning, and remove the suffering of one person in the afternoon. That's enough .... If you and your friends do not despise the small work, a million people will remove a lot of suffering. That is the secret. Start right now."

—Sister Chan Khong, from *The Bodhisattva's Embrace* by Zen teacher Alan Senauke

How can you deal with injustice more effectively, without giving up your integrity? It's tricky. Essentially, it will involve giving up attachments: your attachment to being right, your attachment to being able to change things, your identification with your cause, and your vision of what things would look like if they were put right (among other things). As explained in Chapter 13, an attachment is something you have incorporated into your concept of self, or made a possession of self.

In the case of addressing injustice, if you are attached, you have invested part of your being into correcting the wrong. If the wrong is not corrected, if you are foiled in your efforts, your sense of self is threatened. This is distressing in a way that is very different from the pain you feel because of your sense of empathy, sympathy, sadness, or compassion for the beings affected by injustice. When your sense of self, your very existence, is threatened, a deep fear and opposition is triggered in you. This turns your cause into, "Things must change, *or else* ...." You may leave this "or else" unspecified, but internally you know that it more or less means total catastrophe. It's a scenario that is utterly unacceptable, if not impossible.

It may seem counterintuitive, but it's best to hold even your fight against injustice lightly. By this I mean you hold it the same way you hold any other desires you have, thinking, "It would be wonderful if..." instead of, "This must happen, or else ...." In the case of terrible wrongs, where people and things are facing injury and even destruction, this may seem like giving up the fight, but it's not. Rather, you can continue the fight with less agitation, anger, resentment, outrage, and resistance—and therefore with more perspective, energy, and wisdom.

Your hope for change will be set against a background of a world without expectations. Instead of looking at the world as a place where people *should* act with wisdom and compassion, where they *should* pay attention to the long-term effects of greed and selfishness, where they *should* realize that their well-being is not independent of the well-being of their fellow creatures, you look at the world just as it is. It's a crazy mix of beauty and ugliness, incredible generosity, and incredible selfishness.

There's no rule book of the world that says it's supposed to be a peaceful, wonderful place. So when people opt for justice, clarity, kindness, and selflessness, it's cause for celebration. Your work to encourage this may look the same from the outside, but inside your approach can be transformed. People will notice that you're hoping for the best from them, rather than judging them for being wrong or ignorant, and they will probably respond better. Your efforts will not feel so frustrating, and you will feel more gratitude for your successes, however small they may be.

Illness, Pain, and Old Age

Nothing challenges your sense of self, and your ability to appreciate your life, like problems with your body. The most enlightened Zen master is still dependent on her body and inevitably identified with it to some extent. When you're faced with physical pain or the loss of physical abilities, your life can be radically altered. Depending on the severity of the problem, you may be uncomfortably reminded of your mortality, or you may essentially lose almost everything you have ever cared about.

In either case, life is prying your attachments out of your hands whether you are inclined to work on letting them go or not. At the same time, your physical challenges can make it difficult to do formal Zen practices like attending a Zen group or meditation retreats, or sitting still for longer than a few minutes. So just when you could really use Zen, it can seem like your practice is being taken away from you, too.

 CONSIDER THIS

From a Zen point of view, illness, pain, and old age are wonderful opportunities for learning. Of course, "wonderful" doesn't mean you should look forward to them, or enjoy them. Still, there are certain spiritual lessons you can't possibly understand fully until you are personally faced with physical problems, and with your own mortality. In ancient Buddhism, it was understood that individuals could attain enlightenment, or nirvana, while they were still alive and healthy. But it was only when they died that they attained *parinirvana*, or complete nirvana. Only when they faced and passed through the experience of physical dissolution did they completely let go and attain ultimate liberation.

Worst-Case Scenario

In this section I'm going to talk about how to do Zen practice when you're faced with what, for most of us, is the worst-case scenario: when problems with your body cause you to lose just about everything. The same ideas still apply when your physical problems are not so severe, but it will be easier for you to put them into practice. Also, your minor bodily issues remind you of your mortality, or the fact that eventually you will indeed face this worst-case scenario, so the issue is actually relevant for everyone.

I have learned a great deal from several Zen practitioners who have practiced with severe physical illness. Their lives are constrained by the needs and limitations of their bodies, to the point where their daily life consists largely of just taking care of themselves. Waking up, getting dressed, and having breakfast is enough work for a whole morning and subsequently requires a nap. Showering or doing laundry are major undertakings that have to be carefully planned in order to avoid facing major physical setbacks. Doctor's appointments may require a recovery period of several days or more.

Given such conditions, activities most of us take for granted, like taking a hike, going shopping, or visiting friends, are pretty much impossible. My friends have to depend on help from others, despite the fact that they were formerly extremely competent and independent people. When they talk to others, they have to be careful not to be too honest about just how miserable and discouraged they feel, because then people will start to avoid them. To say that their situations can be depressing is understating the matter. Given their physical challenges, how do they practice?

Essentially, they continue to do their very best to practice in that most profound sense of the word: paying careful attention to their lives, seeking constantly for clarity and wisdom, and trying to decrease suffering and increase happiness for themselves and others. Sometimes they can do formal Zen practice, and sometimes they can't, but they never give up the intention to try.

They also cultivate the perfection of forbearance, the quality of character described in the first section of this chapter. Giving up all comparisons, dreams, and expectations, they try to be present in their life as it is. They try to appreciate the view outside their bedroom window, the taste of their tea, the rare visit from a good friend. They acknowledge their pain and discouragement, and try not to fight it or dwell on the way things *should* be. Sometimes being afflicted with physical problems can feel like an injustice, in which case the practices discussed in the previous section become important.

The Universe in a Cup of Tea

If you have significant physical challenges and you want to find peace of mind, it is essential that you work on letting go of your attachment to who you think you are, what you think your life should be, and what you think a meaningful life should look like. When bodily pain, illness, or limitations get bad enough, the perceived dimensions of your life shrink. Before your challenges, your sphere of operation included many different physical places like work, beautiful outdoor locations, favorite places in your city, friends' houses, and perhaps even places all over the world. Now your sphere may include only your own house and your doctor's office, or perhaps even just one room.

Before your physical limitations, you probably interacted with all kinds of different people and engaged in all kinds of different activities and projects. Now you may just see one or two people on any regular basis, and your activities are limited to taking care of your own basic needs. If this is the case, any comparison of your life with before, or with the lives of others, is going to be a cause for despair. Fortunately, Zen practice can give you enough freedom of mind to work on changing the way you think and letting go of thoughts and stories that only cause you more difficulty and pain.

Even more importantly, letting go of comparisons and ideas about the way things should be allows you to sincerely appreciate your life just as it is. It's not simply that you play mind games with yourself to make yourself feel better, it's that you try to wake up to the reality of your life. Viewed without any expectations or comparisons, it is precious. The view that your life is small compared to the lives of other people, or less impactful or beneficial to others, is an illusion. There is no absolute truth to such comparisons, only relative truth.

Through Zen practice you can experience the way the whole universe is manifest right here, right now. The limited sphere of operation imposed on you by your physical limitations is the same kind of limited sphere intentionally sought out by Zen monks in monasteries, and Zen practitioners during meditation retreats. By simplifying your environment and doing without all the activities that usually give you your sense of identity, purpose, and pleasure, you are forced to find these in whatever is right in front of you. Amazingly, everything you need is right there, and nothing is lacking. It's like the universe can change sizes, and be wholly present in single moments and tiny things.

ZEN WISDOM

"Actually, 'accepting' pain sounds to me too passive to accurately describe the process of successfully dealing with chronic pain. It fails to convey the tremendous energy and courage it takes to accept physical pain as part of your life. Truly accepting pain is not at all like passive resignation. Rather, it is active engagement with life in its most intimate sense. It is meeting, dancing with, raging at, turning toward. To accept your pain on this level, you must cultivate particular skills. After you have developed some proficiency, dealing with pain feels more like an embrace, or the bond that forms between sparring partners, than like resignation."

—Zen Teacher Darlene Cohen, from *Turning Suffering Inside Out*

Remember: this teaching that everything you need is right there, so your life is precious no matter how much pain you are in, is meant to be *experienced*, not just adopted as a belief. If you just take it on as something you *should* feel or understand, you will just be adding another layer of dissatisfaction onto your life. Forbearance is about being authentically present with your life, and sometimes the physical or emotional pain will be too great for you to be able to feel wonder and gratitude for your cup of tea, or to ponder how precious your life is.

However, if you can base your life in something deeper than your feelings, you will be able to endure the really tough times and experience joy and gratitude again. There's no denying this is very hard work, but the alternative to the hard work is despair. Every day—actually, every moment—that you are able to feel some contentment instead of despair, you are offering a gift to the world.

In Chapter 19 I talked about how any work can be offered as a gift, and that includes your work to take care of yourself and keep on living with the best attitude you can muster. Because, whether you know it or not, other people are watching you. When they see from your example that it's possible to remain undefeated by physical problems, their confidence will be increased. When they finally face such problems of their own, your generosity will manifest.

Loss

One of the traps it's easy to fall into in Zen practice is believing that you shouldn't feel the pain of loss. After all, you are doing all this work on yourself in order to give up self-attachments, and to allow things to flow freely in and out of your life without depending on them for your ultimate happiness. Surely, if you were just skilled enough in practice, or dedicated enough, you would be able to shift your thinking so the loss of a job, a home, an ability, a relationship, a pet, or even a loved one wouldn't feel so devastating. Ideally, you could see all of it within the bigger context of emptiness and perfection, and let it go, right?

Unfortunately, Zen practice does not protect you from the pain of loss. It also may not have the best tools or teachings for encouraging you to acknowledge, process, and be patient with your grief (you may want to turn to therapy for help with that; see Chapter 20). However, Zen's main emphasis is on being completely present for your life just as it is, so it follows that you should be attentive to the pain of loss if that's what's going on for you, and not fight, deny, or just try to get rid of it.

> **POTENTIAL PITFALL**
>
> Cultural understandings and traditions around grief may not give you adequate time to acknowledge, understand, process, and heal from loss. Even in the case of the loss of a loved one, other people may not be inclined to hear about or honor your ongoing grief six months or a year after your loss. If your grieving process seems to take a long time—perhaps many, many years—try not to wonder what's wrong with you, or to withdraw your care and attention from your grief. It may be helpful to get support in your grieving, but try to accept that you cannot control the process or how long it's going to take.

A Zen View of Grief

Here's why loss can be legitimately painful, and not just something that challenges your attachments: as discussed in Chapter 11, your true self-nature is a flow of causes and conditions. It arises and is shaped by everything around you, including your work, your family of origin, your culture, your relationships, and your environment. Actually, not only is your self shaped by these things, there is no clear boundary between self and the rest of the world. In a sense, the things and beings in your life are part of you.

This "being part" is very different from attachment, where you conceive of yourself as having an enduring self-essence, and you appropriate things into your self-concept (see Chapter 13). The *real* way in which things are part of who you are is not at all self-centered; in fact, it challenges your sense of self, because these things that are part of you are not under your control, and they can be lost.

The pain you feel when you lose something that was a part of your life is similar to the physical pain and disorientation you would feel if part of your body was amputated. It is grief, or love in the face of loss. A hole has appeared in your self and in your life, a hole where something or someone you valued used to be.

This hole is a wound and may be extremely painful, or at the very least uncomfortable. It will take time for the wound to heal—and it may never heal entirely. Your self has been permanently changed in a substantial way. You need to rebuild a healthy sense of self—one that allows you to function effectively in the world—and you have to do it without the thing or being you have lost.

Loss as Teacher

If the wound of a loss always remains, even when you have more or less rebuilt your conventional and functional sense of self, this is not necessarily a bad thing. Over a lifetime, you will inevitably experience more and more of these wounds, but they can just make you more compassionate, understanding, patient, and humble.

Of course, this requires that you accept and embrace the wounds as part of you. If you just try to fill the holes left in your life by loss because grief is uncomfortable, you won't be seasoned by your wounds. If you deny or fight the fact that you feel the pain of loss, you won't be able to experience the deep, bittersweet peace of acceptance that still honors what you have lost.

Loss is also an incredibly valuable teacher when it comes to seeing the true nature of self. Few things so challenge your delusion of having an inherent, enduring, unchanging self-essence as experiencing a loss that radically alters your life. It will probably occur to you at some point, "If losing this can shake my entire sense of self, what else am I depending on that I can also lose?" It may seem like the solid ground you thought you were standing on is becoming very unstable, or even disappearing.

If you can stay with and explore this experience rather than running away from it (by trying to forget it, or by desperately searching for more solid ground), you have the potential to gain profound insight into the emptiness of self and phenomena. The basic point is that, indeed, there is no solid ground, and there is nothing concrete on which you can depend. And yet, it is possible to stand firmly without any ground under your feet at all.

 ZEN WISDOM

"The journey into a life of awareness begins for most of us in a moment of help-lessness ... a child falls ill, a lover disappoints, or some vast, neutral power of the earth, such as a hurricane or fire, strips us of everything we have relied upon to stay the same .... We find ourselves plunging unprepared, a weakness in every limb. Yet this unexpected fall is also a gift, not to be refused—an initiation ordeal preparing us for new life .... Pitching headlong into this first descent of the journey, we struggle, we suffer untellable grief, but we also wake up—we begin to see our-selves and our lives for what they are."

—Zen Teacher John Tarrant, from *The Light Inside the Dark: Zen, Soul, and the Spiritual Life*

The Least You Need to Know

- There are no circumstances in which Zen practice does not apply. There are conditions where it is extremely challenging to practice, but if you do, the rewards are great.
- Zen practice gives you a greater ability to change the way you think about things—and this can make all the difference when it comes to facing adversity.
- Forbearance, or attentive endurance, is considered a Buddhist perfection. It acknowledges that sometimes life is difficult and painful, but it allows a calm dignity and gratitude in the midst of hardship.
- Extremely distressing experiences like physical illness and pain, or the loss of something or someone important to you, are profound opportunities for learning. They require you to let go of all kinds of attachments, and directly challenge your delusion of inherent, enduring self-nature.

Zen FAQs

It's worth spending some time and energy identifying the questions you have about Zen and Zen practice. Your questions are not expressions of your limitations, nor evidence of your lack of understanding. They are the edge of your experience—the places for growth, insight, and challenge. It may sound trite to say, "There are no stupid questions," but it's true, especially in Zen. Your willingness to question, explore, ponder, and acknowledge your own "not-knowing" is crucial to your Zen practice.

Any difficulties you encounter in Zen have been encountered before, by other people. Any aversion you feel to Zen tools or teachings has been experienced by others, and discussed by Zen teachers and practitioners. As long as you're respectful, you should be able to ask a Zen teacher or sangha anything. However, the answers may or may not satisfy you. If they don't satisfy, keep searching and asking. There *is* an answer to your question somewhere, but it may take some effort to make sure you really know what your question is—and you may have to answer it for yourself.

In This Chapter

- How to address common problems with meditation
- Answers to some typical questions about enlightenment
- What if Zen practice seems shallow or boring?
- Integrating Zen practice into your life—peacefully
- Considering the things you may worry about giving up

Meditation

Zen meditation, or zazen, is a deceptively simple practice: just sit there and be alert and present, and let go of commentary. If you've tried it, you know that this is not always easy to do. In fact, you may not even know what "be alert and present" really means, and you may not know how to get your mind to let go of commentary. The first years of practicing zazen—or maybe all your years of practicing zazen, even if you do it all your life—involve studying the mind and learning through experience all the things zazen is *not*. If you're doing it right, questions will constantly arise.

What If I Can't Concentrate?

Sitting zazen presents quite a paradox. Zazen is certainly not just sitting around like you normally would, allowing your mind to wander, get distracted, numb out, or obsess on things. On the other hand, it's also not about controlling your mind and getting rid of thoughts. Many people think that because they have lots of thoughts in their mind during zazen they're no good at meditation, but this is an unfortunate misunderstanding.

What you want to do is pay close, diligent, energetic attention to your experience during meditation, and sometimes this includes thoughts. Much of the time it includes thoughts, in fact. Thoughts in and of themselves are no problem. You just want to work on the habit of *not concentrating on the individual thoughts!* Your usual mental habit is to latch on to a thought, follow it on to the next thought, and the next, until you're experiencing a "train of thought."

In zazen you're learning to return your attention to the whole of your present experience, instead of latching on to thoughts. When you find you've latched on, you just let go and return to the present, hopefully without the slightest judgment (which just agitates your meditation).

Another way to think about this is that you're trying to get familiar with the space through which your thoughts move. Believe it or not, there is some space between the end of one thought and the beginning of another. When you notice this, you become aware of being larger than your thoughts and feelings. You can be more objective about them because you know they arise and pass away within your larger experience.

What If Seated Meditation Hurts?

If meditation hurts, change your posture. It can be extremely helpful to get some advice on how to do this from a Zen teacher or long-term practitioner (we give this kind of advice all the time). If pain occurs in a cross-legged posture, make sure your spinal alignment is correct (see Chapter 4; you may be slouching slightly) and your knees are lower than your hips. You may be able to achieve better posture sitting on a higher, sturdier cushion, or propping up stiff legs by placing additional cushions underneath them. If you still have pain, try a meditation bench or chair.

If you have upper back pain or sore shoulders while sitting on a meditation bench, it may help to put a cushion on your lap on which to rest your hands. You can't rest your hands on your legs in this posture, so sometimes the effort to keep them together in front of you can cause pain between your shoulder blades. As an alternative, you can rest one hand on each thigh.

If neither a floor cushion nor a bench is comfortable, try sitting in a chair. You can place a cushion on top of the chair to make it higher, so your knees will be lower than your hips. If you need back support, choose a firm cushion to place behind you to make sure you're sitting upright with correct spinal alignment. Some people sit effectively in a chair without any additional props, but you'll want to choose your chair carefully so it makes you sit up straight without leaning back.

What If I Keep Falling Asleep?

If you have trouble with drowsiness in meditation, join the club. If you don't, thank your lucky stars. It's very easy to fall asleep when you're sitting zazen. Many people are busy or distracting themselves with something from the time they wake up in the morning until the time they go to bed, so when they sit down and do absolutely nothing, the body says, "Hey! Time to go to sleep!" It can be very frustrating.

First, be patient with yourself and keep in mind that it's still useful to sit zazen. This may not seem to make sense, but the act of sitting down to meditate is important in and of itself, and if you can be as present as possible for your drowsy zazen, it's still zazen.

That said, you would probably prefer alert zazen, and you need to be alert if you want to cultivate insight in meditation. There are various methods you can try for encouraging alertness in your zazen, like sitting up straighter, breathing more deeply, making sure your eyes are open, sitting in a brighter space, or sitting at a different time of day. You might also call to mind your deepest spiritual aspirations to try to motivate yourself, or recall that your life is of limited length and it is passing by, moment after moment.

 CONSIDER THIS

Zen practitioners have been having trouble staying awake in zazen since there was anything to be called "Zen." There is evidence of this in a famous Chinese myth that says Zen master Bodhidharma, who brought the Zen form of meditation from India to China in the fifth century A.D., was having trouble with falling asleep in zazen. To stay awake he tore off his eyelids. Where his eyelids landed, tea plants sprouted—which subsequently provided Zen students with caffeine to stay awake, so they didn't have to resort to such drastic methods as Bodhidharma.

However, probably the most useful thing you can do is try to get more sleep. People throughout the industrialized world are notoriously sleep deprived. If you have regular problems with falling asleep in zazen, you're probably one of those people who need more sleep. Your poor body is so relieved when you sit down for meditation, it gets right to work—putting you to sleep. Getting more sleep may not be an option for you, but at least it can put your sleepiness into perspective.

I struggled with sleepy zazen for years, dozing off in just about every meditation period. I refused to consider the possibility that I needed more sleep, although my teacher suggested that might be the case. I couldn't give up any of my time each day. However, I finally decided to try giving up a little of my greediness, and came to realize that as long as I get nine hours of sleep a night, I rarely fall asleep in zazen. The process of accepting this limitation was a challenging practice opportunity, as I essentially had to accept a day that was two to three hours shorter than many other people's days. A good chance to give up comparison!

How Can I Make Myself Sit Regularly?

Regular meditation is just like any other healthy habit, such as eating well or getting exercise: it can be hard to start, build, and maintain. If you have trouble making yourself do it, there are two things you can try. First, try to sit every single day for at least five minutes. You probably have much higher aspirations than that, so you may feel an aversion to adopting this practice. (For example, you have a strong desire to sit for 30 minutes at a time, several times a week, and you're sure you'll start next week ....)

But if you're not sitting, you're not sitting. Doing a little each day is helpful in and of itself, and will let you start forming a habit. Chances are good you'll enjoy your five minutes of zazen, and when you have the time you'll feel like sitting longer than that. Five minutes is a short enough time that you can't possibly come up with a legitimate excuse to not do it, except on the very, very rare day.

The other thing you can try is to get some social support from other meditators. Attend meditation with a group at least once a week. Even if you aren't interested in other aspects of Zen Buddhism, you can usually attend just the zazen part of a group's schedule.

An additional way to get social support is to use an application called Insight Timer on a smart phone or tablet. It costs a few dollars, and gives you a nice timer for your meditation, with a selection of different bell tones. It also lets you create a profile on Insight Connect, which means you can see when other people all over the world are meditating with Insight Timer. You can become friends with people (including people you know) who meditate; friends can see each other's meditation sessions, including when and how long each person has meditated (even if you don't meditate at the same time). Many people have found this simple app surprisingly useful for motivating them to sit zazen regularly.

What About Weird Experiences?

Sometimes people experience strange sensations during meditation. These are called *makyo*, and can be as simple as noticing funny patterns in the wall or carpet you are staring at, or as complex as hallucinations of smells or sounds, weird physical sensations like your limbs being very heavy, or feelings of energy flowing or concentrating in certain areas of the body.

Generally speaking, these experiences are uncommon, so don't let worrying about them keep you from meditating. I only mention them here because they can be quite disconcerting and distracting if they happen to you, and you should know they are no big deal and should eventually go away. If they don't, or they are troublesome, talk to a Zen teacher.

Very rarely, people who sit a great deal will have some problems with the flow of energy around their bodies. It's difficult to describe how this feels, but it can manifest as a sense of electrical buzzing or charge, which may be uncomfortable or may result in involuntary movements. If this kind of experience gets painful or distracting or starts to interfere with your daily life, you may want to consult a body worker of some kind, such as a yoga or qigong teacher, or an acupuncturist who specializes in energy work.

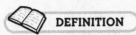

> **DEFINITION**
>
> **Makyo** are unusual, sometimes weird, sensations or perceptions that may be experienced in meditation, particularly if you meditate a great deal. They are simply side effects of meditation and are usually momentary or go away with time. They are not a sign that you are meditating poorly, or that you are meditating well.

Most of the time, however, any weird sensations and perceptions you experience in meditation will just be side effects of learning to use your mind in new ways. Usually by just letting them be, they will go away. The important thing is to not let yourself get too distracted by them. Sometimes people get rather excited about their weird meditation experiences, as if they have tapped into something supernatural or achieved a special meditative power. Zen teachers throughout the ages have admonished their students to just get over far-out experiences and get back to their practice.

If you're having ongoing makyo, it may help to lower your attention in the body to the lower abdomen, as sometimes it seems to be caused by concentrating too much energy in the head. You want to ground your meditation in the here and now, and settle your energy.

Awakening

Awakening, liberation, enlightenment—there are many terms for one of the most intriguing of human experiences. If the concept seems elusive to you, don't be surprised. In fact, it *should* be an elusive concept; wrestling with the idea of enlightenment is part of the Zen path.

Could I Achieve Enlightenment? *Me?*

First of all, enlightenment or awakening in Zen is a direction we take in practice, toward greater insight and liberation from delusion. It isn't something anyone would claim to have achieved more than a small part of, because the amount you can understand about the universe is infinite. (Beware of anyone who does claim complete enlightenment.) Still, the small part you can experience may make a huge difference in your life, so it's still worth asking whether this Zen goal is really achievable, even by you.

The answer is an emphatic "Yes!" In fact, Zen teachers throughout history have worked hard to encourage their students to *go for it!* Sometimes the teachers criticize or complain about their students, but it's never for their inherent aptitude for spiritual realization. It's because their students are failing to take advantage of the opportunity to awaken that is right in front of them. In one of the chants done regularly at Zen centers, Zen master Dogen says, "Intelligence or lack of it is not an issue; make no distinction between the dull and the sharp-witted. If you concentrate your effort single-mindedly, that in itself is wholeheartedly engaging the way." The only thing that matters with awakening is how badly you want to wake up.

 ZEN WISDOM

"Hey! What are you gawking at? Don't you see, it's about you?"

–Kodo Sawaki Roshi (1880-1965), from *The Zen Teaching of Homeless Kodo*, translated by Kosho Uchiyama

Did I Have an Enlightenment Experience?

My first inclination is to say, "No, you didn't," but that's not all there is to it. I'm inclined to say "No" because most often when people new to Zen ask this question they are either referring to makyo (see the question about this in the last section) or to what Zen tends to call an "opening." An opening can be very profound, wonderful, disorienting, and life-changing, but it is not a kensho experience, which is seeing the true nature of the self in a dramatic way, as discussed in Chapter 14.

People have openings all the time, whether they practice Zen or not, but this is not to diminish the value of openings in any way. They are often those pivotal moments when you understand something in a new way—a way that changes your relationship to the world. In this sense, you may indeed have had an enlightenment experience, but I would rather call it an *enlightening* experience. Treasure what it taught you, and even talk to a Zen teacher about it, but beware of trying to enshrine a past experience rather than just learning from it.

Also, whatever it was, it's unlikely to get you any kind of Zen badge of recognition unless you put in some extended, dedicated work in your Zen practice to demonstrate that you have processed and integrated your insight.

What If I Don't Care About Enlightenment?

I recommend you read the parts of this book on enlightenment (Chapters 12 and 16) to be sure you really don't care about experiencing some of it for yourself. It's pretty great when you do. Still, what most people mean when they ask this question is that they're okay with their life as it is, and don't feel any burning desire to experience some dramatic shift in the way they look at the world or live their life.

If you don't care about enlightenment, that's fine; you can still practice Zen. Try to be even more aware and appreciative of your life. Cultivate gratitude, and work with the precepts to become more skillful and generous with people. You can always become more attentive, appreciative, compassionate, and wise. If you spend time in Zen circles and hear about enlightenment, think of it as something people need when they aren't as happy as you are. Still, work on creating strong habits of meditation and mindfulness, because these will serve you well during difficult times in your life.

Do I Have to Go to a Monastery or Become a Monk?

If you're asking this question, it's usually because you are interested in awakening, or in fully absorbing and embodying Zen. Clearly, you don't need to go to a monastery or get ordained as a monk in order to use the Zen tools described in this book and make Zen an important part of your life. Even if you want awakening and full absorption, the answer is still no, you don't have to go to a monastery or get ordained as a monk to do this. There are highly realized and skillful Zen teachers and practitioners who have spent the bulk of their practice in the midst of busy lives, and are lay people.

 ZEN WISDOM

"Learned Audience, those who wish to train themselves [spiritually] may do so at home. It is quite unnecessary for them to stay in monasteries."

—Zen Master Hui Neng (638–713 A.D.), from the *The Sutra of Hui Neng,* as tranlated by A.F. Price and Wong Mou-Lam

However, most of those highly realized and skilled Zen folk *have* spent a significant amount of time in sesshin, or meditation retreats (see Chapter 9). In a way, this is like doing monastery or monk practice for a week at a time. Many lay people have also gone to residential practice intensives that last one to three months or more.

It's not so much that there's something magical about this monastic way of training, it's just that it's very focused, intensive, and supported. Think of it like going to an intensive training for anything else—playing a sport or a musical instrument, or learning a language. You can do these things gradually, working the study into your everyday life, or you can immerse yourself in intensive training that lets you experience and absorb a great deal in a relatively short period of time. It might be hard to make the time for this kind of concentrated training, but it can be very transformative.

How Can I Deepen My Practice?

What do you really want? Is it deep intimacy with other people, or being able to listen deeply to them? Is it the unimpeded performance of your creative or athletic skills? Is it the ability to work for a cause you are passionate about, without burning out? Zen can help you with any of these things, and you can use your desire for them to intensify and fuel your practice.

The thing is, to tap your deepest aspiration you have to find something you *really* care about, not just something you casually think would be nice. Everyone has something that touches, inspires, troubles, intrigues, or confuses them at a deep level. Focusing on serving, understanding, resolving, mastering—whatever you care about the most—makes practice into something personal, rather than something healthy you think you *should* want to deepen.

Of course, this doesn't mean Zen is a miracle-working path that will bring you wealth and fame, or anything else you want. What Zen does is help you access and unlock your own potential, which is probably more vast and amazing than you can imagine. It's not an easy, instant, or necessarily straightforward process, but that's why you have to want the end result so much.

What If My Practice Has Gotten Boring?

If you practice for a while—a year, or 5 years, or 10 years—your Zen practice may become boring. You can sit zazen okay, but don't experience any new insights. You keep the precepts well enough, and it's hard to motivate yourself to care about keeping them perfectly. Zen study and other practices no longer seem fascinating, or even enjoyable. Maybe you're still committed to practicing because you know it helps you maintain your relatively happy, healthy life, but doing it feels about as exciting or rewarding as cleaning your house or going grocery shopping.

If you're practicing Zen correctly, nothing should be boring. Boredom is actually just a lazy, vague state of dissatisfaction. Some part of you thinks that the real, rewarding stuff is over, or is happening somewhere else, and you write off your current experience. You probably think boredom is a sign that you need a change: the problem lies outside you, in the inherent inadequacy of a situation, relationship, practice, etc. However, things perceived directly, without the filter of your self-concern, are never boring. Whatever you are currently experiencing, you have never experienced before. The depth of every situation and experience is infinite; there is always more to appreciate and perceive.

CONSIDER THIS

If you're bored with your Zen practice, it may be a sign that you were expecting to get something special out of it. That is, you might have been hoping that it would make you into a different person, give you a different life, or grant you insights that would make it seem like you were living in a different world. Zen practice *is* very rewarding, but it's beneficial because it wakes you up to your life just as it is.

If you are bored with your Zen practice, boredom is your koan—the issue bringing you up against the limit of your understanding, or your ability to manifest what you understand. You can engage it as you would any koan (see Chapter 15), although you may find it difficult to rouse the energy you need to do it because boredom is a kind of laziness. If you manage to get to the bottom of your boredom, you will definitely learn something.

This is not to say that Zen practice will then become exciting again; excitement is not the opposite of boredom, it's just what you might tend to seek in order to jolt yourself out of feeling bored. Non-boredom means appreciation, which is something Zen can help you access and awaken.

Zen Practice and Your Life

Ideally, the distinction between Zen practice and your life fades away. There is no Zen practice without your life to explore and manifest it in. Still, especially early on in practice, using Zen tools and studying Zen teachings can feel like a special part of your life that can sometimes seem to be in opposition to everything else—especially your relationships, or your habitual ways of being in the world.

Why Has Practice Seemed to Make Things Worse?

Sometimes people think meditation should help relieve stress and make them calmer and more compassionate right off the bat, but instead practice has seemed to make their life more difficult. If this is the case for you, it may be that things aren't actually worse, you're just paying more attention and starting to notice how things have been all along.

You may have been avoiding thinking too much about certain difficult things, like dysfunction in your relationships, dissatisfaction with your job, or harmful patterns of behavior. You may have been suppressing troubling memories or emotions that practice can start to bring to the surface.

Facing these kinds of things can be painful, and may require you to make some tough choices or give up some attachments, so perhaps without even realizing it, you may have been ignoring them or keeping yourself busy with distractions so you didn't have to face them.

On the other hand, you may have always been aware of your problems and issues, but practice has seemed to make things worse because you have finally made some of the changes and decisions to take care of them. This can cause things and people in your environment to shift, perhaps making things more difficult for a while. Making amends, changing habits, and facing consequences all take work, and can be uncomfortable. Try to have faith that you will manage to clean up your life and get things on track, and cultivate patience for this incredibly important process.

What If Practice Causes Relationship Problems?

Sometimes Zen practice can cause some problems in your closest, intimate relationships. There are two primary reasons for this. The first is that you are spending lots of time and energy doing your Zen practice, and the people in your life feel neglected or threatened by it. This is pretty natural, especially if your significant others don't understand or relate to Zen.

Assuming you want to maintain harmony in your relationships, it can help just to be aware of the possibility that the people in your life need a little more time, attention, and appreciation as you deepen your Zen practice, so they can learn to be comfortable with it. It may help to designate a weekend day that you always spend with your partner or family, no matter what Zen event you'd like to attend.

You might also negotiate being able to spend a weekend at a retreat in exchange for spending a weekend with your significant other where you don't meditate or read any Zen books at all. When people see that you're able to pick up and put down your Zen tools out of compassion for them, they're likely to feel more supportive of your practice.

The second reason Zen practice might cause some friction in your closest relationships is that you are changing. People get used to one another acting in certain ways and fulfilling certain roles. People also end up validating one another's behaviors in subtle or obvious ways, such as engaging in gossip or complaining together, overindulging in alcohol or food together, or encouraging one another's anger or resentment.

If, for personal reasons, you change your behavior, it can make the people around you feel confused, worried, criticized, or even threatened. For example, perhaps you and a close friend used to spend most of your time together engaged in critical commentary about your other friends, and people in general. This was a connecting behavior for the two of you. If you suddenly lose your appetite for it, your friend will probably wonder whether you feel judgmental of her for continuing the old style of conversation. She may also wonder whether your friendship is going to last.

If you want a relationship in your life to continue through your Zen practice, it may be helpful to be slower and gentler when making changes. As long as you maintain mindfulness, you don't have to stop or change your behaviors overnight. Maintaining some awareness of the effects of your actions on others may help you make changes in your life in such a way that others are able to change along with you.

POTENTIAL PITFALL

You may find yourself becoming judgmental of other people when you start practicing Zen. As you pay attention to your own life, you start realizing how harmful certain behaviors are, and how liberating it can be to face the truth or give up attachments. At the same time you notice how other people are stuck in their greed, delusions, or anger—and how rarely they seem to want to do anything to change! At least, this is how it can appear to you. If you find yourself feeling judgmental, remember the Zen admonition to "do your own practice." Over time you will tend to notice more about other people's circumstances, and be able to feel more understanding, compassion, and patience.

Do I Have to Give Up Strong Emotions?

If you are asking this question, you're probably somewhat identified with your emotions. Perhaps they make you feel alive, or are synonymous, for you, with caring deeply about the people and things in your life. If this is the case, then to some extent you will have to give up your strong emotions. Or, to be more accurate, you have to give up your *attachment* to your strong emotions.

As discussed in Chapter 13, an attachment is something you have incorporated into your self-concept, or think of as a possession of self. This means you are personally invested in its existence. In the case of strong emotions, this means that you will start to feel your sense of self threatened when you *don't* feel strong emotions. You will start to worry about what's happening, you'll probably look around for something that will trigger strong emotions in you so you can feel normal again.

Giving up attachment to strong emotions does not mean you never experience strong emotions again, and it does not mean you are permanently opting for some emotionally neutral or bland state (as if that were healthy or even possible). When you are no longer attached to strong emotions, it's simply that you can allow them to come and go.

Sometimes you will feel strong emotion, and sometimes you won't. You are no longer *dependent* on experiencing powerful feelings to know you are alive. This allows you to appreciate more subtle feelings and experiences, which can become as rich and rewarding as the dramatic emotions used to. A moment of calm while drinking a cup of tea can seem precious and validating, where it probably used to get lost amidst all the searching for excitement. However, non-attachment to emotion will still leave you open and ready for being deeply moved by people and things, so don't worry that Zen will make you boring or numb.

Is It Still Okay to Want Things?

If you can want things without it making you miserable, go ahead! In fact, if you are refraining from wanting anything at all, it's probably just about protecting yourself from disappointment by holding back from life, which is not the Zen way. Still, if you want things in the way that is habitual for most people, chances are there will be some unhappiness mixed in with your desire. You probably believe, to some extent, that obtaining the thing you want will make you happier, or that until you get it, you're somehow incomplete. These beliefs mean that until you get what you want, you won't really be happy. They also mean that if you can't get what you want, you'll feel at least a little suffering.

If you can maintain gratitude for, and contentment with, your life just as it is, it's possible to want things without it causing problems. It's helpful to say to yourself, "It would be nice if [insert the outcome you desire here]." You can acknowledge that you would really enjoy such-and-such, or even that a certain outcome would make peace of mind, happiness, health, etc., very easy for you to access. Still, your ultimate happiness is not dependent on obtaining the object of your desire.

What About Zen and Pleasure?

If you are attached to experiencing pleasure, it presents the same problems as attachment to anything else (see the discussion about strong emotions earlier in this chapter). Assuming you are not particularly attached to pleasure, what is the relationship between Zen practice and enjoying the sensual, aesthetically pleasing aspects of life?

CONSIDER THIS

Zen has been associated with forms of artistic expression over the millennia, perhaps because of its ability to help increase your powers of attention and appreciation. For example, Zen had significant influence on the formal Japanese tea ceremony, which involves a highly developed sense of aesthetic and a sincere appreciation of grace, beauty, generosity, being with others, and the delicious taste of green tea.

For many people, pleasure is associated primarily with expensive experiences or possessions, rich foods, sex, excitement, novelty, and overindulgence in enjoyable activities or intoxicants. There is nothing inherently wrong with these sources of pleasure, but they often are obtained at a cost. At some point the cost may put them out of your reach, or impact your health or relationships. It's also easy to become dependent on such sources of pleasure, because they are so extreme, rich, intoxicating, or exciting. This will require that you spend lots of your time and money seeking special opportunities for pleasure, and the time in between pleasurable experiences will seem dull in comparison.

Zen does not in any way advocate giving up pleasure. In fact, your ability to enjoy the precious-ness of life provides a big part of your motivation to practice Zen. What Zen recommends is *simplifying your tastes.* There are wonderful opportunities for experiencing pleasure all around you, and most of them are free and have no side effects!

Waking up in the morning with the ability to breathe and move is a pleasure. Giving your loved one a kiss before he or she leaves for work is a pleasure. Cherry blossoms, the smell of fresh-cut grass, a completed project, and a new insight are all sources of pleasure. If these sound pretty lame or boring to you, you still have some work to do in order to be able to tap the real pleasure in them. The delight and appreciation you can experience in simple things can be every bit as intense and exquisite as what you get from more glamorous sources of pleasure.

Will Zen Change Me Too Much?

The answer to this question depends on what you mean by "too much." Maybe you'd like to get rid of your problems, but you don't like the idea of changing so much that you lose track of who you are. Maybe you like your sense of humor, your personality, your creativity, or your critical thinking, and you are a little worried that you will lose them in the process of deep Zen practice. While it's true that you will need to give up your attachment to being any particular way, generally speaking the only aspects of your personality that go away are the ones you are better off without.

As discussed earlier, attachment means you have made acting or being a certain way part of your self-identity. In order to open up to the deepest kind of Zen liberation, you will need to loosen your grip on your attachments and become more familiar with the true nature of the self, which isn't fixed any particular way.

However, your basic flavor will remain because of your karma (genetics, upbringing, experiences, conditions, past actions, etc.). In fact, the good parts of yourself—the parts that don't contribute to suffering and delusion—will probably come out even more strongly as you gain confidence and stop second-guessing yourself so much. When you meet someone who really embodies Zen, they tend to be very much an individual, even quirky, not because they are trying to be different or special, but just because they are completely themselves.

Still, certain things may have to go, particularly behaviors that break precepts. For example, when I started practicing Zen I was quite attached to my sense of humor, which was based on wry, sarcastic comments about the things I encountered. Over time I saw how these comments cut me off from people and things because they required a certain kind of rejection, and placing myself above others.

CONSIDER THIS

There is a rather humorous Zen metaphor for how you can work on yourself and transcend your self-concern, but still be a unique individual with plenty of personality. It's as if you are a cloth bag containing a bunch of fish. As you practice, you empty out the bag and wash it clean. However, no matter how clean you get it, there still lingers the stain and smell of fish. Maybe not a glamorous view of individuality, but the idea is that you end up with affection—but not attachment—for your stinking fish bag.

I gradually stopped employing my sarcasm, and, frankly, I wasn't nearly as funny anymore. It was still worth changing, and I realized that my sarcastic sense of humor had been something I used to make people want to be around me, and I really didn't need it for that purpose anymore. (Amazingly, people are attracted to being around *nice* people—who would have thought?) I still have a sense of humor, but now it can manifest in ways that aren't negative and mean.

The Least You Need to Know

- The questions you have about Zen are vital to your Zen practice—keep looking for them and asking them.
- There are ways to address all the various challenges you face in zazen, including physical discomfort, drowsiness, or a busy mind.
- Wrestling with the concept of enlightenment can be frustrating, but also rewarding. It's meant to be challenging.
- It's natural to experience some awkwardness as you make Zen practice part of your life; change can be difficult for you—and for the people you are close to.
- You'll have to do lots of letting go of attachments in Zen, but you'll find that all the best parts of life are completely compatible with realizing and manifesting Zen.

Mastering the Art of Living

This chapter is about taking your mastery of the art of living to the next level: actively participating in the world, grounded in your Zen practice. The importance of doing this is illustrated by the classic Zen image of the enlightened sage coming out of the monastery or forest where he has trained, and "returning to the marketplace." This sage, if he is truly a sage, does not stand out when he returns. He does not necessarily impress people. Instead, he blends in and quietly goes about manifesting enlightenment, shoulder to shoulder with other people, contributing in whatever way he can.

An essential aspect of the Zen path is helping others. This is not only a sign of enlightenment, it's an *enactment* of enlightenment, so it's important to do it whether you have "realized" anything special or not. When you have seen there's no real separation between you and all other beings, compassion manifests naturally. You feel greater intimacy with all things, because you are no longer caught up in self-concern and defensiveness. Your energy is freed up to work in a way that helps others, not just yourself. You aren't getting in your own way by clinging to ideas and attachments, so you can find the best way for you, personally, to benefit the world.

In This Chapter

- Opening up to more intimacy in your life
- Learning to respond from your true self
- Discovering the best work you can do in the world
- Helping others as a natural outcome of practice
- Keeping your aspirations high but grounded

Allowing Intimacy

Intimacy is about not being separate. People usually think of intimacy in terms of being close with your partner, friends, and family, but it's also rewarding to experience intimacy with each moment of your life. It's precious to feel no separation from your morning routine, your drive to work, your career, your own behavior, and the challenges you face. You can feel intimate with the person waiting at the bus stop with you, your neighbor, and your co-worker. When you feel intimate with people, things, and circumstances, they appear more open and clear to you. It feels like there's a meeting between you and what you're encountering, like there's dialogue and connection—even if nothing is said, or what you're meeting is inanimate.

 ZEN WISDOM

"If we actually wake up to who we are, we will discover a great and compelling intimacy ... with our own hearts, our own environment, our own lives. The call is to tumble into the stream, to learn the current, to flow toward the great ocean. And, I've noticed, as we discover this truth, as we tumble into the Way, we are changed. Our hearts become larger. We care more, and our actions can become the work of God, even if we're only tending a tiny corner of the vineyard."

—Zen Teacher James Ishmael Ford, from *If You're Lucky, Your Heart Will Break: Field Notes from a Zen Life*

The sense of separation most people walk around with can be subtle but pervasive. You may not even realize it's there until you start deliberately examining it. Then you may see, as I once did, that it feels like there's a filter of self between you and everything else.

For example, I remember being given a task at a meditation retreat that involved going out-side to meditate on a flower. We were asked to be very still while looking at the flower, and see if we could drop our sense of separation from it, or realize "not-two." I sat there staring at my flower, longing desperately to be able to "be one" with it—or with anything!—but I still felt such a strong sense of self that intimacy seemed very far away. In fact, my very longing to experience "no separation" seemed to put even more distance between myself and everything else. I began to conceive of my "self" as being a huge obstacle that needed to be dismantled, renounced—or even destroyed.

Fortunately, over time I was able to feel much more intimacy with flowers and everything else—but the route to that intimacy wasn't what I expected it to be. Essentially, I had to take care of my own internal suffering and delusion so I could relax and simply *allow* the intimacy to be. This involved many years of meditation, karma work, and cultivating insight that helped me understand my own body and mind, resolve my most distressing issues, let go of my biggest attachments, and start to appreciate my true, empty self-nature (see Chapter 12).

I did enough work that I attained some measure of peace, and was able to sit and look at a flower without being overwhelmed by self-concern. I was able to just sit and look at a flower, and consequently discovered that intimacy is usually a quiet, subtle thing that is easily missed.

The more Zen practice you do, and the more you work on understanding and liberating yourself, the more intimacy you will be able to feel with everything. It's like you manage to get your house more or less in order, so you can finally look outward and take notice of all the wonder around you. It's not the same thing to simply ignore the troubles in your life, or the fears deep in your psyche, and try to focus on others. That's like closing the door of your house and pretending you don't care about the problems inside it.

To further develop this metaphor, your "house" is the flow of causes and conditions that manifests as *you*, so you really can't ignore what's going on in it. Only when you've done your housecleaning, repaired the leak in the roof, and paid the mortgage can you wholeheartedly turn your energy outward. The more thorough a housecleaning you do, the less you have to worry about your life. Even when everything looks okay on the surface, you open closets and explore basements to make sure there isn't anything moldering or lurking in there that can eventually cause damage. When your house is in order, it functions to support you as you turn your attention to your work.

 POTENTIAL PITFALL

> If you would like more intimacy with people, and with your life, you might need to let go of your ideas about what intimacy looks or feels like. The popular conception of intimacy is what is portrayed in movies, where experiences of closeness are usually intense, emotional, and explicitly recognized as intimate by all parties involved. Occasionally intimacy feels like this, but if you limit your perception of intimacy to this kind of experience, it may feel like life has very few moments of special closeness interspersed with long periods of dry isolation. Deep intimacy is usually much more subtle, like not needing to ask a friend how she's feeling because you are so in tune with her.

The intimacy you experience when you've dropped a lot of your self-concern becomes the basis for how you choose to live your life. Instead of being caught up in lots of ideas, hopes, and fears about what your life will be, you start to listen to what the world is telling you. You can start to trust that you will encounter a need you can meet, and then go from there.

Because your self-concern is so much lighter, it doesn't matter if circumstances seem to be moving you in a different direction than you expected to go. What matters is your ongoing dialogue or dance with your life, and whether you're showing up for it wholeheartedly. You don't compare your activity with that of other people, or judge whether it is significant in the grand scheme of things—it is personal, it is yours, and the universe asked you to do it. How can you refuse?

Expressing Your True Self

Ironically, it's a very personal manifestation in the world that exemplifies a transcendence of self-concern, and a letting go of self-attachments. It may seem strange, but ultimately, after all that stillness and silence, you have to say something. If you don't, you're hiding out, still trying to protect yourself. But if you're ready to step forward and say something, how do you know the right thing to say? How do you find your authentic voice, or position, or work? How can you know when you're responding to the world's intimate request without self-concern?

Expressing your true self in a Zen way is much different than the popular conception of "expressing your true self." Most people think this involves forming unique ideas, opinions, and agendas, and then asserting them in the world. In this kind of expression, you base your communication and actions on the belief that you have—and yes, here it is again!—an inherent, enduring self-essence. There is a special, unique *you* that is making itself known in the world. What drives the expression are your desires and ideas—what you *really* want, what you *really* believe, what you are determined to bring about.

This may not sound so bad, and in a way it's not (depending on what you are determined to bring about), but the problem is that this is looking at your "true self" in shallow terms. It's basing your life on things that are subject to change and are likely to be self-attachments, such as opinions, skills, and roles. When you do this, your "true self" can be a source of suffering, a point of conflict with others, and likely to change (which is disorienting, because you didn't just identify it as *self*, you identified as especially *true*).

A deeper kind of true self can be discovered through Zen practice, as discussed in Chapters 12 and 14. This self is an acceptance of, and responsibility for, the flow of causes and conditions that is your life. It's based in your experience of the present moment, where a response from your true self is dynamic, and free from fear and self-concern. You've ended up with this remarkable set of causes and conditions that give you a unique point of view and set of skills and knowledge to draw from.

A true expression from this self is entirely conditional and unselfconscious. Your true response to a particular circumstance or need today may be different from your true response tomorrow. It's not about maintaining a particular persona, set of ideas, patterns of behavior, preferences, beliefs, or desires. Instead, it's about being as centered, aware, dignified, and ready as you can be, at all times. You can't draw a boundary around this deeper true self and all the things that belong to it.

Your true self-nature is fundamentally without characteristics of its own. In the course of living your life, you may indeed have a flavor, tendencies, style, and things you adopt and take care of. But these things are the *result* of your expression of true self; they do not define it.

When you say or do something from the place of true self, you are often surprised at the results. Your response arises naturally, all by itself (that is, without the apparent direction of an inherent, enduring self-essence), and generally represents the best you have to offer at that given moment. When you subsequently say something that benefits someone, or create something beautiful, or skillfully complete a project, you aren't inclined to take credit. Instead, you stand back and say, "Wow, look at that!"

Another way to describe expressing your true self is responding without self in the way. The self that gets in the way is "small" self, your self-concept and its associated self-concern. As the ancient Zen masters said, your true self is no-self (see Chapter 14). Acting from the place of no-self is something people often do spontaneously when they're engaged in an activity they're passionate about, and for which they have trained extensively.

This is what athletes, artists, and others refer to as "the zone"—a way of being where you are entirely focused, present, and ready, and are at your very best in terms of performance. In the zone, you do not anticipate what you are going to do next. You don't worry about the results, or dwell in self-consciousness about what the results are going to mean for you. You just *do*, wholeheartedly, without the small self in the way.

Being able to get self out of the way at will, rather than only while doing a particular specialized activity, is a challenging process that requires diligent practice. As described elsewhere in this book, you can work on this by gaining insight into the functioning of your own body and mind through meditation and mindfulness, working on your selfish habits of mind and body with karma and precept work, learning to recognize and let go of attachments, and ultimately seeking a personal experience of the true nature of self.

Finding What Is Yours to Do

Learning to respond from true self (which is no-self) is one thing, but what about active expression—action that doesn't feel so much like simply responding to circumstances, but instead involves stepping forward, taking the lead, creating, building, or affecting change? How do you know when to take this kind of action? How do you decide what actions you should take, or what you should commit yourself to? My teachers described the process of answering these questions as finding "what is yours to do."

The Search

Typically, people look out at the world and try to decide what course of action to take—what career to strive for, whether to have a family, what cause to devote themselves to—by considering such things as what they are good at, what they enjoy, what might be worthy of respect and admiration, and what might be lucrative.

Decisions about what to do with your life energy can be very difficult to make. You may feel drawn to many things, or to mutually exclusive things. You may worry that you'll commit yourself to something and then discover it makes you miserable. You may try to plan and antici-pate all the possible pros and cons of each option. When you decide on something, you may feel doubt and grief about roads not taken.

Finding what is yours to do is much more of a receptive, responsive process than you might expect. Your preferences and skills certainly enter into the equation, but in equal measure with patience and attentiveness to opportunity. You try to respond to circumstances from no-self, as described in the previous section, so your attention ends up being on the present rather than on the future. When you have to make decisions, you make them right here and now. They are a response to the present, and not actually about the future.

For example, let's say you have to decide whether or not to seek an advanced degree, and con-sequently take on a great deal of debt. This is a very tough decision to make. Will the degree be worth it? Will you be able to pay off your debt? Will you actually enjoy the work that the degree will allow you to do? So many things to consider and worry about! Now, it's very neces-sary to gather all the information you can and make an informed decision, and the process can't be rushed. Still, ultimately you make the best decision you can *right now* and then let all the worrying go. There are never any guarantees, so taking your next step is always a risk and an adventure.

 CONSIDER THIS

> Discovering what is yours to do, or your life's work, can take a long time. It's very rewarding to find it, but if you feel like it's beyond your grasp you shouldn't be too hard on yourself. It might help to think of your true calling as being a seed within you that requires time and the right conditions to germinate, grow, and finally break through the soil into the light. It may not feel like there's an answer to your question, "What should I do?" because there actually isn't one—yet.

Finding what is yours to do, in this deep Zen sense, is not actually about you. It certainly involves and affects you, but the process is not focused on making you happy, or fulfilling your vision for your life, or making sure you end up in a lucrative, respectable position. Coming from no-self, you recognize no inherently real separation between yourself and the rest of the world, so your benefit is not separate from the benefit of others. You naturally want to do what you can for the sake of others, and for the world in general.

This leaves you open to suggestion, as well as to possibilities you have never considered before. Life may end up pointing you in a direction you never expected or envisioned. If you feel enough compatibility with that direction, the fact that life seems to be asking it of you will be enough to make it rewarding.

Embracing Your Work

You may or may not be an idealist, but if you are, what is yours to do will probably end up looking smaller than your ambitions or aspirations. Viewed from the outside, what you finally commit yourself to may seem like compromising or settling. Fortunately, finding what is truly yours to do is not about compromising or settling, it's about wholeheartedly meeting and embracing the reality of your life.

For example, for many years I held the ideals of Mother Teresa, Dr. Martin Luther King Jr., and Gandhi front and center in my mind. The brave actions of these individuals seemed, to me, to go right to the heart of the matter, and to exemplify selflessness. Doing anything less dramatic with my life looked to me like cowardice or selfishness. And yet, given my life circumstances, I didn't see any way to enact my ideals in the pure and concrete way I saw demonstrated by the remarkable individuals I admired. Sure, I could have given everything away and lived in poverty in order to work with people in need—but to do so felt to me like rejecting my life and going away to live someone else's.

Eventually I realized that it is not so much up to me what I do, and it is definitely not up to me what kind of effect I have in the world. Mother Teresa, Dr. King, and Gandhi were responding to their lives from their true self. Who they happened to be and their circumstances came together to make their stories remarkable, and their actions so impactful. You or I might be faced with a similar confluence of need, opportunity, inspiration, and ability, and end up making a big change in the world. Or we might not. It doesn't matter how your work compares to the work of others, it only matters that it is yours.

 ZEN WISDOM

"The sutras say, 'The Dharma includes no being because it's free from the impurity of being, and the Dharma includes no self because it's free from the impurity of self.' Those wise enough to believe and understand this truth are bound to practice according to the Dharma. And since that which is real includes nothing worth begrudging, they give their body, life, and property in charity, without regret, without the vanity of giver, gift, or recipient, and without bias or attachment."

—Zen Master Bodhidharma, fifth century, as translated by Red Pine in *The Zen Teaching of Bodhidharma*

What is yours to do is often taking care of something that no one else can, or that few other people even see needs care. My teacher once told me a story of when she was in the monastery and felt frustrated because the windows in a particular part of the building were getting grimier and grimier. People were supposed to thoroughly clean the monastery, but for some reason no one ever thought to take care of the windows. Eventually my teacher realized the windows were hers to take care of. She saw them, she cared about them, and she knew what needed to be done.

What is yours to do may be similarly subtle and humble. Your work may go largely unnoticed or unappreciated by people. Perhaps your work is to take care of your neighborhood, or educate people about a particular environmental problem, or raise your children to be good people. You can tell it's yours to do because when you do it, things come together. Things flow. You are the right piece for that part of the puzzle, and if you listen carefully, you can perceive the gratitude of the universe for your contribution.

Helping Others

If you withdraw from active engagement with the world in order to do Zen practice, it should only be temporarily—as long as it takes you to transcend your self-concern. This may take years, of course, but then you should get back to work. Perhaps your work is to stay in a monastery and help others to awaken, but in any case you wake up from your stupor of self-interest and start responding naturally to the world around you in the ways I have been discussing in this chapter.

Without deliberately setting out to *be someone who is helpful to others* (because this is just self-attachment), you get to work helping others. Or, perhaps more appropriately, you get to work *helping*, because there is no real separation between you and others. Still, it is useful to focus on helping others, because it runs counter to your habitual self-concern.

What Is Helpful?

What does it mean to help others? Chances are you can think of a number of jobs or activities that help people, or help the environment. You probably think of serving people who are explicitly in need, working for positive change in our political system or culture, or helping out friends and family who are in trouble. Ideas about helping usually involve someone who (or something that) needs help, the help given, and someone who (or something that) receives the help. It's seen as an explicit, identifiable process.

The Zen view of helping is different. Actually, you help others and yourself by doing your Zen practice, when the focus of your effort is on self-study and—to use the metaphor from earlier in this chapter—getting your own house in order. In your efforts you are challenging your own delusions and selfishness, and moving gradually toward causing less suffering and attaining more happiness.

As you return to more active engagement with the world and look for what is yours to do, you help others, regardless of what your work looks like (unless it is actually harmful), by transforming your work into a gift (see Chapter 19). You benefit others by simply being at peace, joyful, generous, and appreciative of your life.

However, how do you know if your peace, joy, and appreciation are helping others, versus simply serving your own self-interests? This is actually a tough question. It requires repeated self-examination and continued practice. You never get to rest comfortably in certainty that you're doing enough, that you're awake as opposed to complacent, or that you've made good choices that mean your life is beyond reproach. This is why Zen Buddhists frequently chant the four bodhisattva vows:

Beings are numberless, I vow to free them all.

Delusions are inexhaustible, I vow to end them all.

Dharma [truth] gates are boundless, I vow to master them all.

The buddha way is unsurpassable, I vow to attain it.

Clearly, these vows are impossible to keep, so what is the value of making them? If you can't even count how many beings there are, how can you free them all? For that matter, can you truly free anyone, or do they have to free themselves? If it is impossible to exhaust delusions and their associated negative effects like hatred and selfishness, how do you end them *all?* There is no limit to the truth, or what can be learned and mastered, and the path of awakening never actually ends—so what are these vows about mastery and attainment about?

The answer to all these questions is simply this: these vows are about the direction of your life and the orientation of your heart. Do you change that direction and orientation just because it's impossible to completely achieve your goal? Of course not. And in the meantime, you can repeat your intention in order to stay honest about your life. If you've been getting complacent and selfish, it will probably become obvious to you if you call to mind noble aspirations like the four bodhisattva vows.

CONSIDER THIS

According to Buddhist teachings, there are three levels of giving, or helping others. The first level reflects a rather limited understanding, when you want to make others happy but you are still rather self-centered: you give others what *you* would like to receive. At the next level you have learned to be more attentive to others, and you give them what they want. At the third level (and this requires some clarity and wisdom), you give them what is most beneficial.

How Wisdom Helps

The most effective kind of helping requires the cultivation of wisdom. Too often you try to help, only to have the help rejected or to find out that what you did wasn't as helpful as you had hoped. In order to know *how* to help—or what is the most beneficial thing to offer—you need to meet your circumstances from a place of no-self, as discussed in the first section of this chapter. This allows your best understanding to manifest without the obscurations of your own agenda or ideas. You become able to let people and situations "tell" you what is needed and when it would best be given.

Another important reason to cultivate wisdom as you help others is that the whole project can become very discouraging if you don't keep emptiness in mind. Remember those impossible bodhisattva vows? They can start to seem pretty relevant when you're trying to do anything positive in the world. Even the biggest, noblest project can seem like a drop in a bucket when it comes to addressing the injustice and suffering in the world. At the last minute, the beneficial effects you were anticipating don't come to pass, and you wonder if your effort was wasted. When you devote yourself to one cause, you neglect all the others. You may start to doubt whether you are really helping at all.

Fortunately, recognizing the emptiness of self, other, and all phenomena can help your effort stay sincere, energetic, and wholehearted. Understanding emptiness can keep you from making your helping into a self-attachment: something that *must* have enough of a positive effect to make it worthwhile.

The Buddhist sutra *The Perfection of Wisdom in Eight Thousand Lines* describes the activity of bodhisattvas, or beings who cultivate wisdom and then take those vows mentioned earlier: bodhisattvas "engender in themselves the great compassion, which is, however, free from any notion of a being … when the notion of suffering and beings leads [them] to think: 'Suffering I shall remove, the weal of the world I shall work!' Beings are then imagined, a self is imagined, [and] the practice of wisdom, the highest perfection, is lacking."

As soon as you return to operating out of your self-concept, your great work is compromised. The sutra goes on to say that "all words for things in use in this world must be left behind, all things produced and made must be transcended." Essentially, you wholeheartedly and selflessly continue your beneficial activity without getting stuck in abstractions or comparisons. You don't decide what is helpful by calculating the payoff at some future date; you know what is helpful by being fully aware of reality in the moment of helping.

The Least You Need to Know

- Intimacy is not something you have to seek for, it's something you open up to more and more when you start learning to transcend self-concern.

- Your true self is no-self, so expressing your true self is actually responding to the world without self in the way.

- Despite all the letting go Zen asks you to do, ultimately practice includes wholeheartedly embodying your unique manifestation in this world.

- There is something (or many things) in your life that is yours to do. Finding it involves responding to a need you are particularly well positioned or equipped to address.

- Helping others is good practice, but it is also the manifestation of enlightenment.

Glossary

Awakening *See* enlightenment.

bodhisattva The Buddhist ideal of a being who diligently cultivates his or her own discipline and wisdom in order to attain enlightenment, but who also has great compassion for all living beings and works for their happiness as well. The bodhisattva is not satisfied with his or her own attainment of peace and liberation, but only accepts the reward of final nirvana once all other beings are also freed.

buddha Literally "one who is awakened," buddha means a person who has completely woken up to the truth and dispelled all of his or her delusions. Whether there has ever been a human being who is a complete buddha is a matter of debate, although many Buddhists believe there was at least one: Shakyamuni Buddha, originally Siddhartha Gautama, who lived over 2,500 years ago.

dharma The Buddhist teachings, but also simply fundamental truth. The Buddhist or Zen dharma includes all of the teachings and practices in those traditions that point to the truth, but dharma as truth itself is larger than any particular tradition.

dokusan Also called *sanzen*, dokusan is a formal, one-on-one meeting between a Zen student and an authorized Zen teacher. The student presents his or her practice by asking a question or sharing his or her experience, and the teacher responds in such a way as to encourage or deepen the student's Zen. Dokusan is usually brief, about 5 to 10 minutes or less, and focused on one pivotal issue.

dukkha Alternatively translated as suffering, stress, dissatisfaction, or unease, dukkha refers to the full spectrum of human unhappiness from acute suffering to a subtle sense of things not being quite right.

enlightenment A deliberately elusive and complex concept, enlightenment in Zen essentially means waking up to reality. This means you realize there is no real separation between self and other, except in your own mind. You realize all things are empty of inherent, enduring self-nature, and that all things are interdependent. Therefore there is no need to hold on to self-concern, and compassion arises naturally.

five aggregates   The elements that compose the self: physical form, sensations (or feelings, particularly sensing pleasant, unpleasant, or neutral), perceptions (or cognition, naming and identifying things), formations (volition and associated conceptions and mental habits), and consciousness (awareness of all of the elements and the world). Also called the five skandhas.

four bodhisattva vows   Four vows recited regularly in Zen centers and monasteries: Beings are numberless, I vow to free them all; delusions are inexhaustible, I vow to end them all; dharma [truth] gates are boundless, I vow to master them all; the buddha way is unsurpassable, I vow to attain it.

four noble truths   Shakyamuni Buddha's first teaching, which summarizes the essence of Buddhist thought. Translations differ, but they can be expressed like this: 1) recognize the existence of dukkha in your life; 2) learn the causes of that dukkha; 3) let go of the causes of that dukkha; and 4) in all areas of your life, do what supports your ability to take the other three steps. *See* dukkha.

jukai   The ceremony at which people take vows to follow the Zen precepts and formally become a Zen Buddhist. The precepts have to be given by an authorized Zen teacher.

kanzeon   The bodhisattva who embodies compassion, Kanzeon is one of the most popular Buddhist images apart from Shakyamuni Buddha. Kanzeon (or Kuan Yin in China, and Avalokiteshvara in India and Tibet) is described as the "one who hears the cries of the world," and is always ready to respond to need.

karma   Literally "action" or "deed," but also the chain of cause and effect that results from that deed when effects in turn become causes.

kensho   Literally "seeing the true nature of self," kensho generally refers to a dramatic awakening experience where someone suddenly realizes there is no inherent, enduring self-nature. However, the same thing can be understood more gradually, with lots of smaller insights. Another word for seeing this truth is *satori*.

kinhin   Walking meditation that can be done slowly and timed with your breathing, or very quickly. In either case the goal is to keep the attention entirely on your movement. Kinhin is often done in Zen groups between periods of zazen (seated meditation).

koans   Teachings a Zen student contemplates and engages intensively until reaching a deep personal understanding of them. Formal koans are usually stories of historical interactions between teacher and student and present an essential, non-intellectual teaching. Informal koans are challenges that arise in life and practice that require you to *live out* the answer; it's not enough to just have an idea about what the answer is.

kshanti   One of the six perfections, or paramitas, kshanti can be translated as forbearance, tolerance, ability to bear, or composure. It is particularly applicable when you are experiencing difficulty.

law of karma The moral law of the universe, a natural law rather like the law of gravity, which states that selfish or harmful actions—especially ones that are intentionally so—always result in at least some negative consequences for the doer (as well as others).

lineage The Zen term for the transmission of teachings and practices from teacher to student over time. It's like Zen genealogy. There is great emphasis on lineage in Zen because of the idea that true understanding and manifestation of Zen teachings can only be recognized by a person who has attained them him- or herself; the teacher recognizes the student's attainment and empowers her or him to carry on the tradition. Every lineage ends up with a slightly (or very) different style and flavor.

makyo Unusual, sometimes unnerving, physical sensations or minor hallucinations that may be experienced in meditation, particularly if you meditate a great deal. Makyo are side-effects of meditation and are usually momentary or go away with time. They are not a sign that you are meditating poorly, or that you are meditating well.

mindfulness The practice of returning your attention to what's in front of you and keeping it there, particularly when you are engaged in some kind of movement or task.

nirvana Liberation from samsara, achieved by putting an end to the grasping and aversion that keep you bound to the cycle of birth and death. *See* samsara.

noble eightfold path The fourth Noble Truth, which outlines the essential components of Buddhist practice: right speech, right action, right livelihood, right concentration, right mindfulness, right effort, right view, and right intention.

paramita A perfection, or basis for enlightenment. There are different lists of paramitas in Buddhism, but Zen usually uses a list of six: generosity (*dana*), morality (*sila*), diligence or energy (*virya*), forbearance (*kshanti*), meditation or concentration (*dhyana*), and wisdom (*prajna*).

rakusu A bib-like cloth garment that may be received during Jukai or a formal student ceremony, along with a Buddhist name. It is subsequently worn during sangha practice events.

Rinzai Zen A school of Zen Buddhism that arose in China in the ninth or tenth century A.D. that tends to emphasize dramatic awakenings to the true nature of reality and employs traditional teaching stories, or *koans*, to facilitate such awakening.

roshi A Japanese title meaning "old teacher," that implies a mastery of Zen generally understood to come only with many decades of practice.

samadhi An ancient Pali and Sanskrit term for the experience of one-pointed concentration, alternatively translated as absorption, or collectedness.

samatha Translated as tranquility or calm abiding, samatha is the aspect of meditation that involves letting go of any volitional engagement with thinking in order to experience reality as a whole.

samsara   An ancient pre-Buddhist term referring to the endless cycle of birth and death, happiness and suffering, good fortune and bad fortune experienced by living beings.

sangha   A community of Zen and/or Buddhist practitioners. From the beginning of Buddhism, the value of learning from, practicing with, and teaching others has been strongly emphasized; sangha is considered one of the three treasures of Buddhism, along with buddha and dharma.

sanzen   *See* dokusan.

satori   Comprehension or understanding, particularly of the true nature of self. *See* kensho.

seiza   Kneeling posture in which, unless you are using a bench, you sit on your heels.

seiza bench   A short bench you sit on while kneeling on the floor in the seiza position.

sensei   A Japanese title for a teacher, used to indicate respect for someone's authority within their realm of expertise.

sesshin   Intensive, communal, silent meditation retreats, usually of at least three days duration and involving a 24-hour schedule. The schedule includes formal Zen practices like zazen, chanting, and study, but also all of the basic activities of daily life like eating, working, and sleeping.

Shakyamuni Buddha   The name for Siddhartha Gautama after he attained enlightenment around 500 B.C. Shakyamuni subsequently taught what he realized, and his teachings became Buddhism.

shikantaza   Only (*shikan*) precisely (*ta*) sitting (*za*). This refers particularly to themeless zazen, as opposed to meditating with koans.

Soto Zen   A school of Zen Buddhism that arose in China in the ninth century A.D. that tends to emphasize that there is nothing separate from your experience to awaken to, and eschews the koans of the Rinzai school in favor of a themeless, goalless approach to meditation.

sutra   A Buddhist scripture, generally one claiming to contain the direct teachings of Shakyamuni Buddha. Some sutras are known to have been passed down orally from the time of Shakyamuni and then written down (most of the ones in the Pali Canon), while others are known to have been composed later.

three treasures   The three treasures of Buddhism are buddha, dharma, and sangha. These three things have been considered central and essential to Buddhist practice for over 2,500 years.

vipassana   Meaning "insight" or "wisdom," vipassana is meditation in which you begin from a state of tranquility (samatha) and then judiciously employ volitional thinking to contemplate teachings or questions. (Alternately *vipasyana*.)

wagessa   A narrow strip of cloth with the two ends united by a decorative knot, which is sometimes received during the Jukai ceremony and subsequently worn during sangha practice events.

zabuton   A rectangular mat you sit on during meditation. It's usually about 2 feet by 3 feet and stuffed with cotton to cushion your legs from the floor.

zafu   A sturdy round cushion made specifically for sitting on in a cross-legged posture.

zazen   Literally, "seated (*za*) meditation (*zen*)," zazen is a silent, introspective form of meditation that is the central practice of Zen.

Zen   Zen has multiple meanings: (1) meditation itself; (2) the school (or sect) of Buddhism that uses meditation as its primary method, or Zen Buddhism; (3) an adjective describing a spare, clean, elegant, and/or nature-based aesthetic; and (4) an adjective describing the mind-state or approach to life that is supposed to be the result of meditation or Zen practice.

Resources

Books

Aitken, Robert. *The Mind of Clover: Essays in Zen Buddhist Ethics.* New York, NY: North Point Press, 1984.

———. *Taking the Path of Zen.* New York, NY: North Point Press, 1982.

Anderson, Reb. *Being Upright: Zen Meditation and the Bodhisattva Precepts.* Berkeley, CA: Rodmell Press, 2001.

———. *The Third Turning of the Wheel: Wisdom of the Samdhinirmocana Sutra.* Berkeley, CA: Rodmell Press, 2012.

Aoyama, Shundo. *Zen Seeds: Reflections of a Female Zen Priest.* Tokyo, Japan: Kosei Publishing Co., 1983.

Barasch, Marc Ian. *Field Notes on the Compassionate Life: A Search for the Soul of Kindness.* Emmaus, PA: Rodale, Inc., 2005.

Batchelor, Stephen. *Buddhism Without Beliefs: A Contemporary Guide to Awakening.* New York, NY: Riverhead Books, 1997.

Bays, Jan Chozen. *How to Train a Wild Elephant: And Other Adventures in Mindfulness.* Boston, MA: Shambhala Publications, 2011.

Beck, Charlotte Joko. *Everyday Zen: Love and Work.* New York, NY: Harper Collins Publishers, 1989.

Carlson, Kyogen. *Zen in the American Grain: Discovering the Teachings at Home.* Barrytown, NY: Station Hill Press, 1994.

———. *Zen Roots.* Portland, OR: Dharma Rain Zen Center, 1989.

Chögyam, Ngakpa, with Kandro Déchen. *Spectrum of Ecstasy: Enbracing the Five Wisdom Emotions of Vajrayana Buddhism.* Boston, MA: Shambala Publications, 2003.

Cleary, Thomas, trans. *Classics of Buddhism and Zen, Volume 1: The Collected Translations of Thomas Cleary*. Boston, MA: Shambala Publications, 1997.

————. *The Flower Ornament Scripture: A Translation of the Avatamsaka Sutra*. Boston, MA: Shambala Publications, 1993.

Cohen, Darlene. *The One Who Is Not Busy: Connecting with Work in a Deeply Satisfying Way*. Salt Lake City, UT: Gibbs Smith, 2004.

————. *Turning Suffering Inside Out: A Zen Approach to Living with Physical and Emotional Pain*. Boston, MA: Shambala Publications, 2000.

Conze, Edward, trans. *The Perfection of Wisdom in Eight Thousand Lines & Its Verse Summary*. San Francisco, CA: Four Season Foundation, 1973.

Einstein, Albert. *The World As I See It*. San Diego, CA: The Book Tree, 2007.

Field, Rick. *How the Swans Came to the Lake: A Narrative History of Buddhism in America*. Boston, MA: Shambhala Publications, 1986.

Fischer, Norman. *Training in Compassion: Zen Teachings on the Practice of Lojong*. Boston, MA: Shambhala Publications, 2013.

Ford, James Ishmael. *If You're Lucky, Your Heart Will Break: Field Notes from a Zen Life*. Boston, MA: Wisdom Publications, 2012.

————. *Zen Master Who? A Guide to the People and Stories of Zen*. Boston, MA: Wisdom Publications, 2006.

Frankl, Viktor E. *Man's Search for Meaning: An Introduction to Logotherapy*. New York, NY: Simon and Schuster, Inc., 1984.

Fronsdal, Gil. *The Dhammapada: A New Translation of the Buddhist Classic with Annotations*. Boston, MA: Shambala Publications, 2011.

Hanh, Thich Nhat. *Anger: Wisdom for Cooling the Flames*. New York, NY: Riverhead Books, 2001.

————. *Cultivating the Mind of Love: The Practice of Looking Deeply in the Mahayana Tradition*. Berkeley, CA: Parallax Press, 1996.

————. *The Miracle of Mindfulness: An Introduction to the Practice of Meditation*. Boston, MA: Beacon Press, 1999.

————. *Present Moment Wonderful Moment: Mindfulness Verses for Daily Living*. Berkeley, CA: Parallax Press, 1990.

————. *Stepping into Freedom: An Introduction to Buddhist Monastic Training*. Berkeley, CA: Parallax Press, 1997.

Harada, Shodo. *The Path to Bodhidharma*. Boston, MA: Tuttle Publishing, 2000.

Hilbert, Harvey Daiho. *The Zen of Trauma: A Practice for Life*. Amazon Digital Services, Inc.: Order of Clear Mind Zen, 2012.

Kapleau, Philip. *Awakening to Zen: The Teachings of Roshi Philip Kapleau*. Boston, MA: Shambala Publications, 2001.

————. *The Three Pillars of Zen: Teaching, Practice, and Enlightenment*. New York, NY: Anchor Books, 2000.

Katagiri, Dainin. *You Have to Say Something: Manifesting Zen Insight*. Boston, MA: Shambhala Publications, 1998.

Larkin, Geri. *Tap Dancing in Zen*. Berkeley, CA: Celestial Arts, 2000.

Leighton, Taigen Dan, trans. *Cultivating the Empty Field: The Silent Illumination of Zen Master Hongzhi*. Boston, MA: Tuttle Publishing, 2000.

Loori, John Daido. *The Heart of Being: Moral and Ethical Teachings of Zen Buddhism*. Boston, MA: Charles E. Tuttle Co., Inc., 1996.

————. "The Whole Earth Is Medicine." Featured in *Mountain Record* 22.3. Mt Tremper, NY: Zen Mountain Monastery, 2004.

————. *Zen Mountain Monastery Liturgy Manual*. Mt. Tremper, NY: Mountains and Rivers Order. 1998

Maezumi, Taizan, and Bernie Glassman, ed. *On Zen Practice: Body, Breath, and Mind*. Boston, MA: Wisdom Publications, 2002.

Magid, Barry. *Ending the Pursuit of Happiness: A Zen Guide*. Boston, MA: Wisdom Publications, 2008.

————. *Ordinary Mind: Exploring the Common Ground of Zen and Psychoanalysis*. Somerville, MA: Wisdom Publications, 2005.

Malone, Calvin. *Razor-Wire Dharma: A Buddhist Life in Prison*. Boston, MA: Wisdom Publications, 2008.

Martin, Philip. *The Zen Path Through Depression*. New York, NY: HarperCollins Publishers, 1999.

Nearman, Rev. Hubert, trans. *The Denkoroku: The Record of the Transmission of the Light*. Mount Shasta, CA: Shasta Abbey Press, 2001.

Nishijima, Gudo, and Chodo Cross. *Master Dogen's Shobogenzo* (in four volumes). London: Windbell Publications, 1994.

Okumura, Shohaku. *Realizing the Genjokoan: The Key to Dogen's Shobogenzo*. Boston, MA: Wisdom Publications, 2010.

Packer, Toni. *The Work of This Moment.* Boston, MA: Shambala Publications, 1990.

Pine, Red, trans. *The Zen Teaching of Bodhidharma.* New York, NY: North Point Press, 1987.

Price, A.F., and Wong Mou-lam, trans. *The Diamond Sutra and The Sutra of Hui Neng.* Boston, MA: Shambala Publications, 2005.

Richmond, Lewis. *Work as a Spiritual Practice: A Practical Buddhist Approach to Inner Growth and Satisfaction on the Job.* New York, NY: Broadway Books, 1999.

Rockwell, Irini. *The Five Wisdom Energies: A Buddhist Way of Understanding Personalities, Emotions, and Relationships.* Boston, MA: Shambala Publications, 2002.

Sahn, Seung. *Only Don't Know: Selected Teaching Letters of Zen Master Seung Sahn.* Boston, MA: Shambala Publications, 1999.

Senauke, Alan. *The Bodhisattva's Embrace: Dispatches from Engaged Buddhism's Front Lines.* Berkeley, CA: Clear View Press, 2010.

Senzaki, Nyogen, and Ruth Strout McCandless. *Buddhism and Zen.* New York, NY: The Wisdom Library, 1953.

Sheng, Yen. *The Method of No-Method: The Chan Practice of Silent Illumination.* Boston, MA: Shambala Publications, 2008.

Suzuki, Shunryu. *Zen Mind, Beginner's Mind.* New York, NY: Weatherhill, 1999.

Tanahashi, Kazuaki, trans., ed. *Moon in a Dewdrop: Writings of Zen Master Dogen.* New York, NY: North Point Press, 1985.

Thanissaro, Bhikkhu. *The Wings to Awakening: An Anthology from the Pali Canon.* Barre, MA: Dhamma Dana Publications, 1996.

Uchiyama, Kosho. (Thomas Wright, trans.) *From the Zen Kitchen to Enlightenment: Refining Your Life.* New York, NY: Weatherhill, 1983.

———. (Shokaku Okumura, trans.) *The Zen Teachings of "Homeless" Kodo.* Tokyo, Japan: Kyoto Soto-Zen Center, 1990.

Watson, Burton, trans. *The Zen Teachings of Master Lin-Chi.* New York, NY: Columbia University Press, 1993.

Yen, Sheng. *The Method of No-Method: The Chan Practice of Silent Illumination.* Boston, MA: Shambala Publications, 2008.

Websites

http://www.accesstoinsight.org

Access to Insight. This website is a wonderful resource. It contains a large selection of texts from the Pali Canon (the main texts for Theravadin Buddhism, but also the oldest and most traditional Buddhist writings), plus many great articles and commentaries. The whole site is searchable and also has an extensive index.

http://www.americanzenteachers.org

The American Zen Teachers Association (AZTA), a professional organization of Zen teachers from different Zen lineages, including Ch'an (Chinese) and Son (Korean) Buddhism. The website includes information on these different Zen lineages, or schools, and links to Zen center led by AZTA members.

http://www.dharmanet.org

DharmaNet. Includes a directory of Buddhist centers all over the world, plus access to online courses in Buddhism and lots of articles on Buddhist topics.

http://global.sotozen-net.or.jp/eng

Japanese Sotoshu. Sotoshu means Soto school, and this link is to their English language website. There is a wealth of resources here, including translations of traditional chants and texts, descriptions of practices, information on temples worldwide, and news about the organization.

http://www.secularbuddhism.org

Secular Buddhist Association. Articles, podcasts, links, and meditation support from a non-religious point of view.

http://www.szba.org

The Soto Zen Buddhist Association (SZBA), a professional organization of Soto Zen priests. The website contains information about Soto Zen, the activities of the SZBA, and profiles and links for affiliated Soto Zen teachers and Zen centers all over the world.

http://www.sweepingzen.com

Sweeping Zen offers the latest news and developments in Zen worldwide, bios of Zen teachers, and brief descriptions of and links to Zen centers, plus interviews, articles, and blogs.

http://www.tricycle.com

Tricycle is a Buddhist magazine. On the website you can subscribe to articles, or read previews and blogs for free.

Index